TIDINGS
OUT OF THE
Northeast

A GENERAL HISTORICAL
SURVEY OF DANIEL 11

MICHAEL & ANGIE:
GOD BLESS & GOD SPEED !!

MARC ALDEN SWEARINGEN

M A S...

Dedication

This book is dedicated to my younger brother, Jason Scott
Swearingen (March 18, 1977–July 20, 2005), whom I hope
to see again on the beautiful resurrection morning.

—*Marc Swearingen*

Copyright © 2006
by Marc Alden Swearingen
All Rights Reserved
Printed in the USA

Published by
Remnant Publications
649 East Chicago Road
Coldwater MI 49036
517-279-1304
www.remnantpublications.com

Note: All Bible quotations are
taken from the *King James Version*.

The author assumes responsibility for
the accuracy of all footnotes and references.

Cover design by Haley Trimmer
Text design by Greg Solie • Altamont Graphics

Library of Congress Cataloging-in-Publication Data

Swearingen, Marc Alden, 1968–
  Tidings Out of the Northeast : a general historical survey of Daniel Eleven /
by Marc Alden Swearingen.
    p. cm.
  Includes bibliographical references.
  ISBN 1-933291-02-8 (alk. paper)
  1. Bible. O.T. Daniel XI--Criticism, interpretation, etc. I. Title.
  BS1555.52.S94 2006
  224'.5077--dc22
                                    2006033966

06 07 08 09 10 • 5 4 3 2 1

—— TIDINGS ——

Table of Contents

— ONE —
An Introduction
The Author's Preface

Every faithful student of Bible prophecy will agree that the human race is on the fast track toward the end of this earth's history. This sobering reality creates an urgent necessity for an understanding of the prophecies of Daniel and Revelation; these two prophetic books of the Bible are inspired sources that are absolutely essential for end-time survival. A proper understanding of their contents will provide a powerful impetus to motivate the true, born-again Christian to prepare for the final events of human history. Ellen White also confirmed this assertion with the following observation:

> When the books of Daniel and Revelation are better understood, believers will have an entirely different religious experience. They will be given such glimpses of the open gates of heaven that heart and mind will be impressed with the character that all must develop in order to realize the blessedness which is to be the reward of the pure in heart.[1]

Therefore, as we realize the importance of an overall understanding of Daniel and Revelation, it goes without saying that this would obviously include the powerful and yet difficult line of prophecy found in Daniel 11. Ellen White actually articulated that those who live in the end of time will see its complete fulfillment:

> We have no time to lose. Troublous times are before us. The world is stirred with the spirit of war. Soon the scenes of trouble spoken of in the prophecies will take place. The prophecy in the eleventh of Daniel has nearly reached its complete fulfillment. Much of the

---

1 Ellen G. White, *Testimonies to Ministers and Gospel Workers* (Mountain View, CA: Pacific Press, 1962), 114.

history that has taken place in fulfillment of this prophecy will be repeated.[2]

Now, given what we have just discussed, I must say that, as a pastor and evangelist, I have preached numerous sermons on many of the prophecies found in Daniel and Revelation. Yet, up until just recently, Daniel 11 was one particular prophecy that I had never even dared to touch. And, if I was to be honest with myself, the reason for my avoidance of this chapter stemmed from the fact that I just did not understand it. To take this point even further, I had an inherent fear of even approaching Daniel 11 because of the possibility of failing to understand its meaning.

Yet, eventually the day would come where I would decide that this specific chapter would not intimidate me any longer; I purposed to study it and not rest until I had a basic understanding of its general chronology. Thus began my own personal quest for developing a workable interpretation of this vitally important chapter. This document that you now hold in your hand is the result of this personal quest. It is my hope that as you traverse through the pages of this particular book, you too will also come to a basic understanding of Daniel 11.

Furthermore, through this particular document, I hope to offer encouragement by emphasizing that we need not be afraid or intimidated by the apparent complexity of Daniel 11. God has allowed its entrance into the Bible for a specific reason, and I don't believe that it would be with the stipulation that His followers would not be able to understand it. God has placed this chapter in the Bible for our review and examination; and, with the divine aid of the Spirit of God, through an examination of its passages, we will see the path of human history clearly outlined in the prophetic chronology of this specific chapter.

Now, when we examine the scope of church history, a variety of interpretations on Daniel 11 have been produced by Christian scholars and theologians over the centuries;[3] yet, the purpose of this work will not be to

---

2   Ellen G. White, *Manuscript Releases*, 21 vols. (Legacy of Light, 2000), 13:394. See also Ellen G. White, "The Day of the Lord is Near, and Hasteneth Greatly," *Review and Herald*, 24 Nov 1904, paragraph 8, and Ellen G. White, *Testimonies for the Church*, 9 vols. (Boise, ID: Pacific Press, 1948), 9:14.

3   See LeRoy E. Froom, *The Prophetic Faith of Our Fathers*, 4 vols. (Washington, DC: Review and Herald, 1946–1954), 1:456–457, 894–895, 2:156–157, 528–529, 784–785, 3:252–253, 744–745, 4:392–393, 396–397, 846–847, and 4:1118–1119. These sources offer a review on the major Christian theologians over the centuries and their respective interpretations on the prophecies of

review each of these particular interpretations, but rather allow both the Bible and the record of history to dictate the actual chronological structure. In doing so, we will divide this chapter into manageable sections that will hopefully prove easy to understand. As we use this approach, we will examine each particular verse and outline the major trends of human history that each passage is trying to emphasize. Our end result will be the establishment of a basic prophetic chronology that can hopefully be easily understood.

Furthermore, it will make sense that, before we attempt to understand Daniel 11, we must also have a basic understanding of the prophetic chronology outlined in the earlier prophecies of Daniel. These earlier prophecies will prove to be invaluable in understanding the eleventh chapter. In fact, we will discover that Daniel 11 is actually a repetition and enlargement of these prior prophecies.[4] It will also be profitable to review the chronology of both Revelation 13 and Revelation 17, as we will find that these two chapters will also prove to be a tremendous supplement in understanding Daniel 11.

After reviewing these specific chapters, we will also take the time to highlight certain transitional passages in Daniel 11 that demonstrate specific historical trends, which in turn will give us an idea as to where we are in the stream of prophetic history. Therefore, we will review the particular prophecies of Daniel 2, Daniel 7, Daniel 8, Revelation 13, and Revelation 17, and then highlight the transitional passages of Daniel 11 that give a clear demonstration of certain periods in prophetic history. After we accomplish these preparatory tasks in order to establish a solid foundation, we will then divide chapter 11 into the following sections:

(1) **Daniel 11:1–4**—an outline of Media-Persia, Greece, and the four Hellenistic Empires that arose after Alexander the Great (one chapter);

(2) **Daniel 11:5–15**—the "Five Syrian Wars" between Hellenistic Syria and Hellenistic Egypt over the territory of ancient Israel (one chapter);

(3) **Daniel 11:16–30**—highlights in the career of pagan Rome, who eventually subjugated each of the kingdoms from Alexander's former empire (divided into three chapters);

Daniel and Revelation, which would include their views on Daniel 11.

4   Louis F. Were, *The King of the North at Jerusalem* (St. Maries, ID: LMN Publishing, 2002), 47.

(4) **Daniel 11:31–39**—the Dark Age career of papal Rome, from A.D. 538–1798 (one chapter);

(5) **Daniel 11:40–45**—the career of a resurrected, resurgent papal Rome after A.D. 1798, labeled in this section as the "king of the north," which would parallel both the composite "beast" whose "deadly wound was healed" of Revelation 13:1–3, and the "scarlet coloured beast" who "was," "is not," and "shall ascend out of the bottomless pit" and go "into perdition" of Revelation 17:8–11 (divided into six chapters);

After our examination of the general sections of Daniel 11 mentioned above, we will relate this chapter with Daniel 12, offer a paraphrase rendition of chapter 11 in its entirety, and then provide some final thoughts on what we have discovered overall from our quest to understand this seemingly complex prophecy. Hopefully, at the end of this study, you as the reader will have had a rich experience through the discussion presented in this book, and ultimately have a basic working knowledge of the chronology of Daniel 11.

—— TWO ——
A Review of Daniel 2
"An Ancient King's Dream"

Τ he first line of prophecy that we should review before tackling Daniel 11 can be found in Daniel 2. This particular prophecy will outline a solid historical chronology that will serve as a foundation for the later prophecies of Daniel. As it turned out, King Nebuchadnezzar of ancient Babylon, who reigned from 604–562 B.C.,[5] had a nightmarish dream one evening; yet, after he awoke, the king realized that he could neither remember the dream nor ascertain its interpretation. The prophet Daniel would later stand before the famous king and provide both the dream and its respective meaning. We will now examine this particular vision, which can be found in verses 31–45; we will first examine verses 31–35, which discuss the actual dream itself, and then move to verses 36–45, which will provide the interpretation of the dream.

> Thou, O king, sawest, and behold a great image. This great image, whose brightness was excellent, stood before thee; and the form thereof was terrible. This image's head was of fine gold, his breast and his arms of silver, his belly and his thighs of brass, His legs of iron, his feet part of iron and part of clay. Thou sawest till that a stone was cut out without hands, which smote the image upon his feet that were of iron and clay, and brake them to pieces. Then was the iron, the clay, the brass, the silver, and the gold, broken to pieces together, and became like the chaff of the summer threshingfloors; and the wind carried them away, that no place was found for them: and the stone that smote the image became a great mountain, and filled the whole earth. (Daniel 2:31–35)

---

5   Edwin R. Thiele, *The Mysterious Numbers of the Hebrew Kings* (Grand Rapids, MI: Kregel Publications, 1983), 227.

Daniel explained to King Nebuchadnezzar that he had dreamed of a "great image" consisting of a head of gold, chest and arms of silver, belly and thighs of brass, legs of iron, and feet of both iron and clay. He then described that a stone cut without hands had come and smashed the feet of the statue, turning the entire image into powder. As the wind carried this powder away, the stone then became a great mountain that would fill the entire earth. Daniel then conveyed the meaning of what this dream would symbolize; he explained that each successive metal of the statue would symbolize a specific empire that would arise through the progressive course of human history. This sequence of empires would actually begin with King Nebuchadnezzar's kingdom of ancient Babylon:

> This is the dream; and we will tell the interpretation thereof before the king. Thou, O king, art a king of kings: for the God of heaven hath given thee a kingdom, power, and strength, and glory. And wheresoever the children of men dwell, the beasts of the field and the fowls of the heaven hath he given into thine hand, and hath made thee ruler over them all. Thou art this head of gold. (Daniel 2:36)

Thou art this head of gold. In confirmation of God's revelation, the record of history will confirm that King Nebuchadnezzar and the armies of ancient Babylon had annihilated the ruling Assyrian Empire by destroying both its capital of Nineveh in 612 B.C. and an Egyptian garrison at Carchemish in 605 B.C.; these convincing victories would raise ancient Babylon to the level of superpower status in that time period, while at the same time causing the Assyrian Empire to vanish from the scene of human history.[6] Turning due south from Carchemish in 605 B.C., King Nebuchadnezzar would come from the north to conquer the kingdom of Judah, besieging Jerusalem in the same year, destroying the temple and the city in the process. Soon after conquering Judah, he would return to Babylon with the spoils of war, which would include the precious vessels of the temple and several young princes of Judah, of which Daniel and his three friends were a part.[7]

---

6   See Charles Freeman, *Egypt, Greece, and Rome: Civilizations of the Ancient Mediterranean* (Oxford: Oxford University Press, 1996), 70–71, 587, and *Seventh-day Adventist Bible Commentary*, 12 vols. (Hagerstown, MD: Review and Herald, 1957–2000), 8:179.

7   See Freeman, 587–588, 70–71, and Thiele, 185, 227. Like both Jeremiah and Ezekiel (Jeremiah 21:2, 7, 25, 24:1, 25:1, 9, 29:21, 32:1, 28, 35:11, 37:1, 39:1,

Although ancient Babylon enjoyed its most prosperous years from 625 to 539 B.C., most Bible scholars generally agree on the years 606–605 B.C. as the beginning of ancient Babylonian supremacy, due to the fact that this year included both the defeat of the powerful Assyrian Empire and the first involvement of ancient Babylon in the affairs of ancient Israel. Therefore, Daniel clearly related to King Nebuchadnezzar that he and his Babylonian empire were symbolized by the head of gold in the "great image."[8] Yet, Daniel must have surprised the inquisitive monarch when he conveyed to the king that his mighty empire would eventually be overthrown and succeeded by later kingdoms that would arise after the fall of ancient Babylon:

> And after thee shall arise another kingdom inferior to thee, and another third kingdom of brass, which shall bear rule over all the earth. And the fourth kingdom shall be strong as iron: forasmuch as iron breaketh in pieces and subdueth all things: and as iron that breaketh all these, shall it break in pieces and bruise. (Daniel 2:39–40)

And after thee shall arise another kingdom inferior to thee, and another third kingdom of brass, which shall bear rule over all the earth. Daniel related next that the ancient Babylonian kingdom would be succeeded by kingdoms of silver, brass, and iron; in ascertaining the identity of these respective empires, we find that the Bible actually reveals that the Media-Persian Empire conquered ancient Babylon through the strength of the armies of Cyrus the Great, a future king of Persia.[9]

Thus, the chest and arms of silver would symbolize the era of Media-Persian rule, which would last from 539 B.C. through to the year 331 B.C.;[10]

11, 43:10, 44:30, 46:2, 13, 26, 49:28, 30, 50:17, 51:34, 52:4, 12, 28–30, Ezekiel 26:7, 29:18–19, 30:10), Charles Freeman actually called King Nebuchadnezzar by the name of "Nebuchadrezzar." See also Daniel 1:1–2, 2 Kings 24:1–20, 25:1–30, 2 Chronicles 36:6–23, and Jeremiah 46:1–2, 25:8–9, 4:6–7.

8   See Jacques Doukhan, *Secrets of Daniel: Wisdom and Dreams of a Jewish Prince in Exile* (Hagerstown, MD: Review and Herald, 2000), 29–30, Freeman, 70–71, 587–588, Stephen N. Haskell, *The Story of Daniel the Prophet* (Brushton, NY: Teach Services, 1999), 33–35, C. Mervyn Maxwell, *God Cares*, 2 vols. (Boise, ID: Pacific Press, 1981), 1:35–36, Gerhard Pfandl, *Daniel: The Seer of Babylon* (Hagerstown, MD: Review and Herald, 2002), 26–27, *SDA Bible Commentary*, 4:771–772, Uriah Smith, *Daniel and the Revelation* (Nashville, TN: Southern, 1944), 39–44, and Thiele, 227.

9   See Daniel 5:25–31, Isaiah 44:27–28, 45:1.

10 See Doukhan, *Daniel*, 30–31, Freeman, 73–75, 588, Haskell, *Daniel the Prophet*, 35, Maxwell, 1:36, Pfandl, 26–27, *SDA Bible Commentary*, 4:772–773,

subsequently, their demise took place when they were defeated on the plain of Gaugamela near the town of Arbela in 331 B.C. by a powerful, well-trained Greco-Macedonian army under the command of the famous Greek general Alexander the Great. Therefore, because Alexander's Greek Empire would end the rule of Media-Persia, we can conclude that Greece would be the next kingdom, symbolized by the belly and thighs of brass.[11]

And the fourth kingdom shall be strong as iron: forasmuch as iron breaketh in pieces and subdueth all things: and as iron that breaketh all these, shall it break in pieces and bruise. The Greek Empire, which would include the surviving Hellenistic monarchies forged by the former generals of Alexander, lasted until the "iron" kingdom, the pagan Roman Empire, defeated and ended the Greco-Macedonian monarchy at the Battle of Pydna in 168 B.C.; in effect, this notable victory served as a pivotal point in the ascendancy of this great "iron" empire as the next superpower of prophecy.[12] Pagan Rome would also endure much longer than its predecessors, lasting until its final collapse in A.D. 476, which resulted in the formation of the divided European nations; this formation of a divided Europe would also be explained in the next few verses of this vision:

> And whereas thou sawest the feet and toes, part of potters' clay, and part of iron, the kingdom shall be divided; but there shall be in it of the strength of the iron, forasmuch as thou sawest the iron mixed with miry clay. And as the toes of the feet were part of iron, and part of clay, so the kingdom shall be partly strong, and partly broken. And whereas thou sawest iron mixed with miry clay, they shall mingle themselves with the seed of men: but they shall not cleave one to another, even as iron is not mixed with clay. (Daniel 2:41–43)

And whereas thou sawest the feet and toes, part of potters' clay, and part of iron, the kingdom shall be divided; but there shall be in it of

---

Smith, 44–52, and Thiele, 227–228.

11 See George Willis Botsford and Charles Alexander Robinson, Jr., *Hellenic History* (New York: MacMillan Company, 1950), 287–345, Doukhan, *Daniel*, 31–32, Freeman, 258–267, Haskell, *Daniel the Prophet*, 35, Maxwell, 1:36, Pfandl, 26–27, *SDA Bible Commentary*, 4:773–774, Smith, 54–55, and Thiele, 71, 227–228.

12 See Botsford and Robinson, 451–455, Doukhan, *Daniel*, 32–33, Freeman, 319–535, Haskell, *Daniel the Prophet*, 35, Maxwell, 1:36, Pfandl, 26–28, *SDA Bible Commentary*, 4:774–775, and Smith, 54–55.

the strength of the iron, forasmuch as thou sawest the iron mixed with miry clay. After the fall of pagan Rome, a kingdom of iron and clay would emerge and unsuccessfully try to unify itself. When the western pagan Roman Empire collapsed in A.D. 476, several tribal peoples that occupied the various regions of Western Europe would then crystallize into ten independent nations. These ten nations consisted of the Franks (France), Alemanni (Germany), Suevi (Portugal), Visigoths (Spain), Lombards (Italy), Burgundians (Switzerland), Saxons (England), Heruli (overthrown, A.D. 493), Vandals (overthrown, A.D. 534), and Ostrogoths (overthrown, A.D. 555).[13] Furthermore, ever since this division of Europe, no ruler has been successful in unifying this continent under a single ruling authority for any significant period of time. Thus, the ten toes on the feet of iron and clay symbolize a divided Europe that began in A.D. 476 and continues to the present time.

And whereas thou sawest iron mixed with miry clay, they shall mingle themselves with the seed of men: but they shall not cleave one to another, even as iron is not mixed with clay. In addition to being a symbol of divided Europe, the feet of iron and clay also has a deeper and more significant meaning; the "iron" actually symbolizes the fragmented political elements of the pagan Roman Empire that would remain after the fall of Western Europe, while the clay is also a symbol of the people of God, the church. Isaiah wrote "But now, O LORD, thou art our father; we are the clay, and thou our potter; and we all are the work of thy hand" (Isaiah 64:8). Daniel also referred to the potter's clay as "miry clay," which, according to David, can be dirty clay (Psalm 40:1–2).

Therefore, as we piece these concepts together, we can conclude that the "miry clay" of this prophecy can symbolize a muddy, dirty, slimy "church," i.e., an unfaithful, apostate church that would attempt to unify with the fragmented political elements of the collapsed pagan Roman Empire. In essence, the feet of iron and clay, while in one sense symbolizing divided Europe after A.D. 476, can also symbolize the rise of an unfaithful, apostate church that would attempt to unify Europe through the political remnants of the pagan Roman Empire. The record of history will clearly confirm that the papal Roman Empire did in fact succeed pagan Rome and attempt to unify the various nations of Europe under the spiritual umbrella of Roman Catholicism.

---

13 See Alonzo T. Jones, *The Two Republics* (Ithaca, MI: A. B. Publishing, Inc, n.d.), 532–535, 549–553, and Nicolas Cheetham, *A History of the Popes* (New York: Dorset Press, 1982), 29, 32–34.

Thus, history will demonstrate that the Roman Church would attempt to "cleave" to the states of Europe in order to control the conscience of its subjects. In the Bible, the word "cleave" is used within the context of marriage (Genesis 2:24); yet, even though Christ taught that the church and the state should not unify, or "marry" (Matthew 22:15–22), papal Rome would attempt to enter into an illegal, unholy, "fornicating" relationship with the European nations in order to wield its power over European affairs. The papacy actually grew out of the ruins of paganism to become a religio-political power; between A.D. 493 and 555, all the national enemies of the Catholic Church, i.e., the Herulian, Vandal, and Ostrogothic kingdoms, were subdued,[14] and the papacy would maintain a powerful influence in the political affairs of Europe until revolutionary France, through the hand of Napoleon Bonaparte, would neutralize this power in February of A.D. 1798.[15]

Furthermore, in the year 1929, the papal Roman Empire would be revived through the famous Lateran Treaty, which would return political power to the Roman Catholic Church, thus restoring temporal sovereignty to the Vatican as not just a religious power, but a "state," or political power, as well.[16] We will discover later in our review of both Revelation 13 and Revelation 17 that a resurgent, resurrected papal Rome will launch one final effort at the end of time to control the world in a global union of church and state.[17] This end-time scenario is clearly confirmed by a compelling reference from Ellen White:

> We have come to a time when God's sacred work is represented by the feet of the image in which the iron was mixed with the miry clay. ... The mingling of churchcraft and statecraft is represented by the iron and the clay. This union is weakening all the power of

---

14   See Jones, 532–535, 549–553 and Cheetham, 29, 32–34.

15   Cheetham, 242–246. See also Jones, 532–535, 549–553, and Steve Wohlberg, *End Time Delusions: The Rapture, the Antichrist, Israel, and the End of the World* (Shippensburg, PA: Destiny Image Publishers, Inc., 2004), 95–99.

16   Ibid, 278–280. See also Jacques B. Doukhan, *Secrets of Revelation: The Apocalypse through Hebrew Eyes* (Hagerstown, MD: Review and Herald, 2002), 114–116, Cheetham, 279–280, Stephen N. Haskell, *The Story of the Seer of Patmos* (Brushton, NY: Teach Services, 2004), 232, J. Derek Holmes, *The Papacy in the Modern World: 1914–1978* (New York: Crossroad Publishing, 1981), 33–75, *SDA Bible Commentary*, 7:817–818, Smith, 146–147, 567, and Wohlberg, 95–104.

17   Ellen G. White, *The Great Controversy* (Mountain View, CA: Pacific Press, 1940), 447–450, 578–579, 603–612.

the churches. This investing the church with the power of the state will bring evil results.[18]

Therefore, we may conclude in a general sense that the feet of iron and clay serve as a symbol of both divided Europe (A.D. 476) and the papal Roman Empire; this symbol of papal Rome would include both its past influence over European affairs (A.D. 538–1798) and its future resurgence as a major force in the final events of Bible prophecy.[19]

> And in the days of these kings shall the God of heaven set up a kingdom, which shall never be destroyed: and the kingdom shall not be left to other people, but it shall break in pieces and consume all these kingdoms, and it shall stand for ever. Forasmuch as thou sawest that the stone was cut out of the mountain without hands, and that it brake in pieces the iron, the brass, the clay, the silver, and the gold; the great God hath made known to the king what shall come to pass hereafter: and the dream is certain, and the interpretation thereof sure. (Daniel 2:44–45)

And in the days of these kings shall the God of heaven set up a kingdom, which shall never be destroyed: and the kingdom shall not be left to other people, but it shall break in pieces and consume all these kingdoms, and it shall stand for ever. Forasmuch as thou sawest that the stone was cut out of the mountain without hands, and that it brake in pieces the iron, the brass, the clay, the silver, and the gold. Daniel described that this "great image" would eventually be pulverized by a "stone" cut "without hands." Christ actually referred to Himself as "The stone which the builders rejected" (Matthew 21:42), relating that "whosoever shall fall in this stone shall be broken: but on whomsoever it shall fall, it will grind him to powder" (Matthew 21:44).[20] Therefore, Christ Himself is described as this "stone."

Furthermore, the phrase "without hands" refers to Christ in His resurrected, glorified state. Before His crucifixion, His false accusers stated that "We heard him say, I will destroy this temple that is made with hands, and within three days I will build another made without hands" (Mark 14:58). Yet, when Christ said "Destroy this temple, and in three days I will raise it

---

18 Ellen G. White, *Manuscript Releases*, 21 vols. (Legacy of Light, 2000), 15:39.
19 See Doukhan, *Daniel*, 33–36, and Haskell, *Daniel the Prophet*, 35–36.
20 See Isaiah 28:16, Matthew 21:42–44, Acts 4:8–12, Romans 9:30–33, 1 Corinthians 3:6–9, 10:1–4, Ephesians 2:18–22, and 1 Peter 2:1–10.

up" (John 2:19), He was speaking of the "temple of his body" (John 2:21). Therefore, the phrase "without hands" refers to Christ in His glorified, resurrected state, having been raised by the power of the Holy Spirit (1 Peter 3:18). And, because Christ came forth from the tomb in His resurrected, glorified body made "without hands," He will return again to give His faithful followers this same glorified, resurrected body. Referring to this glorified, resurrected body that the righteous will receive when Christ returns, the apostle Paul stated that "we know that if our earthly house of this tabernacle were dissolved, we have a building of God, an house not made with hands, eternal in the heavens" (2 Corinthians 5:1).

Overall, the Bible clearly demonstrates that the "stone" made "without hands" is a symbol of the resurrected, glorified Christ who will return the second time to earth from the "mountain" of God's kingdom;[21] when this takes place, He will pulverize the "great image," resurrect His faithful followers with glorified bodies "not made with hands," and eventually allow them to populate the new earth in the eternal world.[22]

The great God hath made known to the king what shall come to pass hereafter: and the dream is certain, and the interpretation thereof sure. Daniel assured Nebuchadnezzar that God had desired to show the king what would take place in the future. This prophecy also gives us the same assurance that we can trust that God has revealed the great empires of history beforehand. It also shows us where we are in the stream of time, because the next event to take place in this vision will be the second coming of our Lord Jesus Christ.

Daniel 2	Interpretation
Gold	Babylon (605–539 B.C.)
Silver	Media-Persia (539–331 B.C.)
Brass	Greece (331–168 B.C.)
Iron	Pagan Rome (168 B.C.–A.D. 476)
Ten Toes	Divided Europe (A.D. 476–Present)
Iron/Clay	Papal Rome (A.D. 538–1798 & Future)
Stone	Second Advent and Eternity (Future)

---

21 Ezekiel 28:12–16, Isaiah 14:12–14, Isaiah 11:6–9, 65:17–25, and Psalm 48:2 each equate God's kingdom to a "mountain."

22 See 2 Timothy 4:1, Revelation 21:1–7, and 2 Peter 3:13.

── THREE ──
A Review of Daniel 7
"Four Great Beasts from the Sea"

As we review the prophetic chronology of Daniel 7, five foundational principles must be understood: (1) "beasts" in Bible prophecy symbolize kings and/or kingdoms (Daniel 7:17); (2) "seas" in Bible prophecy, which can also be referred to as "waters," symbolize both the nations of the earth and highly populated areas (Revelation 17:15); (3) the vision of Daniel 7 is a repetition, expansion, and enlargement of the vision given in Daniel 2; (4) the "four great beasts" described in Daniel 7 are actually parallels to each of the four metals that make up the "great image" of Daniel 2; and (5) like Daniel 2, the prophetic chronology given in Daniel 7 also begins with the ancient Babylonian empire. Having a basic understanding of these five principles will now help us to understand Daniel 7.

> Daniel spake and said, I saw in my vision by night, and, behold, the four winds of the heaven strove upon the great sea. And four great beasts came up from the sea, diverse one from another. The first was like a lion, and had eagle's wings: I beheld till the wings thereof were plucked, and it was lifted up from the earth, and made stand upon the feet as a man, and a man's heart was given to it. (Daniel 7:2–4)

And four great beasts came up from the sea, diverse one from another. The first was like a lion, and had eagle's wings. The first "beast" that arises from the "sea" is described as a "lion." Since the vision of Daniel 7 parallels the vision of Daniel 2, we must conclude that the "lion" would also be a symbol of ancient Babylon. This conclusion is confirmed by the prophet Jeremiah: "The king of Babylon hath heard the report of them. … Behold, he shall come up like a lion from the swelling of Jordan unto the habitation of the strong" (Jeremiah 50:43–44). Thus, the first kingdom described in the vision of Daniel 7 would be the empire of ancient Babylon

(605–539 B.C.), which would arise out of the nations of the earth in a highly populated area.[23]

> And behold another beast, a second, like to a bear, and it raised up itself on one side, and it had three ribs in the mouth of it between the teeth of it: and they said thus unto it, Arise, devour much flesh. (Daniel 7:5)

And behold another beast, a second, like to a bear, and it raised up itself on one side, and it had three ribs in the mouth of it between the teeth of it. The second "beast" that arises from the "sea" is described as a "bear" that is "raised up" on "one side" with three "ribs" in its mouth. We discovered in our review of Daniel 2 that the empire succeeding ancient Babylon would be Media-Persia; thus, this "bear" would also be a symbol of the Media-Persian Empire.

In fact, the Bible describes that, under the leadership of Cyrus the Great, (Isaiah 44:27–45:1), Media-Persia would overthrow ancient Babylon on the night of the great feast of Belshazzar, the grandson of Nebuchadnezzar (Daniel 5:25–31). This "bear" is raised up on one side because Media-Persia was a dual power; the Median side had emerged first, and later the Persian side would arise and become more powerful. The "three ribs" in its "mouth" are Egypt, Lydia, and Babylon, the three kingdoms it conquered on the rise to dominance; this ancient superpower would last from 539 B.C. to 331 B.C., until its eventual subjugation by Alexander the Great and the Greco-Macedonian Empire.[24]

23 See Jacques Doukhan, *Secrets of Daniel: Wisdom and Dreams of a Jewish Prince in Exile* (Hagerstown, MD: Review and Herald, 2000), 101–102, Stephen N. Haskell, *The Story of Daniel the Prophet* (Brushton, NY: Teach Services, 1999), 90, C. Mervyn Maxwell, God Cares, 2 vols. (Boise, ID: Pacific Press, 1981), 1:106–111, Gerhard Pfandl, *Daniel: The Seer of Babylon* (Hagerstown, MD: Review and Herald, 2002), 62, *Seventh-day Adventist Bible Commentary*, 12 vols. (Hagerstown, MD: Review and Herald, 1957–2000), 4:820, and Uriah Smith, *Daniel and the Revelation* (Nashville, TN: Southern, 1944), 39–44, 107.

24 See Doukhan, *Daniel*, 102–104, Haskell, *Daniel the Prophet*, 91–92, Maxwell, 1:106–111, Pfandl, 62–63, *SDA Bible Commentary*, 4:821, and Smith, 44–52, 107–108. See the following sources that show Media-Persia conquering the "three ribs" of Egypt, Lydia, and Babylon: George Willis Botsford and Charles Alexander Robinson, Jr., *Hellenic History* (New York: MacMillan Company, 1950), 115–116, Doukhan, 103, Charles Freeman, *Egypt, Greece, and Rome: Civilizations of the Ancient Mediterranean* (Oxford: Oxford University Press,

After this I beheld, and lo another, like a leopard, which had upon the back of it four wings of a fowl; the beast had also four heads; and dominion was given to it. (Daniel 7:6)

After this I beheld, and lo another, like a leopard, which had upon the back of it four wings of a fowl; the beast had also four heads; and dominion was given to it. The third "beast" that emerges in the vision of Daniel 7 is described as a "leopard" with "four wings" and "four heads." As we continue to remain consistent with the fact that Daniel 2 and Daniel 7 are parallels, we must conclude that this "leopard" would also be a symbol of the Greco-Macedonian Empire, led by Alexander the Great.[25] The "four wings" would be a symbol of speed in the four directions of the compass (Habakkuk 1:8, Ezekiel 1:4–12), and describe the swiftness and military efficiency of Alexander as he conquered a vast territory in a relatively short amount of time. Again, he would defeat the Media-Persian Empire with a victory in the Battle of Gaugamela near the town of Arbela in 331 B.C.

The "four heads" actually symbolize the four former generals of Alexander that had emerged after the famous Battle of Ipsus and had consolidated kingdoms for themselves (301 B.C.); these former generals would consist of Cassander (Greece, Macedonia), Lysimachus (Thrace, Asia Minor), Seleucus (Syria, Eastern Territories), and Ptolemy (Egypt, Judeo-Palestine).[26] Later, after the Battle of Corupedium (281 B.C.), Seleucus would defeat and kill Lysimachus and annex his kingdom into the Seleucid-Syrian Empire. After this key battle, three of these four empires would remain (Greco-Macedonia, Syria, Egypt), and grow to dominate the Hellenistic Era of ancient history, which would consist of the interim time period between the death of Alexander (323 B.C.) and the rise of the pagan Roman Empire (168 B.C.). After the famous Battle of Pydna in 168 B.C., the

---

1996), 73–75, *SDA Bible Commentary*, 4:821, and Smith, 108.

25 See Doukhan, *Daniel*, 104–105, Haskell, *Daniel the Prophet*, 92, Maxwell, 1:109–111, Pfandl, 63, *SDA Bible Commentary*, 4:821–823, and Smith, 108–109.

26 See Botsford and Robinson, 381 and *SDA Bible Commentary*, 4:822–825. See the following sources on the emergence of Alexander's four generals: Edwyn R. Bevan, *The House of Seleucus: A History of the Hellenistic Near East under the Seleucid Dynasty*, 2 vols. (Chicago: Ares, 1985), 1:57–62, Haskell, *Daniel the Prophet*, 92, Maxwell, 1:109–111, Pfandl, 63, *SDA Bible Commentary*, 4:821–823, Smith, 108–109, and F.W. Walbank, *The Hellenistic World* (Cambridge, MA: Harvard, 1992), 46–59.

Greco-Macedonian monarchy would be defeated and terminated by the emerging pagan Roman Empire.[27]

> After this I saw in the night visions, and behold a fourth beast, dreadful and terrible, and strong exceedingly; and it had great iron teeth: it devoured and brake in pieces, and stamped the residue with the feet of it: and it was diverse from all the beasts that were before it; and it had ten horns. (Daniel 7:7)

Behold a fourth beast, dreadful and terrible, and strong exceedingly; and it had great iron teeth. Daniel explains that a "fourth beast" with "great iron teeth" would emerge after the "leopard" power of ancient Greece; parallel to the "legs of iron" from Daniel 2, this "fourth beast" is also a symbol of the pagan Roman Empire. After the general and consul Lucius Aemilius Paullus led the Roman armies to victory over a Greco-Macedonian coalition in the famous Battle of Pydna (168 B.C.), this rising Mediterranean power would also begin the process of subduing the two remaining Hellenistic kingdoms that had survived Alexander's empire, namely Seleucid Syria and Ptolemaic Egypt.

Under the command of Gnaeus Pompeius Magnus, i.e., Pompey the Great, pagan Rome would next subdue Syria in 64–63 B.C.; three decades later, the combined efforts of the famous Roman dictator Gaius Julius Caesar and his grandnephew Gaius Octavian (Caesar Augustus) would bring the final Hellenistic kingdom of Egypt under Roman control (30 B.C.), which would be precipitated by Octavian's famous naval victory over Mark Antony in the Battle of Actium off the coast of western Greece (31 B.C.). Thus, being "dreadful and terrible," "strong exceedingly," and having "stamped the residue" of all rival kingdoms with its powerful military machine, pagan Rome would grow to control nearly all of Europe, the Middle East, and North Africa around the Mediterranean basin and rule interrupted until A.D. 476, "devouring" and "breaking" any kingdom that would challenge its authority.[28]

It was diverse from all the beasts that were before it; and it had ten horns. This "fourth beast" is also described as having "ten horns," which

---

27 See Bevan, *The House of Seleucus*, 2:144, Botsford and Robinson, 381–384, 451–455, Freeman, 274–293, 328–329, 602, Michael Grant, *History of Rome* (New York: Book-of-the-Month Club, 1997), 138–141, 156, 196, Pfandl, 63, *SDA Bible Commentary*, 4:822–825, and Walbank, 90, 239.

28 See Freeman, 371–395, Grant, *History of Rome*, 241–273, and Alonzo T. Jones, *The Two Republics* (Ithaca, MI: A. B. Publishing, Inc., n.d.), 67–85.

would essentially parallel the ten toes of the "great image" of Daniel 2; again, these "ten horns" are also symbolic of the ten independent European kingdoms that would emerge after the collapse of the western Roman Empire.[29] Under the constant pressure of Germanic invasions in the fourth and fifth centuries, pagan Rome would finally collapse in the year A.D. 476 after seeing its last western emperor, Romulus Augustulus, deposed by the notorious Odoacer, a powerful Germanic military leader of an Arian tribal people called the Heruli.[30]

After seizing control of the Italian peninsula and removing Romulus Augustulus from the western emperorship, the rebellious Odoacer asked for permission from the eastern Roman emperor to make himself ruler in Italy;[31] Zeno, the eastern emperor, could only acquiesce to Odoacer's request by default, thus allowing him to become the first "barbarian" king of Italy. This significant historical event would officially mark the end of the western Roman Empire and lead to the subsequent development of the ten tribal nations that would form a divided Europe after A.D. 476.[32] These ten tribal nations would include the following: (1) the Franks (France), (2) the Alemanni (Germany), (3) the Lombards (Italy), (4) the Burgundians (Switzerland), (5) the Saxons (England), (6) the Suevi (Portugal), (7) the Visigoths (Spain), (8) the Heruli (overthrown, A.D. 493), (9) the Vandals (overthrown, A.D. 534), and (10) the Ostrogoths (overthrown, A.D. 555).[33]

I considered the horns, and, behold, there came up among them another little horn, before whom there were three of the first horns

---

29 See Doukhan, *Daniel*, 105–106, Haskell, *Daniel the Prophet*, 93–94, Maxwell, 1:109–111, Pfandl, 63, *SDA Bible Commentary*, 4:823–826, and Smith, 110.

30 See Nicolas Cheetham, *A History of the Popes* (New York: Dorset Press, 1982), 29, Freeman, 518–525, 611, Edward Gibbon, *The Decline and Fall of the Roman Empire*, 6 vols. (New York: Everyman's Library, 1993), 3:518–527, Grant, *History of Rome*, 423–436, 462–470, 522, Jones, 518, John Moorhead, *The Roman Empire Divided, 400–700* (London: Pearson Education Limited, 2001), 42, Smith, 123, 485, and *SDA Bible Commentary*, 4:826.

31 Under the emperor Diocletian (reign 284–305), the Roman Empire had been divided into eastern and western sections. See pages 141–143, 148–149.

32 See Freeman, 518–525, 611, Gibbon, 3:518–527, Grant, *History of Rome*, 423–436, 462–470, 522, Jones, 522, and Smith, 123.

33 See Doukhan, *Daniel*, 105–106, Haskell, *Daniel the Prophet*, 93–96, Maxwell, 1:129, Pfandl, 63, *SDA Bible Commentary*, 4:826, and Smith, 57–63, 110, 119. These ten horns of Daniel 7 would parallel the ten toes of Daniel 2's vision. See page 13.

plucked up by the roots: and, behold, in this horn were eyes like the eyes of man, and a mouth speaking great things. (Daniel 7:8)

There came up among them another little horn, before whom there were three of the first horns plucked up by the roots. As Daniel viewed the "ten horns" of the "fourth beast," he saw the rise of a "little horn" power from "among" the "ten horns." Another kingdom is thus brought into view that would arise among the ten tribal nations of Western Europe sometime after A.D. 476; this kingdom would also overthrow three of the ten kingdoms during its rise to power. As we consider the identity of this "little horn" power, we had discovered that the "feet" of "iron and clay," while in one sense symbolizing a divided Europe, was also a symbol of the papal Roman Empire. The "iron" symbolizes the remaining political elements of the collapsed pagan Roman Empire, i.e., the divided European nations, while the "miry clay" symbolizes an apostate church. These two elements would attempt to "mingle" together in a union of church and state, and history will clearly demonstrate that papal Rome, as an apostate religious power, had used the governments of the European nations to exercise the control of conscience until its eventual removal from power by revolutionary France in the year A.D. 1798.

Therefore, this "little horn" power, a parallel in one sense to the "feet" of "iron and clay," is a symbol of the papal Roman Empire that had emerged out of the ruins of pagan Rome.[34] And, again, Daniel states that this "little horn" of papal Rome would overthrow three of the ten divided European kingdoms on its way to power. As we consider the actual subjugation of these three kingdoms, we must take the time to offer a general historical survey of the events that took place concerning the ascendancy of the "little horn" power.

After the Roman emperor Constantine signed the Edict of Milan into effect (A.D. 313), which ultimately granted religious freedom to the Christians of the empire, Catholicism would eventually arise as the dominant version of Christianity.[35] The bishop of Rome, later to become the papacy, would emerge as the spiritual leader of the Catholic Church, and desire to eliminate Arianism, its chief spiritual rival.[36] Three of the ten

---

34 See Doukhan, *Daniel*, 106–111, Haskell, *Daniel the Prophet*, 94–97, Maxwell, 1:122–143, Pfandl, 59–67, *SDA Bible Commentary*, 4:826–838, and Smith, 110–111, 115–147. .

35 Gibbon, 2:252–253 and Jones, 180–182.

36 To summarize briefly, Arian Christianity essentially denied the divinity of Jesus Christ, while Catholicism advocated a Trinitarian view of God,

kingdoms of Western Europe, the Heruli, Vandals, and Ostrogoths, were all major Arian powers; thus, as the papacy sought to convert the European nations to Catholicism, it would use the military power of these European allies to eliminate all three of these Arian rivals.

We have already discussed that Odoacer, the king of the Arian Heruli, seized control of Italy in A.D. 476, removing the last western Roman emperor from power, Romulus Augustulus, thus causing the collapse of pagan Rome. Having made himself king of Italy, he would later meddle in the affairs of the Roman Church by enacting legislation that would guarantee civil protection over its land-estate affairs. Because this civil protection infringed upon the jurisdiction of the Catholic Church, the bishop of Rome took offense to this action and encouraged the eastern emperor Zeno to hire King Theodoric and his unsettled tribal people, the Arian Ostrogoths, to retaliate by invading Italy in order to deal with Odoacer and eliminate the Arian Heruli.

Desiring to serve the eastern emperor and settle his own people permanently, Theodoric promptly invaded Italy under the authority of Zeno, and in A.D. 489–490 he defeated Odoacer and the Arian Heruli in three separate engagements. After eventually being suppressed in a three-year siege at Ravenna, Odoacer attempted to secure a peace settlement, but was later deceitfully murdered at a banquet by Theodoric as part of a villainous plot with the bishop of Ravenna, and the Heruli were then subsequently massacred (A.D. 493). After securing the complete annihilation of the Arian Heruli, the Arian Ostrogoths established a somewhat permanent settlement in Italy, thus securing peace for several years under the reign of Theodoric.[37] Yet, as time would progress, the doctrinal differences between these Arian Ostrogothic settlers and the Roman Catholic occupants of Italy became more and more apparent, which would eventually lead to an armed conflict between the bishop of Rome and the Arian Ostrogoths.

Meanwhile, Clovis, a powerful pagan king of the Franks, converted to Roman Catholic Christianity after winning a decisive battle against the Germanic Alemanni in A.D. 496. He would later be baptized and subdue the Arian Visigoths through military force in A.D. 507–508, driving the Visigothic presence from Gaul, while at the same time committing his powerful military machine to the side of the rising papal power. By the same year (A.D. 508), Clovis became a powerful Catholic influence in European

---

where Jesus Christ is identified as God the Eternal Son. See footnote 264 on page 154.

37 See Cheetham, 29, 33–34, Freeman, 527, 538, 546, Gibbon, 4:127–139, Jones, 532–535, Moorhead, 42–43, 133, *SDA Bible Commentary*, 4:826–827, and Smith, 123, 127–128, 489.

affairs outside of the Italian peninsula, fully supporting the authority of the bishop of Rome;[38] thus, by A.D. 508, with the complete support of the military strength of Clovis, the papacy would continue to strengthen its religio-political position in Europe and grow to dominate Western European affairs through the spiritual subjugation of kings and the conversion of many tribal settlers to Roman Catholic Christianity.[39]

Later, after the first major Arian power, the Heruli, had been destroyed by Theodoric and his Arian Ostrogoths (A.D. 493), the eastern Roman emperor Justinian, fearing Catholic persecution by both the Arian Vandal threat in North Africa and the Arian Ostrogothic influence in Italy, would eventually give his undivided support to the bishop of Rome. He issued a decree giving the papacy supremacy over all the churches (A.D. 533), charging that the two remaining major Arian powers were to be driven from northern Africa and the Italian peninsula. Dr. Alberto Treiyer made the following observation:

> Actually, in religious matters, Justinian issued a letter in the year 533, by which he engaged himself to make the pope 'the head of all the Holy Churches,' and increase 'the honor and *authority* of your See.' He promised then, 'to preserve the unity of your Apostolic See, and the condition of the Holy Churches of God. … We have exerted ourselves to unite all the priests of the East and subject them to the See of *Your Holiness*. … We have still considered it necessary that they should be brought to the attention of *Your Holiness*.'[40]

Having given the bishop of Rome supremacy over all the churches of Europe, Justinian then promptly commissioned his imperial general, Belisarius, to execute this decree; the famous general first landed in North Africa where he would crush the Arian Vandal Empire (A.D. 533–534).[41]

---

38 Alberto R. Treiyer, *Apocalypse: Seals & Trumpets* (Dr. Alberto R. Treiyer, 2005), 97–104, 114.

39 See Freeman, 529–530, Gibbon, 4:51–71, Grant, *History of Rome*, 462, Jones, 525–527, Moorhead, 73–75, 261, *SDA Bible Commentary*, 4:881, Smith, 271–272, 324–330, and Treiyer, 97–104, 114.

40 See Treiyer, 104–105. In this quotation, Dr. Treiyer quotes Samuel Parsons Scott, *The Civil Law*, Book 12 (Cincinnati, OH: Central Trust Company, 1932), 11–12, concerning Justinian's decree on the primacy of the bishop of Rome. The italics were his specific emphases in the quotation.

41 See Cheetham, 33, Freeman, 545–546, Gibbon, 4:236–267, Grant, *History of Rome*, 464, Jones, 533–534, 549–550, Moorhead, 54–55, 127–128, *SDA Bible*

He then invaded the Italian peninsula to confront the Arian Ostrogoths, and, after a series of regional conquests, liberated Rome by defeating a garrison of four thousand Ostrogothic soldiers (A.D. 536). The remainder of the Ostrogothic army made a valiant attempt to hold and defend Italy; yet, they would eventually exhaust their resources in this defense, and later be driven from Italian peninsula altogether by A.D. 555. Furthermore, although the Ostrogoths were not finally defeated militarily until A.D. 555, we may date the ascendancy of the papacy as beginning in A.D. 538, primarily due to Belisarius' first initial liberation of Rome, Justinian's deposition of the pro-Arian pope Silverius, and his installation of the pro-Catholic bishop Vigilius to the papal seat. These events began the process of ending Ostrogothic control in Italy, thus eliminating all Arian opposition to the bishop of Rome, and eventually resulted in their final subjugation by A.D. 555, which was a mere military formality. Dr. Treiyer confirmed that,

> It was in this same year of 538 when, for the first time since the fall of the empire half a century before, the Ostrogoths were expelled from Rome. For the first time since there were no more emperors in the city of Rome, the pope could be free from the Arians who promoted their faith and opposed the influence of the Roman bishop.[42]

Thus, despite having used the Arian Ostrogothic power to defeat the Arian Heruli, the papacy would conveniently turn on this former ally to end the so-called "Arian heresy," and gain complete political and spiritual control of Western Europe.[43] With this final victory over the Ostrogoths, the pro-Catholic bishop of Rome, Vigilius, was left free to exercise sole spiritual authority over Christendom as dictated by Justinian's decree of A.D. 533; Justinian did not appoint another emperor to rule in the west, thus allowing the papacy to assume this position:

> Down to the sixth century all popes are declared saints in the martyrologies. Vigilius (537-555) is the first of a series of popes who no longer bear this title, which is henceforth sparingly conferred. From this time on [the ascendancy of Vigilius as pope in 537-538]

Commentary, 4:827, and Smith, 127–128.

42 Treiyer, 107.

43 See Cheetham, 33–34, Freeman, 546, Gibbon, 4:267–304, Haskell, *Daniel the Prophet*, 231–234, Jones, 550–553, Moorhead, 133, *SDA Bible Commentary*, 4:827, and Smith, 127–128.

the popes, more and more involved in worldly affairs, no longer belong solely to the Church;—they are men of the state, and then rulers of the state.[44]

Therefore, with the initial liberation of Rome by Belisarius in March of A.D. 538, this very year would begin the ascendancy of the papacy to power. The calculated absence of a political ruler in Western Europe would allow the bishop of Rome, later renamed the "Papal See," or "Papacy" (A.D. 606), to grow to have complete control over European Christendom.[45]

Behold, in this horn were eyes like the eyes of man, and a mouth speaking great things. Daniel described that this "little horn" power would have the "eyes of a man" and a "mouth speaking great things." It is quite obvious that a man, namely the person of the pope, is the visible head of the papal Roman Empire; furthermore, having "a mouth speaking great things," he would speak great things of "blasphemy" against God (Revelation 13:5–6).

After Christ had equated Himself with the Father, the religious leaders sought to stone Him, citing that "For a good work we stone thee not; but for blasphemy; and because that thou, being a man, makest thyself God" (John 10:33). Christ is God and equal with the Father (Philippians 2:6); yet, when a mere human being claims to be equal with God, he or she commits blasphemy. Foreseeing the rise of the papal power, Paul stated that the papacy, as the "man of sin" and the "son of perdition," would commit blasphemy against God by exalting himself "above all that is called God, or that is worshipped; so that he as God sitteth in the temple of God, shewing himself that he is God" (2 Thessalonians 2:3–4).

There is also a second definition of blasphemy; before healing a paralytic, Christ first offered forgiveness for the man's sins (Mark 2:1–5). Once again, the religious leaders criticized Jesus for offering forgiveness to the man, saying, "Why doth this man thus speak blasphemies? Who can forgive sins but God only?" (Mark 2:7). Christ does in fact have the authority to forgive sins; yet, when mere human beings claim to have the power to forgive and absolve men of sin, they commit blasphemy.

Several Roman Catholic sources state that the office of the papacy claims infallibility and equality with God. In one such source, Pope Leo

---

44 Charles Bemont and G. Monod, *Medieval Europe from 395 to 1270* (New York: Henry Holt and Company, 1906), 120–121.

45 See John Dowling, *The History of Romanism* (Pensacola, FL: Vance, 2002), 541–542, Jones, 532–553, *SDA Bible Commentary*, 4:826–828, and Smith, 111, 121–128, 268.

XIII (reign, 1878–1903) proclaimed that "We hold upon this earth the place of God Almighty."[46] *The Catholic National* also stated that "The Pope is not only the representative of Jesus Christ, but he is Jesus Christ Himself, hidden under veil of flesh."[47] Lucius Ferraris penned that "The pope can modify divine law, since his power is not of man, but of God, and he acts in the place of God upon earth, with the fullest power of binding and loosing his sheep."[48]

The Church of Rome also claims that its clergy have the power to forgive sins. The 1997 edition of the *Catechism of the Catholic Church* states that "bishops and priests, by virtue of the sacrament of Holy Orders, have the power to forgive all sins 'in the name of the Father, and of the Son, and of the Holy Spirit.'"[49] Peter Geiermann, in his 1949 edition of *The Convert's Catechism of Catholic Doctrine*, clearly stated that one must "Confess his sins to the priest" and then "Perform the penance that the priest imposes."[50] In confirmation with these references just mentioned, please notice these next three quotations that demonstrate the blasphemous claims of the Catholic Church:

> In order to preserve the Church in the purity of the faith handed on by the apostles, Christ who is the Truth willed to confer on her a share in his own infallibility. ... Christ endowed the Church's shepherds with the charism of infallibility in matters of faith and morals.[51]

46 Pope Leo XIII, "The Reunion of Christendom," *Encyclical Letter*, 20 June 1894, quoted in Kevin Morgan, *Sabbath Rest* (Brushton, NY: Teach Services, 2002), 63. See also Cheetham, 317–320.

47 *The Catholic National*, 1 July 1895, in Morgan, 63.

48 Lucius Ferraris, "Papa," in *Prompta Bibliotheca*, Volume 6 (1772), article 2, page 29, in Morgan, 63.

49 *Catechism of the Catholic Church*, 2nd Ed. (Washington, DC: United States Catholic Conference, 1997), 367. This very same source also stated that "any priest ... can absolve from every sin and excommunication" (page 368). There are a number of statements in this particular source that demonstrate this point.

50 Peter Geiermann, *The Convert's Catechism of Catholic Doctrine* (St. Louis, MI: B. Herder Book Company, 1949), 82–83.

51 *Catechism of the Catholic Church*, 235. Notice also the following statement: "All dogmatic decrees of the Pope, made with or without his general council, are infallible. ... Once made, no pope or council can reverse them. ... This is the Catholic principle, that the Church cannot err in faith" (*The Catholic World*, June 1871, 422–423, in Morgan, 62).

'The Roman Pontiff, head of the college of bishops, enjoys this infallibility in virtue of his office, when, as supreme pastor and teacher of all the faithful—who confirms his brethren in the faith—he proclaims by a definitive act a doctrine pertaining to faith or morals.' ... This infallibility extends as far as the deposit of divine Revelation itself.[52]

The Pope is an infallible Teacher in Faith and Morals because the Attributes of a divine Church are necessarily found in their fulness [sic, fullness] in her headship, which the Pope inherits from St. Peter. ... The Pope teaches with the infallible guidance of the Holy Ghost only when he acts in his official capacity as Vicar of Christ, that is, when he publicly teaches a doctrine of Faith or Morals to be held by all the faithful.[53]

These statements all prove that this blasphemous "little horn" power can be none other than papal Rome, a spiritual empire that clearly claims to possess equality with God and the power to forgive sins.

For the sake of efficiency, we will skip over verses 9–24 of Daniel 7, and move to verse 25 and examine some other details that will confirm the actual identity of the "little horn" power as the papacy.

And he shall speak great words against the most High, and shall wear out the saints of the most High, and think to change times and laws: and they shall be given into his hand until a time and times and the dividing of time. (Daniel 7:25)

He shall speak great words against the most High, and shall wear out the saints of the most High. Having already commented on the "great words" of "blasphemy" that papal Rome would speak against God, we also see that this power would "wear out the saints of the Most High." The

---

52 Ibid, 235–236. See also the following statement: "The Roman Pontiff, when he speaks *ex cathedra*—that is, when in the exercise of his office as pastor and teacher of all Christians he defines, by virtue of his supreme Apostolic authority, a doctrine of faith or morals to be held by the whole Church—is ... possessed of that infallibility with which the Divine Redeemer wished His Church to be endowed ... and consequently that such definitions of the Roman Pontiff are irreformable of their own nature" (*The Catholic Encyclopedia*, Volume 7 [1910], 796, in Morgan, 63).

53 Geiermann, 30.

record of history will clearly demonstrate that the Church of Rome has sent an uncountable number of people to their deaths for the supposed crime of heresy.

Surprisingly, the 1907 edition of the *Catholic Encyclopedia* indicates that "For professing faith contrary to the teachings of the Church of Rome, history records the martyrdom of more than one hundred million people."[54] William E. H. Lecky, in the second volume of his work entitled *The History of the Rise and Influence of the Spirit of Rationalism in Europe*, observed that "the Church of Rome has shed more innocent blood than any other institution that has ever existed among mankind," a point that "will be questioned by no Protestant who has a competent knowledge of history."[55] In his work entitled *The History of Romanism*, John Dowling also noted that,

> From the birth of popery ... to the present time, it is estimated by careful and credible historians, that more than fifty millions of the human family, have been slaughtered for the crime of heresy by popish persecutors,—an average of more than 40,000 religious murders for every year of the existence of popery.[56]

These statements prove beyond the shadow of a doubt that papal Rome clearly fulfilled its prophetic role as a fierce persecutor of God's faithful followers. More recently, the late Pope John Paul II sponsored a "Day of Pardon," offering a formal apology for the past centuries of persecution against suspected heretics committed by the Inquisition:

> [We] cannot fail to recognize the infidelities to the Gospel committed by some of our brethren, especially during the second millennium. Let us ask pardon for the divisions which have occurred among Christians, for the violence some have used in the service of the truth and for the distrustful and hostile attitudes sometimes taken towards the followers of other religions.[57]

---

54 *The Catholic Encyclopedia*, Volume 12 (1907), 266. See the following references for information on the Catholic Inquisition and persecution of Christians: *Bible Readings for the Home* (Nashville, TN: Southern, 1944), Christian Edwardson, *Facts of Faith* (Nashville, TN: Southern, 1943), and Benjamin G. Wilkinson, *Truth Triumphant* (Mountain View, CA: Pacific Press, 1944).

55 William E. H. Lecky, *The History of the Rise and Influence of the Spirit of Rationalism in Europe*, vol. 2 (University Press of the Pacific, 2001), 32.

56 Dowling, 541–542.

57 See the following website for the above quotation given by Pope John Paul II on

And think to change times and laws. Daniel was also told that this power would "think to change times and laws;" in fulfillment of this particular prophecy, it can be easily demonstrated that the Catholic Church has "thought" to change the ten commandment law of God. God's original ten-commandment law can be found in Exodus 20:3–17; yet, when one examines Rome's version of the Ten Commandments, it can be easily demonstrated that the second commandment forbidding the worship of graven images has been removed altogether. To preserve the number of the Ten Commandments, the tenth commandment has been divided into two commandments, and each commandment has been shifted up one position.

The Roman Catholic Church has also claimed to have changed the Sabbath day of the fourth commandment (which Rome calls the third commandment) from the seventh day (Saturday), to the first day of the week (Sunday), while at the same time admitting that the Bible sanctions no such change. Therefore, papal Rome has (1) changed God's "laws" by removing the commandment that forbids the worship of graven images, while dividing the tenth commandment into two parts, and (2) changed God's "times" by transferring the actual time of the Sabbath day from the seventh day of the week, Saturday, to the first day of the week, Sunday, while admitting that there is no biblical basis for such a change. [58] Please notice the following statements from the Roman Catholic Church herself that claim this alleged power to change God's law:

> The pope can modify divine law, since his power is not of man, but of God, and he acts in the place of God upon earth, with the fullest power of binding and loosing his sheep. [59]

seeking forgiveness for past persecutions: http://www.Aloha.Net/~mikesch/pope_to_seek_forgiveness.Htm. Pope John Paul II did in fact make the above quotation in his "day of pardon" homily on march 12, 2000, formally asking for forgiveness for papal rome's history of persecution. See Ellen G. White, *The Great Controversy* (Mountain View, CA: Pacific Press, 1940), 571, for a commentary on how Rome would apologize for its past acts, but in reality her nature has not changed, nor will ever change.

58 See *Catechism of the Catholic Church*, 498–611, Bertrand L. Conway, *The Question Box* (New York: The Paulist Press, 1929), 409–411, Geiermann, 50–51, John A. O'Brien, *The Faith of Millions* (Huntington, IN: Our Sunday Visitor, 1974), 399–401, *Rome's Challenge: Why Protestants Keep Sunday*, ISBN 0-8280-0378-5, and White, *Great Controversy*, 51–53, 447–449. Catholic sources refer to the Sabbath as the third commandment instead of the fourth commandment.

59 Ferraris, 29, in Morgan, 63.

Which day is the Sabbath day? ... *Saturday* is the Sabbath day. ... Why do we observe *Sunday* instead of Saturday? ... We observe *Sunday* instead of *Saturday* because the Catholic Church *transferred* the solemnity from Saturday to Sunday.[60]

Perhaps the boldest thing, the most revolutionary change the Church ever did, happened in the first century. The holy day, the Sabbath, was changed from Saturday to Sunday. 'The Day of the Lord' (dies Dominica) was chosen, not from any directions noted in the Scriptures, but from the Church's sense of its own power.[61]

And they shall be given into his hand until a time and times and the dividing of time. This passage indicates that the faithful people of God would be persecuted by papal Rome for a "time," "times," and the "dividing" of a "time." A "time" would correspond to one prophetic year, the "times" would be two prophetic years, and the "dividing" of a "time" would be one-half of a prophetic year, totaling 3½ years of prophetic time. Now, as we learn to interpret prophetic time in the Bible, we should understand that a biblical year consists of 360 days; therefore, 3½ years of 360 days per year would equal 1,260 prophetic days, a prophetic period that can be found seven times in the books of Daniel and Revelation.[62] As we seek to unlock the mystery of prophetic time, one prophetic day equates to one literal year of time;[63] therefore, this period of 1,260 prophetic "days" would equal 1,260 literal years of actual time.

As the Bible has accurately predicted, the papal Roman Empire did in fact hold supremacy for 1,260 literal years, and, during that time, had vehemently persecuted the people of God. This 1,260-year period actually began in March of A.D. 538, when the city of Rome was first liberated from Ostrogothic control by Belisarius, together with Justinian's installation of

---

60 Geiermann, 50, emphasis mine.

61 *Saint Catherine Catholic Church Sentinel*, Algonac, Michigan, Volume 50, Number 22, 21 May 1995.

62 Using Daniel 4:16, 25, 32, 34, we can see that "times" can be equal to "years." The following verses demonstrate that a biblical year consists of 360 days: Genesis 7:11, 24, and 8:3–4. See Daniel 12:7, Revelation 11:2–3, 12:6, 14, and 13:5.

63 See Numbers 14:34, Ezekiel 4:6, Genesis 29:20–28, Isaiah 34:8, and Psalm 77:5. For an excellent analysis of the day-year principle, see Steve Wohlberg, *End Time Delusions: The Rapture, the Antichrist, Israel, and the End of the World* (Shippensburg, PA: Destiny Image Publishers, Inc., 2004), 95–99.

the pro-Catholic bishop Vigilius by the imperial armies; it ended when the French general Alexandre Berthier invaded the city of Rome under the authority of Napoleon Bonaparte and revolutionary France, and removed Pope Pius VI from his seat of power on February 10, 1798. This year would signify the end of the 1,260-year supremacy of the papal Roman Empire.[64]

> But the judgment shall sit, and they shall take away his dominion, to consume and to destroy it unto the end. And the kingdom and dominion, and the greatness of the kingdom under the whole heaven, shall be given to the people of the saints of the most High, whose kingdom is an everlasting kingdom, and all dominions shall serve and obey him. (Daniel 7:26–27)

But the judgment shall sit, and they shall take away his dominion, to consume and to destroy it unto the end. Daniel was assured that God's judgment would eventually sit and destroy the "little horn" power. Overall, we can see that the chronology of Daniel 7 confirms and expands on the same chronology from Daniel 2:

Daniel 2	Daniel 7	Interpretation
Gold	Lion	Babylon (605–539 B.C.)
Silver	Bear	Media-Persia (539–331 B.C.)
Brass	Leopard	Greece (331–168 B.C.)
Not mentioned	4 Heads	4 Kingdoms (301 B.C.)
Legs of Iron	4th Beast	Pagan Rome (168 B.C.–A.D. 476)
10 Toes	10 Horns	Divided Europe (A.D. 476)
Iron/Clay	Little Horn	Papal Rome (A.D. 538–1798)
Not mentioned	Judgment	Pre-Advent Judgment
Stone	Kingdom	Second Advent, Eternity

---

64 See Doukhan, *Daniel*, 108–110, Maxwell, 1:130–131, Pfandl, 59–66, *SDA Bible Commentary*, 4:833–838, Smith, 143–145, Treiyer, 89–118, White, *The Great Controversy*, 54–55, 266–268, 306, 356, 439, and Wohlberg, *End Time Delusions*, 95–99. See the following supplementary sources: William Barry, *The Papacy and Modern Times: A Political Sketch, 1303–1870* (New York: Henry Holt and Company, 1911), 196, Frank J. Coppa, *The Modern Papacy since 1789* (London: Longman, 1998), 31, and Williston Walker, *A History of the Christian Church* (New York: Charles Scribner's Sons, 1918), 133.

—— FOUR ——
A Review of Daniel 8
"The Cleansing of the Sanctuary"

W e will discover that the vision of Daniel 8 is actually a reiteration and expansion of the same prophetic chronology that we have already established from our review of Daniel 2 and Daniel 7. Using the symbol of a "great image" consisting of different metallic elements that would equate to the successive empires of history, Daniel 2 outlined a series of kingdoms that have directly affected the people of God. While covering the same historical chronology as Daniel 2, Daniel 7 had used an entirely different set of prophetic symbols, i.e., "beasts," to describe each successive empire. In like manner, Daniel 8 will also use its own distinct set of prophetic symbols to describe the same basic chronology. Yet, while Daniel 2 and Daniel 7 began their respective chronological sequences with ancient Babylon, Daniel 8 will begin its chronological sequence with Media-Persia.

> Then I lifted up mine eyes, and saw, and, behold, there stood before the river a ram which had two horns: and the two horns were high; but one was higher than the other, and the higher came up last. I saw the ram pushing westward, and northward, and southward; so that no beasts might stand before him, neither was there any that could deliver out of his hand; but he did according to his will, and became great. (Daniel 8:3–4)

There stood before the river a ram which had two horns: and the two horns were high; but one was higher than the other, and the higher came up last. I saw the ram pushing westward, and northward, and southward. Daniel first describes a "ram" with "two horns" that pushed "westward," "northward," and "southward." One of these "two horns" would arise first, and then the second horn would come after and rise "higher" than the first horn. The angel would later give the identity of this two-horned ram by telling Daniel that the "ram which thou sawest having two horns are the kings of Media and Persia" (Daniel 8:20), thus beginning the chronology of Daniel 8 with the Media-Persian Empire (539–331 B.C.).[65] Media arose as the first of the two horns, and the Persian "horn" came later and grew higher, becoming the stronger partner of this dual power. Geographically, Media-Persia was an "eastern" empire in reference to Israel, and pushed "west" to conquer Lydia (546 B.C.), "north" to conquer Babylon (539 B.C.), and "south" to conquer Egypt (525 B.C.).[66] As we have already demonstrated, Media-Persia would begin its supremacy after invading and destroying ancient Babylon (539 B.C.), under the authority of Cyrus the Great (Daniel 5:28–31), who would serve as the first king of Persia.[67]

> And as I was considering, behold, an he goat came from the west on the face of the whole earth, and touched not the ground: and the goat had a notable horn between his eyes. And he came to the ram that had two horns, which I had seen standing before the river, and ran unto him in the fury of his power. And I saw him come close unto the ram, and he was moved with choler against him, and smote the ram, and brake his two horns: and there was no power in the ram to stand before him, but he cast him down to the ground, and stamped upon him: and there was none that could deliver the ram out of his hand. Therefore the he goat waxed very great: and when he was strong, the great horn was broken; and for it came up four notable ones toward the four winds of heaven. (Daniel 8:5–8)

65 See Jacques Doukhan, *Secrets of Daniel: Wisdom and Dreams of a Jewish Prince in Exile* (Hagerstown, MD: Review and Herald, 2000), 122, Stephen N. Haskell, *The Story of Daniel the Prophet* (Brushton, NY: Teach Services, 1999), 104–106, Dave Hunt, *A Woman Rides the Beast* (Eugene, OR: Harvest House, 1994), 40–41, C. Mervyn Maxwell, *God Cares*, 2 vols. (Boise, ID: Pacific Press, 1981), 1:155–159, Gerhard Pfandl, *Daniel: The Seer of Babylon* (Hagerstown, MD: Review and Herald, 2002), 77–79, *Seventh-day Adventist Bible Commentary*, 12 vols. (Hagerstown, MD: Review and Herald, 1957–2000), 4:840, and Uriah Smith, *Daniel and the Revelation* (Nashville, TN: Southern, 1944), 149–151.

66 See George Willis Botsford and Charles Alexander Robinson, Jr., *Hellenic History* (New York: MacMillan Company, 1950), 115–116, and Charles Freeman, *Egypt, Greece, and Rome: Civilizations of the Ancient Mediterranean* (Oxford: Oxford University Press, 1996), 73–75.

67 See Edwin Thiele, *The Mysterious Numbers of the Hebrew Kings* (Grand Rapids, MI: Kregel Publications, 1983), 227–228. God names Cyrus as the deliverer of Israel from Babylonian captivity (see Isaiah 44:27–45:1).

Behold, an he goat came from the west on the face of the whole earth, and touched not the ground: and the goat had a notable horn between his eyes. And he came to the ram that had two horns, which I had seen standing before the river, and ran unto him in the fury of his power. Next, Daniel describes the rise of a "he goat," or male goat, that would come "from the west" to conquer the "whole earth," i.e., a vast territory. This male goat would have a "notable horn," a powerful king, who would destroy the ram "in the fury of his power." We know from the record of history that the Greek Empire, under the leadership of Alexander the Great, would be the actual power to conquer Media-Persia. Thus, this male goat would symbolize Greece, and the "notable horn" would symbolize Alexander (356–323 B.C.). He would come from the "west" of Judeo-Palestine, i.e., Greece and Macedonia, to conquer Media-Persia (331 B.C.) and press eastward to control "the whole earth."

In confirmation, the angel would later reveal to Daniel that the "rough goat is the king of Grecia: and the great horn that is between his eyes is the first king" (Daniel 8:21). After routing the Media-Persian Empire through his victory at Gaugamela near Arbela (331 B.C.), Alexander's Greco-Macedonian Empire would endure through the reign of the Hellenistic kingdoms that formed after his death in 323 B.C., until its eventual domination by pagan Rome (168 B.C.).[68]

Therefore the he goat waxed very great: and when he was strong, the great horn was broken; and for it came up four notable ones toward the four winds of heaven. After the death of Alexander the Great (323 B.C.), the Greco-Macedonian empire would be divided into four distinct kingdoms, symbolized by the "four notable horns." These "four notable" horns would parallel the "four heads" of the "leopard" beast of Daniel 7 (Daniel 7:6). The angel would later confirm this future four-fold division, stating that, after Alexander was "broken," "four kingdoms" would "stand up out of the nation, but not in his power" (Daniel 8:22). To review, these four kingdoms would actually stabilize after the Battle of Ipsus (301 B.C.), and each specific kingdom would be controlled by a former general of Alexander: (1) Greece and Macedonia would be ruled by Cassander, (2) Thrace and Asia Minor would be ruled by Lysimachus, (3) Egypt and Palestine would be ruled by Ptolemy, and (4) Syria and the Eastern Territories would be

---

68 See the following sources that discuss the various aspects of the Greco-Macedonian defeat of the Media-Persian Empire in 331 B.C. under Alexander the Great: Botsford and Robinson, 298–341, Doukhan, *Daniel*, 123, Freeman, 257–272, Haskell, *Daniel the Prophet*, 104–109, Hunt, 40–41, Maxwell, 1:155–159, Pfandl, 77–79, Smith, 151–155, and Thiele, 227–228.

He lived only 33 yrs.

When Alexander was only 25 yrs. old

ruled by Seleucus.[69] After the Battle of Corupedium (281 B.C.), these four kingdoms would be reduced to three dynasties—Antigonid Greco-Macedonia, Seleucid Syria, and Ptolemaic Egypt. As mentioned earlier, the Greco-Macedonian kingdom would continue until its eventual demise and subjugation by the rising power of pagan Rome after the Battle of Pydna (168 B.C.).[70]

> And out of one of them came forth a little horn, which waxed exceeding great, toward the south, and toward the east, and toward the pleasant land. And it waxed great, even to the host of heaven; and it cast down some of the host and of the stars to the ground, and stamped upon them. (Daniel 8:9–10)

Out of one of them came forth a little horn, which waxed exceeding great, toward the south, and toward the east, and toward the pleasant land. And it waxed great, even to the host of heaven. While viewing the "four horns," Daniel saw a "little horn" emerge from one of the "four horns" that would "wax exceeding great." Simply put, another power would arise out of the four-fold division of Alexander's former empire and grow to be very powerful. Some Bible scholars and theologians have identified this "little horn" as Antiochus IV Epiphanes, a Seleucid-Syrian king who reigned from 175 to 163 B.C. This position is supposedly justified because Antiochus IV arose "out of" one of the "four horns," namely Seleucid-Syria, and had conquered Judeo-Palestine, plundering Jerusalem in the process (168–167 B.C.), thus having a direct effect on the people of God in that particular time in history.

Even so, a closer inspection of this passage dictates that we must reject this view for two main reasons. First, Daniel 8 is a repetition and expansion of the prophetic chronology we have already established from Daniel 2 and Daniel 7, and neither chapter includes Antiochus IV in this chronology. Second, while Media-Persia would wax "great" (verse 4) and Greece "very great" (verse 8), this "little horn" would wax "exceeding great" (verse 9),

---

69 See Edwyn R. Bevan, *The House of Seleucus: A History of the Hellenistic Near East under the Seleucid Dynasty*, 2 vols. (Chicago: Ares Publishers, 1985), 1:58–59, 61, Botsford and Robinson, 374, 381, Doukhan, *Daniel*, 123, Haskell, *Daniel the Prophet*, 104–109, Maxwell, 1:155–159, Pfandl, 77–79, *SDA Bible Commentary*, 4:824–825, 840–841, Smith, 151–155, and F.W. Walbank, *The Hellenistic World* (Cambridge, MA: Harvard, 1986), 46–47.

70 See Botsford and Robinson, 451–455, Freeman, 326–329, and Michael Grant, *History of Rome* (New York: Book-of-the Month Club, 1997), 138–140.

meaning that it would become more powerful than its Media-Persian and Greek predecessors. History will certainly testify to the fact that Antiochus IV did not exceed the power and greatness of either empire.

Therefore, this "little horn" would have to be a power that would come after the division of Alexander's empire and exceed the greatness of both Media-Persia and Greece. Consistent with the chronology of Daniel 2 and Daniel 7, we have to conclude that this "little horn" must be a symbol of Rome.[71] Rome would certainly exceed the greatness of Media-Persia and Greece, expanding toward the "south" (Egypt), the "east" (Greco-Macedonia), and toward the "pleasant land" (Syria, Judeo-Palestine), thus bringing each of the three remaining Hellenistic kingdoms of Alexander's former empire under its control.

Some commentators have rejected Rome as the "little horn" because it was an entirely different kingdom, i.e., it was not originally one of Alexander's four kingdoms. Yet, a proper understanding of what I will call the "replacement principle" will clearly prove how Rome did in fact arise "out of" one of these four kingdoms in a symbolic sense. When Greco-Macedonia became the first Hellenistic kingdom to fall under its power (168 B.C.), Rome then in a sense "replaced" Greco-Macedonia as one of the four kingdoms. This "replacement" principle will be discussed again when we examine the "king of the north" in Daniel 11.[72]

Next, we must also understand Alexander's policy of Hellenism, i.e., the practice of inculcating Greek culture into the conquered territories of his empire. Because Hellenism was such a powerful cultural force, it would eventually gain tremendous popularity among the sophisticated societies of the ancient Mediterranean world. The success and popularity of Hellenism stemmed from the fact that it was open to what other cultures had to offer. It would avoid the appearance of eradicating the cultural uniqueness of a conquered region by adopting its best cultural attributes, thus forming one synthesized "super-culture." And, as Rome would eventually conquer Greece, it would "Latinize" Greek Hellenism into "paganism." Thus, "paganism" would essentially consist of a "Latinized" version of Greek Hellenism, and, as the backbone of Roman society, it would later have a tremendous influence on papal Roman theology. This is why the "little horn" would symbolize Rome in both its "pagan" and "papal"

---

71 See Paul A. Gordon, *The Sanctuary, 1844, and the Pioneers* (Nampa, ID: Pacific Press, 2000), 107–111.

72 See pages 115–116, 153, 171 for a discussion of the "replacement principle" and the "king of the north."

phases.[73] We should observe that Greek, in addition to Latin, would also become a dominant language in the Roman Empire. Therefore, as Rome would "replace" Greece by both conquest and the "Latinization" of Greek Hellenism, it would "become" one of the "four horns."

And it waxed great, even to the host of heaven; and it cast down some of the host and of the stars to the ground, and stamped upon them. Rome would "wax great" as the most dominant empire the world had ever seen up to that point in history. The deified Roman Caesars and exalted Roman pontiffs were worshipped as "gods," waxing great, "even to the host of heaven." Both paganism and papalism were also vehement persecutors of Christians, casting "some of the host" and the "stars to the ground." Paganism would especially view Christianity as a growing threat to the stability of the empire. By the first century A.D., Christianity had gained recognition as a powerful spiritual force to be contended with, and would awaken the wrath of several pagan Roman emperors. Later, after his victory at the Milvian Bridge (A.D. 312), won allegedly through the help of Christ, Constantine the Great would nominally convert to Christianity and later take part in the enactment of the famous Edict of Milan (A.D. 313), which would grant religious freedom and toleration to Christians, thus paving the way for Christianity to eventually become the state religion of the Roman Empire.[74]

> Yea, he magnified himself even to the prince of the host, and by him the daily sacrifice was taken away, and the place of his sanctuary was cast down. And an host was given him against the daily sacrifice by reason of transgression, and it cast down the truth to the ground; and it practiced, and prospered. (Daniel 8:11–12)

Yea, he magnified himself even to the prince of the host. This sub-passage states that the "little horn" power would "magnify" itself by claiming to be equal to Christ, the "prince of the host." Because this "little horn" symbolizes a combination of both pagan and papal Rome, its "magnification"

---

73 See Doukhan, *Daniel*, 123–125, Haskell, *Daniel the Prophet*, 109–117, Maxwell, 1:159–194, Pfandl, 77–84, *SDA Bible Commentary*, 4:840–843, and Smith, 155–162.

74 See Freeman, 481–483, 499–500, Grant, *History of Rome*, 409–410, Haskell, *Daniel*, 224–227, and Alonzo T. Jones, *The Two Republics* (Ithaca, MI: A.B. Publishing, n.d.), 180–182, 246–252. Concerning the destruction of paganism, see Edward Gibbon, *The Decline and Fall of the Roman Empire*, 6 vols. (New York: Everyman's Library, 1993), 3:137–169.

to the level of God would refer to the blasphemous deification of the pagan Caesars and Roman pontiffs, who both demanded the worship and homage of their subjects, thus clearly exalting themselves to the level of God.

And by him the daily sacrifice was taken away, and the place of his sanctuary was cast down. This "little horn" power would also take away the "daily" and cast down the "place" of "his sanctuary." Interestingly, a majority of Seventh-day Adventist pioneers associated the concept of the "daily" with pagan Rome.[75] They had compared this passage with 2 Thessalonians 2:7, which states that "the mystery of iniquity doth already work: only he who now letteth will let, until he be taken out of the way." From this passage they had concluded that the current power in Paul's day, i.e., pagan Rome, was preventing the appearance of the "mystery of iniquity," i.e., the papacy. Yet, when paganism would collapse, i.e., be "taken out of the way," papal Rome would then appear as the next power in historical sequence.

Simply put, the Adventist pioneers concluded that the phrases "taken away" (Daniel 8:11) and "taken out of the way" (2 Thessalonians 2:7) were parallel passages, thus equating the "daily" with paganism. And, although she stated that her writings did not support any particular conclusion as to the identification of the "daily," citing that we shouldn't get into controversy over this issue,[76] Ellen White did infer that our pioneers were led by God in drawing this particular conclusion:

> Then I saw in relation to the 'daily' (Daniel 8:12) that the word 'sacrifice' was supplied by man's wisdom, and does not belong to the text, and that the Lord gave the correct view of it to those who gave the judgment hour cry. When union existed, before 1844, nearly all were united on the correct view of the 'daily'; but in the confusion since 1844, other views have been embraced, and darkness and confusion have followed.[77]

Therefore, an understanding of Adventist history will clearly demonstrate that a majority of Adventist pioneers equated the "daily" with paganism.[78] They also concluded that the "sanctuary" of Daniel 8:11 would

---

75 See Gordon, 111–114.

76 Ellen G. White, *Selected Messages from the Writings of Ellen G. White*, 3 vols. (Hagerstown, MD: Review and Herald, 1980, 1986), 1:164–168.

77 Ellen G. White, *Early Writings* (Hagerstown, MD: Review and Herald, 1945), 74–75.

78 See R.W. Schwarz, *Light Bearers to the Remnant* (Boise, ID: Pacific Press, 1979), 397–398. This source discusses the particular Adventist pioneers who

refer to the "political sanctuary" of the city of Rome, where the "seat" of paganism had been located before its collapse. And, after papal Rome had allegedly caused the demise of paganism, thus "casting down" the "political sanctuary" of its predecessor, it would also locate its "seat," i.e., its own "political sanctuary," in the city of Rome as well. Therefore, the papacy would "replace" paganism by assuming the same location (Rome) and the same religio-political authority that its pagan predecessor had possessed in its time of existence.[79]

As the papacy would occupy the position of the deified pagan emperors, this power would elevate itself to the level of intercessor for mankind. The pagan Caesars and Roman pontiffs had both demanded worship; yet, the papacy especially has claimed to assume the role of man's intercessor before God. This blasphemous claim later led to the spiritual usurpation of Christ's intercessory ministry in the heavenly sanctuary. This power would also corrupt the "spiritual sanctuary" of God's church through persecution and the inculcation of apostate doctrines,[80] with the specific intention of directing Christians to the pope for worship, and away from Christ, our Great High Priest.

And an host was given him against the daily sacrifice by reason of transgression, and it cast down the truth to the ground; and it practised, and prospered. This passage indicates that the "little horn" in both its pagan and papal phases would be successful in casting the truth of God's Word to the ground and gaining control of the conscience of its Christian subjects through persecution and the promotion of false doctrines. As a result, this power would "cast down the truth to the ground," and "prosper" in its desire to be equal with Christ, the "prince of the host."

---

equated the "daily" with paganism.

79 Smith, 159–162. We should also understand that while the papacy would occupy the position that paganism once had, thus in a sense "removing" paganism, it did not totally destroy paganism. Because of the rise of Christianity, paganism would cease to exist as both an independent non-Christian religion and the state religion of the Roman Empire; yet, in order to convert the former pagans to Christianity, Catholicism did in fact incorporate many former pagan practices, which in turn did more to preserve paganism than cause its destruction. In essence, Roman Catholicism is perpetuation and absorption of paganism, but within a Christian context.

80 See 1 Corinthians 3:16–17, 2 Corinthians 6:16, Ephesians 2:18–22, and Revelation 3:12 that equate the church with a "sanctuary."

Then I heard one saint speaking, and another saint said unto that certain saint which spake, How long shall be the vision concerning the daily sacrifice, and the transgression of desolation, to give both the sanctuary and the host to be trodden under foot? And he said unto me, Unto two thousand and three hundred days; then shall the sanctuary be cleansed. (Daniel 8:13–14)

How long shall be the vision concerning the daily sacrifice, and the transgression of desolation, to give both the sanctuary and the host to be trodden under foot? And he said unto me, Unto two thousand and three hundred days; then shall the sanctuary be cleansed. As Daniel pondered the blasphemy of this "little horn" power, he heard a question concerning how long God would allow this power to "trodden" the "sanctuary" and the "host" underfoot through persecution, false doctrine, and the usurpation of Christ's intercessory ministry in the heavenly sanctuary. It is stated that 2,300 prophetic "days" ("evenings" and "mornings") would transpire, and then the "sanctuary" would be "cleansed." In other words, 2,300 literal years would pass,[81] and then God would "cleanse" the "sanctuary."

Now, at the end of chapter 8, Daniel was told that this "vision of the evening and the morning which was told is true: wherefore shut thou up the vision; for it shall be for many days" (Daniel 8:26). He was actually looking forward to Israel's release from Babylon after a 70-year period of captivity prophesied by the prophet Jeremiah,[82] and no doubt equated the "cleansing" of the "sanctuary" with the restoration of ancient Israel and the rebuilding of the earthly sanctuary in Jerusalem that had been destroyed during the invasion of Nebuchadnezzar. Having already waited 70 years for Israel's restoration, Daniel must have been quite discouraged to think that Israel would have to wait an additional 2,300 years for the "sanctuary" to be "cleansed."

Yet, a closer examination of this 2,300-year prophecy will reveal that God was referring to something quite different from Daniel's perspective of rebuilding the earthly sanctuary in Jerusalem. We have already demonstrated that the earthly "sanctuary" of the New Testament dispensation is the spiritual "sanctuary" of the Christian Church, while the literal heavenly

---

81 A "prophetic" day in Bible prophecy translates into a literal year of actual time. See Ezekiel 4:6 and Numbers 14:34.

82 See both Daniel 9:1–2 and Jeremiah 25:12.

"sanctuary" is where our Great High Priest is performing His intercessory ministry in behalf of mankind.[83]

Given these principles, we must conclude that the context of Daniel 8:13–14 is in specific reference to papal Rome's domination of the earthly "sanctuary" of the Christian Church and its usurpation of the heavenly "sanctuary" as the place of Christ's intercessory ministry. Therefore, after 2,300 years would transpire and conclude, both the earthly "sanctuary" of the Christian Church and the heavenly "sanctuary" where Christ is interceding would be "cleansed."

Now, as we consider what it means for the "sanctuary" to be "cleansed," we should observe that all of the prophetic symbols used in Daniel 8 were part of the Old Testament earthly sanctuary services (ram, goat, horns). We can glean some insight from the model of the Old Testament earthly sanctuary and its services as we seek to understand the meaning of the "cleansing of the sanctuary." This sanctuary was actually "cleansed" on the last day of the Hebrew year through a service called the Day of Atonement (Leviticus 16:1–33). In this particular service, the high priest alone would offer the respective sacrifices that would result in the "blotting out" of Israel's sins from the sanctuary for that particular year. This solemn service was viewed by ancient Israel as time of deep heart-searching; they considered this specific day to be a day of judgment.

In the sacred service that was connected with the "Day of Atonement," the high priest would go alone into the most holy place of the sanctuary and perform an atoning work that would result in "cleansing" both the earthly sanctuary and the people of Israel from all their sins for the past year. In other words, Israel as a spiritual church and the actual sanctuary itself were both "cleansed" from sin. Now, these services in the earthly sanctuary of the Old Testament were actually "types" and "shadows" that would provide a vivid illustration of the High Priestly ministry of Christ in the heavenly sanctuary (Hebrews 8:1–5, 9:1–7). As our Intercessor in this celestial sanctuary in heaven, Christ would seek to "cleanse" His church through the "blotting out" of their sins from both their hearts and the books of record (Hebrews 9:11–14) in a solemn time of judgment that would transpire before His return to earth.

Overall, Daniel 8:14 conveys primarily that 2,300 literal years would transpire, and then Christ would begin a period of judgment

---

83   See 2 Corinthians 6:14–18, Ephesians 2:19–22, 1 Corinthians 3:16–17, 6:19–20, and Revelation 3:12–13. See also the following verses that demonstrate the sanctuary of God in heaven: Hebrews 8:1–2, 9:22–28, Revelation 11:19, and 15:5–8.

that would take place in the most holy place of the heavenly sanctuary (Revelation 11:15–19). In this time of judgment, which would conclude before His second advent (Hebrews 9:22–28), He will "cleanse" the heavenly sanctuary through the removal, or "blotting out" of the sins recorded in the record books (Acts 3:19–21), while also "cleansing" the earthly sanctuary of His church by removing sin from the lives of His true followers who live as overcomers through His blood (Revelation 3:5, 12:11). This wonderful "cleansing" truth that God has clearly presented in the Bible has been given in order to inspire hope, confidence, and assurance that Christ ever lives to make intercession for His church (Hebrews 7:25). This is a concept that the Roman Catholic Church has gone to great lengths to obscure in its work to usurp the authority of Christ.

We will now address the actual time element of 2,300 years. We will need a starting point to begin this time period; but, as we examine Daniel 8, no starting point is given. Daniel had actually fainted at the end of the chapter (Daniel 8:26–27), so the angel Gabriel could not explain the time component.[84] Yet, Gabriel returns in Daniel 9 (Daniel 9:20–23) to introduce another time prophecy that will provide the necessary starting point for Daniel 8:14. In this particular time prophecy (Daniel 9:24–27), 70 prophetic weeks are actually introduced, and would be "determined," or "cut off," from the 2,300 years. This means that the first portion of the 2,300-year prophecy would consist of a period of 70 prophetic weeks; thus, the starting point of the 70-weeks' prophecy would also be the starting point for the 2,300-year prophecy.

Since we know there are seven days in a week, the 70-weeks' period translates into 490 prophetic days. And, since a prophetic day translates into a literal year of time, 490 prophetic days would equal 490 literal years of time. This 490-year period would begin with the decree to rebuild and restore Jerusalem by the Persian king Artaxerxes in 457 B.C.,[85] and would end in A.D. 34. The 2,300 years would then continue beyond A.D. 34 to the year A.D. 1844. Thus, in the year A.D. 1844, Christ would begin an investigative judgment in the heavenly sanctuary.[86]

---

84   Ellen G. White, *Prophets and Kings* (Nampa, ID: Pacific Press, 1943), 554.

85   See Ezra 6:14, 7:11–25 for details on the decree of Artaxerxes. It is quite interesting that this third decree by Artaxerxes is the only decree detailed in the Bible.

86   See Acts 3:19–21, Hebrews 9:22–28, and Revelation 22:11–12 for biblical evidence that Jesus will conduct and conclude the judgment before He returns. For some excellent sources concerning the earthly sanctuary, the heavenly sanctuary, and the investigative judgment of the year A.D. 1844: Clifford

We should now relate the "cleansing of the sanctuary" to the reign of the "little horn" power. We have already established that "little horn" power has corrupted God's earthly, spiritual sanctuary, the Church, with both persecution and false doctrine, while at the same time usurping Christ's ministry in the heavenly sanctuary. Thus, the "cleansing of the sanctuary" would involve more than just the removal of sin from both the church and heaven's judgment books; the year A.D. 1844 would also usher in a type of "doctrinal cleansing" for God's church from the false doctrines of papal Rome (which incidentally came from paganism); this would take place through the emergence of God's final prophetic movement, the Seventh-day Adventist Church, which would have a pure doctrinal foundation and proclaim a judgment-hour message to the world that would relate an accurate understanding of the cleansing of the sanctuary found in Daniel 8:14. Even though Christ has always ministered in heaven's sanctuary in behalf of mankind, this final prophetic movement would proclaim the "Sanctuary Message" as a unique teaching that would return Christ to His rightful position, thus redirecting the minds of His people back to His intercession in heaven's sanctuary, while at the same time calling people out of the false system of papal Roman Catholicism (Revelation 14:8, 18:1–4).

Therefore, when the significance of Daniel 8:14 and the year A.D. 1844 were discovered by the Seventh-day Adventist pioneers, the so-called "removal" of Rome's false doctrines took place, as these humble, God-fearing people, led by the guidance of the Holy Spirit, hammered out the doctrinal truths of the Bible that comprise the Adventist message.[87] Through the emergence of these doctrinal truths, the false doctrines of papal Rome were exposed, thus providing a type of "doctrinal cleansing" for God's spiritual church on earth. This "cleansing" would help to direct the minds of the people to the heavenly sanctuary above where Christ would

Goldstein, *1844 Made Simple* (Nampa, ID: Pacific Press, 1988), Steven N. Haskell, *The Cross and Its Shadow* (Brushton, NY: Teach Services, 2002), 173–197, 209–238, and Ellen G. White, *The Great Controversy* (Mountain View, CA: Pacific Press, 1950), 409–432, 479–491. See pages 180–183 for a thorough explanation of Daniel 9:24–27.

87 See White, *Great Controversy*, 409–410, J.N. Loughborough, *The Great Second Advent Movement* (Pacific Press, Adventist Pioneer Library, 1992), Francis D. Nichol, *The Midnight Cry* (Brushton, NY: Teach Services, 2000), P. Gerard Damsteegt, *Foundations of the Seventh-day Adventist Message and Mission* (Berrien Springs, MI: Andrews University Press, 1995), and George R. Knight, *Millennial Fever and the End of the World* (Boise, ID: Pacific Press, 1993).

be serving as the Savior and Intercessor for mankind in a solemn time of investigative judgment.[88]

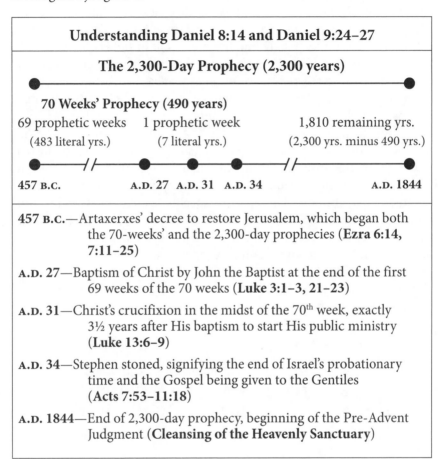

Understanding Daniel 8:14 and Daniel 9:24–27

The 2,300-Day Prophecy (2,300 years)

70 Weeks' Prophecy (490 years)

69 prophetic weeks	1 prophetic week	1,810 remaining yrs.
(483 literal yrs.)	(7 literal yrs.)	(2,300 yrs. minus 490 yrs.)

457 B.C.	A.D. 27 A.D. 31 A.D. 34	A.D. 1844

457 B.C.—Artaxerxes' decree to restore Jerusalem, which began both the 70-weeks' and the 2,300-day prophecies (**Ezra 6:14, 7:11–25**)

A.D. 27—Baptism of Christ by John the Baptist at the end of the first 69 weeks of the 70 weeks (**Luke 3:1–3, 21–23**)

A.D. 31—Christ's crucifixion in the midst of the 70th week, exactly 3½ years after His baptism to start His public ministry (**Luke 13:6–9**)

A.D. 34—Stephen stoned, signifying the end of Israel's probationary time and the Gospel being given to the Gentiles (**Acts 7:53–11:18**)

A.D. 1844—End of 2,300-day prophecy, beginning of the Pre-Advent Judgment (**Cleansing of the Heavenly Sanctuary**)

It should be mentioned that even before the year A.D. 1844 many non-Adventist Protestant reformers had also advocated that papal Rome could never be the intercessor for mankind, and that Christ alone is man's only true mediator (1 Timothy 2:5–6). Furthermore, even though no one Protestant church had possessed a completely pure doctrinal package, many Protestant churches did have several isolated pure biblical doctrines in their belief systems.

---

88   See Doukhan, *Daniel*, 126–156, Goldstein, 1–96, Haskell, *Daniel the Prophet*, 111–153, Haskell, *Cross and Its Shadow*, 187–197, Maxwell, 1:155–265, Pfandl, 75–102, Smith, 162–223, and White, *Great Controversy*, 391–432, 479–491.

Even so, through the emergence of the Seventh-day Adventist Church, God would allow the complete package of doctrinal truth to emerge in one single movement, and, at the very heart of this package would be the beautiful truth of the sanctuary doctrine from Daniel 8:14.[89] This truth would especially focus on the vitally important concept of the High Priestly, intercessory ministry of Christ in the heavenly sanctuary, thus restoring our Lord and Savior to His rightful position as man's only true Mediator, and, in one sense, "ending" the blasphemous claim by papal Rome that it would supposedly hold the position of man's intercessor before God.

Through the rise of the Seventh-day Adventist movement, God has produced a doctrinally pure "sanctuary," so to speak, here on earth that is completely free from any of the doctrinal pollutions of the "little horn" power, thus striking a serious blow to the deceptive teachings that are advocated by papal Rome. Through this specific "sanctuary," God has provided a "cleansed" faith that truly has not been witnessed since apostolic times.[90] Those who desire to abandon the false doctrines of papal Rome and make their stand with this final prophetic movement will in fact receive a type of spiritual "cleansing." Overall, we have demonstrated that Daniel 8 clearly expands on both Daniel 2 and Daniel 7 in its repetition of the same basic chronology:

Daniel 2	Daniel 7	Daniel 8	Interpretation
Gold	Lion	*N/A*	Babylon, 605 B.C.
Silver	Bear	Ram	Media-Persia, 539 B.C.
Brass	Leopard	He-Goat	Greece, 331 B.C.
N/A	4 heads	4 Horns	4 Kingdoms, 301 B.C.
Iron	4th Beast	Little Horn	Pagan Rome, 168 B.C.
10 Toes	10 Horns	*N/A*	Europe, A.D. 476
Iron/Clay	Little Horn	Little Horn	Papacy, 538–1798
N/A	Judgment	Sanctuary	Judgment, 1844
Stone	Kingdom	Kingdom	Second Advent, Eternity

89 White, *Great Controversy*, 409–410.

90 For an excellent synopsis on the doctrinal infrastructure of the Seventh-day Adventist Church, see *Seventh-day Adventists Believe: A Biblical Exposition of 27 Fundamental Doctrines* (Hagerstown, MD: Review and Herald, 1988). While it is not an infallible "creed," this source also summarizes the biblical evidence for Adventist doctrinal beliefs.

── FIVE ──

A Review of Revelation 13
"The Sea Beast and the Earth Beast"

Having established a basic prophetic chronology from chapters 2, 7, and 8 of Daniel, it will now prove quite useful to establish a basic understanding of Revelation 13. An understanding of this specific chapter will be a tremendous help in our quest to establish a chronology of Daniel 11. John's specific vision of Revelation 13 reveals some very important details that will especially complement the vision of Daniel 7. While Daniel saw the rise of "four great beasts" (Daniel 7:2–3), John would see the rise of a single composite "beast" that would parallel Daniel's fourth, non-descript beast (Daniel 7:7); yet, this composite "beast" would be made up of different body parts from the first three beasts (Daniel 7:4–6).

> And I stood upon the sand of the sea, and saw a beast rise up out of the sea, having seven heads and ten horns, and upon his horns ten crowns, and upon his heads the name of blasphemy. (Revelation 13:1)

And I stood upon the sand of the sea, and saw a beast rise up out of the sea. We have already established that "beasts" in Bible prophecy symbolize kings and kingdoms (Daniel 7:17, 23), while "seas," which can also be referred to as "waters," symbolize both the nations of the world and highly populated areas (Revelation 17:15). As a parallel to the fourth, non-descript beast found in Daniel 7 (Daniel 7:17–20), we will see that this "beast," or "kingdom," that emerges from the nations of the earth in the midst of a highly populated area is an actual description of the papal Roman Empire.[91]

---

91 See Jacques B. Doukhan, *Secrets of Revelation: The Apocalypse through Hebrew Eyes* (Hagerstown, MD: Review and Herald, 2002), 114–116, Stephen N. Haskell, *The Story of the Seer of Patmos* (Brushton, NY: Teach Services, 2004), 224–234, C. Mervyn Maxwell, *God Cares*, 2 vols. (Nampa, ID: Pacific

Having seven heads. This "beast" is first described as having "seven heads." Now, in order to identify these "seven heads," we must understand that this same composite "beast" is also mentioned in Revelation 17, and, in that specific chapter, John was first told that these "seven heads" symbolize "seven mountains" (Revelation 17:9), which can also be synonymous with "hills." Interestingly, Rome itself is actually known as the "city of seven hills," which would include the Capitoline, Quirinal, Viminal, Esquiline, Caelian, Aventine, and Palatine hills.[92] Therefore, this detail referring to the "seven heads" as "seven mountains" is a clear reference to the actual city of Rome.

In a dual application, John was told that these "seven heads" also symbolize "seven kings: five are fallen, and one is, and the other is not yet come; and when he cometh, he must continue a short space" (Revelation 17:10). Thus, in addition to symbolizing the seven-hilled city of Rome, these "seven heads" also symbolize "seven kings." As we consider what "kingdoms" these "seven heads" symbolize, we must understand that when prophets receive visions from God, quite often they are shown people and events in far distant times and places; yet, when the visions are explained later, the interpretation is usually given from the context of the prophet's own current day.[93]

Daniel's visions give precedent to this concept. In Daniel 2 and 7, these two visions begin their chronology with Babylon (head of gold, lion), Daniel's current kingdom (Daniel 2:1; 7:1). Daniel was living under the last king of Babylon when he received the vision of chapter 8 (Daniel 8:1), which began with Media-Persia (ram); yet, when he was given the full explanation of this vision in the ninth chapter (Daniel 9:20–27), he was living under Media-Persian rule (Daniel 9:1). Chapter 11 also begins with Media-

Press, 1985), 2:324–331, *Seventh-day Adventist Bible Commentary*, 12 vols. (Hagerstown, MD: Review and Herald, 1955–2000), 7:816–819, Uriah Smith, *Daniel and the Revelation* (Nashville, TN: Southern, 1949), 561–571, and Ellen G. White, *The Great Controversy* (Mountain View, CA: Pacific Press, 1950), 439.

92 "Rome (Italy)," *Microsoft® Encarta® Encyclopedia 2000*. © 1993–1999 Microsoft Corporation. All Rights Reserved. See also *SDA Bible Commentary*, 7:855. See the following passages that use "mountains" and "hills" synonymously: Proverbs 8:25, Song of Solomon 2:8, Isaiah 40:12, 42:15, 54:10, 55:12, 65:7, Jeremiah 4:24, Ezekiel 6:3, Hosea 4:13, 10:8, Micah 4:1, and Luke 23:30. This list is not exhaustive.

93 Jon Paulien, "The Hermeneutics of Biblical Apocalyptic," unpublished paper, 2004, 25. See Daniel 7:17, 23 for a passage that uses "kings" and "kingdoms" synonymously.

Persia because Daniel was well into Media-Persian rule at that point in time (Daniel 11:1). Therefore, using Daniel's visions as precedents, the pivotal point in identifying these seven kingdoms would be John's current day. With this as our point of reference, we can examine both the Bible and the record of history together to determine the identity of these "seven kings."

Since pagan Rome was the actual ruling power in John's day, this specific empire would be the "one" who "is," i.e., the sixth kingdom of the seven kingdoms. Using this pivotal point, we need only go back in history to discover the identity of the five ruling empires prior to pagan Rome who had direct involvement in the history of Israel. The fifth kingdom would be Greece (331–168 B.C.), the fourth kingdom Media-Persia (539–331 B.C.), and the third kingdom Babylon (605–539 B.C.).

Concerning the second and first kings, we need only identify the empires that existed prior to ancient Babylon who had oppressed the people of God. The Bible reveals that both Assyria and Egypt had conquered and enslaved Israel,[94] and would thus constitute the first and second kings. Therefore, the first six kings would be (1) Egypt (fallen), (2) Assyria (fallen), (3) Babylon (fallen), (4) Media-Persia (fallen), (5) Greece (fallen), and (6) pagan Rome ("is," current in John's day).[95]

Now, in order to identify the seventh kingdom, we obviously need only look to the power that would emerge after pagan Rome. According to our established chronology, papal Rome would emerge next and continue a "short space" of time (Revelation 17:10). Now, at first glance, the 1,260-year reign of papal Rome (A.D. 538 to 1798) might not seem like a "short pace" of time. Yet, when we consider the time of Satan's deceptive work on earth, i.e., 2,000 years since Calvary and 6,000 years total (comparatively longer than the reign of papal Rome), we see that the Bible also refers to this period as a "short time" (Revelation 12:7–13). Therefore, a "short space," or

---

94 Again, God will only mention an empire in Bible prophecy if it has a direct effect on either Old Testament Israel or the New Testament church. The Bible demonstrates that both ancient Assyria and ancient Egypt persecuted and held captive the nation of ancient Israel. Egypt at one point held Israel in captivity for over 400 years, as Israel first began to exist as a "nation" during their bondage in ancient Egypt (see Genesis 15:13, Exodus 1:7–14, 12:40–41, Acts 7:6, Galatians 3:17); much later, the Assyrian Empire conquered and occupied ancient Egypt (671–663 B.C.), and persecuted the children of Israel (see 2 Kings 15–18, 1 Chronicles 5); Babylon would eventually conquer Assyria (612, 605 B.C.), while Egypt would be conquered by the Media-Persians (525 B.C.). See Freeman, 65–75, 586.

95 See Louis F. Were, *The Woman and the Beast* (Sarasota, FL: H.K. LaRondelle, 1993), 189–214, 221–224 and *SDA Bible Commentary*, 7:856.

"short time," doesn't necessarily mean a short amount of time as we might think, especially when we consider the entire span of redemptive history from eternity past to eternity future.[96] We can thus identify the seventh king as the papal Roman Empire.

Furthermore, the number "seven" can also symbolize both "perfection" and "completeness." In essence, these seven kingdoms are basically a "perfect" and "complete" description of all the empires in redemptive history that have oppressed and persecuted the people of God. And, because the "beast" would ultimately be "dictated by" and "synonymous with" the current "head" in power, we must conclude that when the seventh head of the papacy would appear, the "beast" in its entirety would also be the papacy; this specific power is the final spiritual conglomeration of all the prior apostate religio-political ideologies that each kingdom had espoused during its time of existence. Each successive empire would hand down bits and pieces of its apostate theology to the next empire in sequence, and the papacy would be the final culmination of this process as the seventh king and final spiritual offspring of these prior ruling powers.

And ten horns. This "beast" is also described as having "ten horns." In considering the identity of these "ten horns," we will discover that, like the "seven heads," they have a dual meaning. John was told later that the "ten horns which thou sawest are ten kings, which have received no kingdom as yet; but receive power as kings one hour with the beast. These have one mind, and shall give their power and strength unto the beast" (Revelation 17:12–13).

First, as a parallel to the "ten toes" of Daniel 2 (Daniel 2:40–44) and the "ten horns" of Daniel 7 (Daniel 7:19–24), these "ten horns" would symbolize the ten European nations that would form a divided Europe after the collapse of pagan Rome in A.D. 476. Again, using John's current day as a reference point, these ten kings would obviously still be future to John's day and would consist of (1) the Franks (France), (2) the Alemanni (Germany), (3) the Lombards (Italy), (4) the Burgundians (Switzerland), (5) the Saxons (England), (6) the Suevi (Portugal), (7) the Visigoths (Spain), (8) the Heruli (overthrown, A.D. 493), (9) the Vandals (overthrown, A.D. 534), and (10) the Ostrogoths (overthrown, A.D. 555). This passage emphasizes that these ten kingdoms would lend their civil and military power to the papacy so that it could enforce its decrees and control the conscience of Europe during the Dark Ages (A.D. 538–1798).[97]

---

96 Ekkehardt Mueller, *The Beast of Revelation 17—A Suggestion* (Biblical Research Institute, May 2005), 8–14.

97 See Doukhan, 105–106, Haskell, 93–96, Maxwell, 1:129, Pfandl, 63, *SDA Bible*

In a second application, these "ten horns" also symbolize a future end-time global coalition of nations that will unite with the papacy. Having ruled for 1,260-years (A.D. 538–1798), papal Rome would receive a "deadly wound" (Revelation 13:3), having its power taken away by France. Napoleon Bonaparte ordered General Alexandre Berthier to invade Rome in 1798 and set up a Roman republic under French rule. When Pius VI protested, he was removed from power and died a year later in exile (A.D. 1799), thus ending the 1,260-year reign of the papacy:

> When in 1797, Pope Pius VI fell grievously ill, Napoleon gave orders that in the event of his death no successor should be elected to his office, and the Papacy should be discontinued. But the Pope recovered. The peace was soon broken: Berthier entered Rome on the tenth of February, 1798, and proclaimed a republic. The aged Pontiff refused to violate his oath by recognizing it, and was hurried from prison to prison in France. Broken with fatigue and sorrows, he died on the 17th of August, 1799, in the French fortress of Valence aged 82 years. No wonder half of Europe thought Napoleon's veto would be obeyed, and that with the Pope, the Papacy was dead.[98]

Yet, this "deadly wound" would eventually be "healed" (Revelation 13:3), meaning that the papacy would later be restored to power through the Lateran Treaty (A.D. 1929).[99] In confirmation, John was told that "the beast that was, and is not, even he is the eighth, and is of the seven, and goeth into perdition" (Revelation 17:11); in other words, a resurrected papacy would be the eighth power, having come from the seven kings, namely the seventh king specifically.

Commentary, 4:826, and Smith, 57–63, 110, 119.

98 Joseph Rickaby, "The Modern Papacy," *Lectures on the History of Religions*, Volume 3 (London: Catholic Truth Society, 1910), Lecture 24, page 1.

99 See William Barry, *The Papacy and Modern Times: A Political Sketch, 1303–1870* (New York: Henry Holt and Company, 1911), 195–196, Nicholas Cheetham, *A History of the Popes* (New York: Dorset Press, 1982), 279–280, Frank J. Coppa, *The Modern Papacy since 1789* (London: Longman, 1998), 175–176, Will Durant, *The Age of Napoleon: A History of European Civilization from 1789 to 1815* (New York: Simon and Schuster, 1975), 544, and J. Derek Holmes, *The Papacy in the Modern World: 1914–1978* (New York: Crossroad Publishing Company, 1981), 33–75.

Thus, the papacy "was" (ruled for 1,260 years), "is not" (received deadly wound in 1798), and will go "into perdition" (be healed of its deadly wound, beginning in 1929 and going into the future). And, just as the nations of Europe gave their power to the papacy during its 1,260-year reign, so will the nations of the world give their power to the papacy at the end of time. Therefore, these "ten horns" also symbolize a future global coalition that would unite with a resurrected papacy to enforce the "mark" of the beast.

In the two quotations below, Ellen White confirmed this second application by observing that, as the "iron and clay" would "mingle" together in a union of "churchcraft" and "statecraft" (Daniel 2:41–44), these ten nations will have "one mind" by giving their power and strength to the "beast" at the end of time:

> Men in authority will enact laws controlling the conscience, after the example of the papacy. ... Every nation will be involved. Of this time John the Revelator declares: [Revelation. 18:3–7; 17:13, 14, quoted]. 'These have one mind.' There will be a universal bond of union, one great harmony, a confederacy of Satan's forces. 'And [they] shall give their power and strength unto the beast.'[100]

> We have come to a time when God's sacred work is represented by the feet of the image in which the iron was mixed with the miry clay. ... The mingling of churchcraft and statecraft is represented by the iron and the clay. This union is weakening all the power of the churches. This investing the church with the power of the state will bring evil results. Men ... have invested their strength in politics, and have united with the papacy.[101]

And upon his horns ten crowns, and upon his heads the name of blasphemy. These "ten horns" are described as having "crowns," thus confirming that they are "kingdoms." Each of the "seven heads" would also have names of "blasphemy." We have already discovered that the papacy commits "blasphemy" against God, claiming to be equal with God and claiming to have the authority to forgive sins. Each of the seven kingdoms symbolized by the "seven heads" have also held the philosophy that their specific rulers were to be worshiped as "gods," whether they were the

---

100 Ellen G. White, *Selected Messages from the Writings of Ellen G. White*, 3 vols. (Hagerstown, MD: Review and Herald, 1980–1986), 3:392.

101 Ellen G. White, *Manuscript Releases*, 21 vols. (Legacy of Light, 2000), 15:39.

Pharaoh's of Egypt, the kings of Babylon, or the pagan Roman Caesars. This concept would be handed down from each kingdom and reach a culmination in the papal power.[102]

> And the beast which I saw was like unto a leopard, and his feet were as the feet of a bear, and his mouth as the mouth of a lion: and the dragon gave him his power, and his seat, and great authority. And I saw one of his heads as it were wounded to death; and his deadly wound was healed: and all the world wondered after the beast. (Revelation 13:2–3)

And the beast which I saw was like unto a leopard, and his feet were as the feet of a bear, and his mouth as the mouth of a lion. The vision of Daniel 7 had described the rise of "four great beasts," i.e., a "lion," "bear," "leopard," and a "fourth beast" (Daniel 7:2–7). Interestingly enough, John would see the rise of a single "beast" that would be composite in nature and parallel the "fourth beast" of Daniel 7 (Daniel 7:7); yet it would also consist of different body parts from the first three beasts of Daniel 7 (Daniel 7:4–6). This "beast" would have the body of a "leopard" (Greece), the feet of a "bear" (Media-Persia), and the mouth of a "lion" (Babylon). Notice also that these three "beasts" (leopard, bear, lion) are mentioned in reverse order to that of Daniel 7 (lion, bear, leopard); this is because Daniel would see the rise of these empires as future to his day, while John would see these three kingdoms as empires of the past. This observation confirms the fact that the apostle John would understand this specific vision from the context of his own current day.[103]

We should also notice that this composite beast has the "body" of a "leopard." In other words, a majority of this composite beast would be made up of the "leopard" power, i.e., the Greek Empire, which had made the largest religio-political contribution to the development of papal Rome. In our review of Daniel 8, we had established the fact that Hellenistic Greek philosophy had made a tremendous impact on the development of Roman society. Remember, Rome's "Latinized" version of Hellenistic Greek philosophy had a major influence on Roman "paganism," which in turn would later make a substantial contribution to Roman Catholic theology.[104]

---

102 See Mark 2:1–7, John 10:27–33, and pages 26–28.

103 *SDA Bible Commentary*, 7:817.

104 See pages 36–38 for an analysis of how Greek philosophy helped to form Roman society. See also Haskell, *The Seer of Patmos*, 227.

The dragon gave him his power, and his seat, and great authority. And I saw one of his heads as it were wounded to death; and his deadly wound was healed: and all the world wondered after the beast. John is told that the "dragon," i.e., Satan (Revelation 12:9, 20:2), would give this papal beast its power and authority, using it as a cloak to inculcate the world with his deceptions. As we had discussed earlier, John also sees that one of the "seven heads" would be "wounded to death" and then later be "healed." When a "kingdom" receives a "wound," it symbolizes a loss of superpower status; conversely, when its "wound" is healed, it would mean that this kingdom would experience a restoration to superpower status once again.

Now, of the seven powers described by the "seven heads" of this beast, six of these powers, namely Egypt, Assyria, Babylon, Media-Persia, Greece, and pagan Rome, would receive a "deadly wound" and never again achieve superpower status; yet, the seventh power, papal Rome, who also received a "deadly wound," would be the only power of the seven to achieve superpower status once again by having its "wound healed." This is further evidence to confirm that the seventh head would be the papacy. A partial "healing" of this "wound" would take place through the Lateran Treaty of 1929,[105] when the papacy would once again be revived from the "deadly wound" it had received in 1798. This "wound" will continue to heal until the papacy once again receives the religio-political power it had possessed in times past.[106]

> And they worshipped the dragon which gave power unto the beast: and they worshipped the beast, saying, Who is like unto the beast? who is able to make war with him? And there was given unto him a mouth speaking great things and blasphemies; and power was given unto him to continue forty and two months. And he opened his mouth in blasphemy against God, to blaspheme his name, and his tabernacle, and them that dwell in heaven. (Revelation 13:4–6)

And they worshipped the dragon which gave power unto the beast. And they worshipped the beast, saying, Who is like unto the beast? Who is able to make war with him? Since the "dragon" (Satan) is the power behind the "beast," those who worship the "beast" will essentially be worshipping Satan. It has been Satan's continual design to disguise his true identity through the use of mediums; his use of the serpent in the Garden

---

105 See Cheetham, 279–280, Coppa, 175–176, and Holmes, 33–75.
106 See Maxwell, 2:346–347, and *SDA Bible Commentary*, 7:817–818.

of Eden is a perfect example of this stealthy approach to secure worship (Genesis 3:1–6, Ezekiel 28:12–16).

Furthermore, ever since his original rebellion in heaven, Satan has desired the worship that is due alone to Christ, and he has especially used the Roman Church as a vessel to achieve his overall goal of securing global worship. Whether through flattery, force, intimidation, or compromise, Satan has empowered the papacy to suppress God's Word and wage an aggressive war against God's faithful followers who attempt to uphold the great truths of the Bible.

Overall, Satan has worked through the various empires of history to turn people away from the worship of the true God, thus securing worship for himself. In using this composite beast, Satan has synthesized all of these powers into one final religio-political system of false worship known as Roman Catholicism. This system has been designed by Satan to secure self-worship through the suppression of the Bible, persecution, deception, and the control of conscience. And, because Satan's deceptions will be quite successful at the end of time, the Bible predicts that nearly the whole world will worship the unrivaled power of the papacy.

And there was given unto him a mouth speaking great things and blasphemies; and power was given unto him to continue forty and two months. And he opened his mouth in blasphemy against God, to blaspheme his name, and his tabernacle, and them that dwell in heaven. Having already discussed "blasphemy," we will now review the concept of "forty and two months." We should remember that a biblical year consists of 360 days; thus, forty-two months would total 3½ years, or 1,260 days, a time period found a total of seven times in the Bible.[107] This forty-two-month period would equate to the period of 1,260 years (A.D. 538 to 1798), when papal Rome would reign supreme over European affairs.[108]

> And it was given unto him to make war with the saints, and to overcome them: and power was given him over all kindreds, and tongues, and nations. And all that dwell upon the earth shall worship him, whose names are not written in the book of life of the Lamb slain from the foundation of the world. (Revelation 13:7–8)

---

107 See Daniel 7:25, 12:7, Revelation 11:2–3, 12:6, 14, 13:5.

108 See Doukhan, *Secrets of Revelation*, 115, Haskell, *Seer of Patmos*, 232, Maxwell, 326–331, *SDA Bible Commentary*, 7:818, Smith, 561–571, and White, *Great Controversy*, 54, 439.

And it was given unto him to make war with the saints, and to over-come them: and power was given him over all kindreds, and tongues, and nations. And all that dwell upon the earth shall worship him, whose names are not written in the book of life of the Lamb slain from the foundation of the world. Once again, history will clearly demonstrate that the papacy, during its 1,260-year Dark Age reign (A.D. 538–1798), had a historical resume of brutal persecution. The Roman popes had ruling authority over the nations of Europe, and had gained the worship of a majority of those nations; yet, God states that those who have rendered Rome the worship it demands do not have their names written in the Lamb's Book of Life. Also, because God clearly states that we will reap what we sow (Galatians 6:7–9), papal Rome was eventually destroyed because this power itself was a destroyer. This first destruction took place in A.D. 1798, and it will receive a second and final destruction, a "second death" so-to-speak, at the second coming of Christ.

> If any man have an ear, let him hear. He that leadeth into captivity shall go into captivity: he that killeth with the sword must be killed with the sword. Here is the patience and the faith of the saints. (Revelation 13:9–10)

He that leadeth into captivity shall go into captivity: he that killeth with the sword must be killed with the sword. Because papal Rome led many people into captivity and killed many people with the sword through the Dark Age period of 1,260 years (A.D. 538–1798), this power itself would be led into captivity and be killed with the sword (Matthew 26:52). Once again, this is another direct reference to the year A.D. 1798, when papal Rome would be taken into captivity and be killed with the sword by the power of revolutionary France.[109]

> And I beheld another beast coming up out of the earth; and he had two horns like a lamb, and he spake as a dragon. And he exerciseth all the power of the first beast before him, and causeth the earth and them which dwell therein to worship the first beast, whose deadly wound was healed. (Revelation 13:11–12)

And I beheld another beast coming up out of the earth; and he had two horns like a lamb, and he spake as a dragon. Around the time of the

---

109 See Christian Edwardson, *Facts of Faith* (Nashville, TN: Southern Publishing, 1943), 57–60. See also pages 31, 171–172.

papacy's deadly wound (A.D. 1798), John was shown that another "beast," or kingdom, would arise out of the "earth." The papal beast emerged out of the "sea," i.e., the nations of the world in the highly populated area of Western Europe (Revelation 17:15); yet, this second beast would arise out of the "earth," which is essentially the opposite of the "sea"—i.e., a sparsely populated area.

This would mean that around the year A.D. 1798, a power would arise in a sparsely populated area; it would have two horns like a lamb, arising as a professed Christian nation, but then eventually speak as a dragon by becoming a world superpower. Concerning the identity of this "earth beast," there is only one nation in all of history that could fit this description—the United States. This power would: (1) arise around the year A.D. 1798, (2) arise in a sparsely populated area (the North American continent), (3) arise as a professed Christian nation with "two horns" (civil and religious liberty, i.e., republicanism and Protestantism), and (4) eventually become a world superpower ("speak as a dragon"). Thus, this "earth beast" would symbolize the United States of America.[110]

And he exerciseth all the power of the first beast before him, and causeth the earth and them which dwell therein to worship the first beast, whose deadly wound was healed. America will eventually grow to exercise all the power that the papacy had exercised in times past. Just as Rome had controlled the conscience of Europe through intimidation and persecution, so will America also eventually grow to exercise the control of conscience on a global sphere through intimidation and persecution. As our great nation continues to strengthen its religio-political ties to Rome with the passing of time, there will come a day in the near future when the entire world will be forced to worship the papacy through the influence of the United States.

> And he doeth great wonders, so that he maketh fire come down from heaven on the earth in the sight of men, And deceiveth them that dwell on the earth by the means of those miracles which he had power to do in the sight of the beast; saying to them that dwell on the earth, that they should make an image to the beast, which had the wound by a sword, and did live. (Revelation 13:13–14)

---

110 See Doukhan, *Secrets of Revelation*, 116–120, Edwardson, 234–242, Haskell, *The Seer of Patmos*, 234–244, Maxwell, 2:340–349, *SDA Bible Commentary*, 819–820, Smith, 571–584, and White, *Great Controversy*, 439–442.

And he doeth great wonders, so that he maketh fire come down from heaven on the earth in the sight of men. This "earth beast" would make "fire come down from heaven on the earth in the sight of men;" as we consider this phrase, we will discover that it can actually represent three different concepts: (1) a counterfeit, spiritualistic religious revival that will take place within the leading churches of Protestant America;[111] (2) a series of counterfeit miracles that are perceived to be of divine origin, but are in reality perpetrated by Satan, which will ultimately deceive the world into receiving the mark of the beast;[112] and (3) a series of natural disasters that will threaten the economic stability of the United States,[113] and be seen by the Protestant majority in America as God's displeasure against prevailing infidelity and sin, thus providing the spiritual impetus to appeal to the American government for legislative religious reform.

And deceiveth them that dwell on the earth by the means of those miracles which he had power to do in the sight of the beast; saying to them that dwell on the earth, that they should make an image to the beast, which had the wound by a sword, and did live. John sees that the satanic power of a false religious revival, coupled with counterfeit miracles and natural disasters, will eventually move the Protestant majority within the United States to lead out in a global agenda to erect an "image" to the papacy. Since papal Rome has used the civil power to enforce religion in times past, Protestant America will follow in these very same footsteps by

---

111 Smith, 584–590. See also White, *Great Controversy*, 588.

112 See 2 Thessalonians 2:3–9. Yet, there will also be true miracles taking place during the Latter Rain of the Holy Spirit. See both Joel 2:28–32 and White, *Great Controversy*, 611–612.

113 See Genesis 19:23–29, Job 1:16, and Luke 9:54–56. See also the following quotation: "Satan works through the elements also to garner his harvest of unprepared souls. He has studied the secrets of the laboratories of nature, and he uses all his power to control the elements as far as God allows. When he was suffered to afflict Job, how quickly flocks and herds, servants, houses, children, were swept away, one trouble succeeding another as in a moment. It is God that shields His creatures and hedges them in from the power of the destroyer. But the Christian world have shown contempt for the law of Jehovah; and the Lord will do just what He has declared that He would—He will withdraw His blessings from the earth and remove His protecting care from those who are rebelling against His law and teaching and forcing others to do the same. Satan has control of all whom God does not especially guard. He will favor and prosper some in order to further his own designs, and he will bring trouble upon others and lead men to believe that it is God who is afflicting them" (See White, *Great Controversy*, 589).

also appealing to the civil power of the United States in order to enforce religious laws that will mandate the worship of the papacy. An "image" is the likeness of an original, and because it will use the civil power to enforce religion, Protestant America will become the "image" to the papacy. The development of this "image to the beast" will inevitably result in religious intolerance, control of conscience, and the eventual persecution of all non-compliant people around the world.[114]

> And he had power to give life unto the image of the beast, that the image of the beast should both speak, and cause that as many as would not worship the image of the beast should be killed. And he causeth all, both small and great, rich and poor, free and bond, to receive a mark in their right hand, or in their foreheads: And that no man might buy or sell, save he that had the mark, or the name of the beast, or the number of his name. (Revelation 13:15–17)

And he had power to give life unto the image of the beast, that the image of the beast should both speak, and cause that as many as would not worship the image of the beast should be killed. John was shown that the United States would give "life" to this "image to the beast" by "speaking" in its behalf. A nation "speaks" through its legislative apparatus and a combination of its civil and military power. As America enacts religious legislation through the influence of the Protestant majority, it will "speak" by enforcing this legislation through the exercise of its civil and military power against all those who are non-compliant. Eventually, those who refuse to submit to the authority of the state will be deemed worthy of death.

We find an excellent biblical parallel of religious intolerance with the example of Shadrach, Meshach, and Abednego, who faced legislated image-worship on the plain of Dura in ancient Babylon. When these three Hebrew boys refused to worship King Nebuchadnezzar's image, some accusing Chaldeans cried out, "Thou, O king, hast made a decree, that every man ... shall fall down and worship the golden image: And whoso falleth not down and worshippeth, that he should be cast into the midst of a burning fiery furnace" (Daniel 3:10–11).

In other words, King Nebuchadnezzar had erected a golden image on the plain of Dura; he then passed a decree, or law, that required those

---

114 Doukhan, *Secrets of Revelation*, 116–120, Edwardson, 234–272, Haskell, *The Seer of Patmos*, 240, Maxwell, 2:343–349, *SDA Bible Commentary*, 819–822, Smith, 590–603, and White, *Great Controversy*, 441–450.

present to worship this image. This "image" therefore involved the enforcement of religious worship through a legislative decree. Again, as the papacy used the legislative and military power base of the nations of Europe to enforce her doctrines on the masses in times past, so will Protestant America appeal to the legislative and military power base of the United States government to enforce worship. In short, America will seek to control conscience by passing laws that will mandate the worship of the papacy; these laws will then be enforced through the use of civil and military power, thus providing the necessary force of arms needed to bring total compliance on both a national and global scale.

And he causeth all, both small and great, rich and poor, free and bond, to receive a mark in their right hand, or in their foreheads: And that no man might buy or sell, save he that had the mark, or the name of the beast, or the number of his name. The United States will force the entire world to receive a "mark" in the "right hand" or "forehead," and without this "mark," buying and selling will be impossible. Through the use of civil penalties and military force, those individuals and nations who refuse to comply with this oppressive legislation will be hit with economic sanctions and will not be able to buy and sell for the basic necessities of life. This enforcement of the "mark of the beast" will cast God's faithful followers into the "great tribulation" (Matthew 24:21, Revelation 7:14), and ultimately lead to the final "time of trouble" (Daniel 12:1).

These penalties will eventually result in a global death decree against all those who refuse to comply with the legislated worship of the papacy; those who are faithful to God in the midst of this tremendous conflict will receive the "seal of God" in their foreheads (Revelation 7:1–3). Conversely, those who capitulate to economic pressure will receive the "mark" of the beast in the "hand;" they have known the truth, but their "actions" demonstrate obedience to the state rather than to God. Those who receive the "mark" in the forehead have actually been deceived into thinking that the laws of the state are the will of God (2 Thessalonians 2:3–9).

Our next task will be to identify the "mark" of the beast; yet, we must first understand that the book of Revelation presents specific truths with their respective counterfeits. Here are several examples of this principle: (1) the pure woman (Revelation 12:1) vs. the harlot (Revelation 17:1); (2) the three angels' messages (Revelation 14:6–12) vs. the three unclean spirits (Revelation 16:13–14); (3) the "holy city," New Jerusalem (Revelation 21:10) vs. the "great city," Babylon (Revelation 17:5); (4) the marriage supper of the Lamb (Revelation 19:6–9) vs. the great supper of God (Revelation 19:11–21); and (5) the Father, Son, and Holy Spirit

(Revelation 1:4–8) vs. the dragon, beast, and false prophet (Revelation 16:13). When we consider the "mark" of the beast, we should realize that it is an opposite and counterfeit to the "seal" of God. Just as the "mark" will be received either in the "forehead" or "hand," the "seal" of God will also go in both of these locations:

> And I saw another angel ascending from the east, having the seal of the living God: and he cried with a loud voice to the four angels, to whom it was given to hurt the earth and the sea, Saying, Hurt not the earth, neither the sea, nor the trees, till we have *sealed* the servants of our God in their *foreheads*. (Revelation 7:2–3, emphasis mine)

> God thundereth marvelously with his voice; great things doeth he, which we cannot comprehend. For he saith to the snow, Be thou on the earth; likewise to the small rain, and to the great rain of his strength. He *sealeth* up the *hand* of every man; that all men may know his work. (Job 37:5–7, emphasis mine)

The apostle Paul revealed that we should "grieve not the holy Spirit of God, whereby ye are sealed unto the day of redemption" (Eph 4:30). The prophet Isaiah also stated that we are sealed with God's law: "Bind up the testimony, seal the law among my disciples" (Isaiah 8:16). When comparing these two passages to this next passage, we will see that the Holy Spirit seals us with the law of God by writing it into our hearts and minds: "Whereof the Holy Ghost also is a witness to us: for after that he had said before, This is the covenant that I will make with them after those days, saith the Lord, I will put my laws into their hearts, and in their minds will I write them" (Hebrews 10:15–16).

We should also note that the concept of the "forehead" is synonymous with both the "heart" and "mind." This is the location where we make our decisions and choose our allegiance, while the "hand" is symbolic of the action that reflects this inward decision.[115] Thus, as we choose to render obedience to God's Law, the Holy Spirit will write this law into our hearts and minds (symbolized by the "forehead"); as a result, we will live out this

---

115 See Genesis 6:5, Proverbs 23:7, Matthew 15:18–19, and Hebrews 4:12, for evidence that associates "thoughts" and "thinking" with the "heart." See also Song of Solomon 8:6. See Hebrews 1:10 for a passage that equates one's "works," or "actions," with the "hand."

choice through the outward action of the life (symbolized by the "hand"). Notice these next few Bible references:

> My son, keep my words, and lay up my commandments with thee. Keep my *commandments*, and live; and my *law* as the apple of thine eye. Bind them upon thy *fingers*, write them upon the table of thine *heart*. (Proverbs 7:1–3, emphasis mine)

> And it shall come to pass, if ye shall hearken diligently unto my *commandments* which I command you this day, to love the LORD your God, and to serve him with all your heart and with all your soul, That I will give you the rain of your land in his due season, the first rain and the latter rain, that thou mayest gather in thy corn, and thy wine, and thine oil. ... Therefore shall ye lay up these *my words* in your *heart* and in your soul, and bind them for a *sign* upon your *hand*, that they may be as *frontlets* between your eyes. (Deuteronomy 11:13–14, 18, emphasis mine)

In essence, God's "seal" is not a literal, visible mark, but rather a spiritual one, based on an internal choice that is ultimately seen in the lifestyle of the believer. Now, we discovered earlier that we are "sealed" on the "hand" (Job 37:7), while the passage above says God will write His Law as a "sign" upon the "hand" (Deuteronomy 11:18). Evidently, the Bible evidence suggests that a "sign" and a "seal" are synonymous concepts and are therefore one and the same thing. The apostle Paul confirmed this principle, saying that Abraham "received the *sign* of circumcision, a *seal* of the righteousness of the faith which he had yet being uncircumcised" (Romans 4:11, emphasis mine). Thus, as Paul equated a "sign" with a "seal," he demonstrated that the "sign" of actual, literal circumcision was an outward reflection of the inner, spiritual "seal" in Abraham's faith experience. The inner "seal" of faith will lead to the outward "sign" of obedience to God's Law (Revelation 14:12, Romans 3:31).

A "seal" also consists of three components, i.e., the name, office, and territory of what that "seal" represents. We see this concept in many modern political seals, including the seal of the president of the United States. Therefore, God's "seal," or "sign," will possess His name, office, and territory; and, as we examine the Ten Commandments, we can see one commandment in particular that has possession of God's name, office, and territory—the specific commandment that articulates the observance of the seventh-day Sabbath:

> Remember the sabbath day, to keep it holy. ... For in six days the LORD [His name] *made* [His office—Creator, Maker] *heaven and earth, the sea, and all that in them is* [His territory—all of creation], and rested the seventh day: wherefore the LORD blessed the sabbath day, and hallowed it. (Exodus 20:8, 11, emphasis mine)

The Bible evidence that we have just examined clearly reveals that the "seal" of God, while including the entire ten-commandment law, will focus on the Sabbath of the fourth commandment in the final crisis at the end of time. It is the only commandment within God's law that contains all three components of a "seal," and, because a "seal" and "sign" are synonymous, it would also be the "sign" between God and His faithful followers:

> And the LORD spake unto Moses, saying, Speak thou also unto the children of Israel, saying, Verily my *sabbaths* ye shall keep: for it is a *sign* between me and you throughout your generations; that ye may know that I am the LORD that doth sanctify you. ... Wherefore the children of Israel shall keep the *sabbath*, to observe the sabbath throughout their generations, for a perpetual covenant. It is a *sign* between me and the children of Israel for ever: for in six days the LORD [His name] *made* [His office—Creator, Maker] *heaven and earth* [His territory—all of creation], and on the seventh day he rested, and was refreshed. (Exodus 31:12–13, 16–17, emphasis mine)

> Moreover also I gave them my *sabbaths*, to be a *sign* between me and them, that they might know that I am the LORD that sanctify them. ... And hallow my *sabbaths*; and they shall be a *sign* between me and you, that ye may know that I am the LORD your God. (Ezekiel 20:12, 20, emphasis mine)

Therefore, at the end of time, those who choose to obey God's Sabbath by faith will receive the inward "seal" of God, and demonstrate the outward "sign" of this experience by keeping the true Sabbath day holy and set apart as a special day of worship.

Now that we have identified the "seal" of God, we can identify the "mark" of the beast. Again, we must remember that the "seal" of God and the "mark" of the beast are opposites; the "mark" of the beast is the actual counterfeit of the "seal" of God. Since the "seal" is not a literal, visible "seal," but a symbolic one, we must also conclude that the "mark" is also symbolic.

It is not a computer chip or laser tattoo or the number 666, but a spiritual "mark" involving the conscious choice of an individual to serve the laws of the state over the law of God.

Now, we have proven the "beast" power to be papal Rome, and we have also shown that this power has "thought" to change "times" and "laws" (Daniel 7:25), which would include the change of Sabbath observance from the seventh day (Saturday) to the first day of the week (Sunday) without any biblical authority. Therefore, if the beast is papal Rome, and the Sabbath is God's "sign" and "seal," then what must be the "mark," i.e., Rome's counterfeit to the true, seventh-day Sabbath? It must be Rome's institution of Sunday sacredness:

> Which day is the Sabbath day? ... *Saturday* is the Sabbath day. ... Why do we observe *Sunday* instead of Saturday? ... We observe *Sunday* instead of *Saturday* because the Catholic Church *transferred* the solemnity from Saturday to Sunday.[116]

> Protestants reject Divine Tradition, the Unwritten Word, which Catholics accept as of equal authority ... The [Catholic] Church is *above* the Bible; and this *transference* of Sabbath observance from Saturday to Sunday is proof positive of that fact.[117]

> Of course the *Catholic Church* claims that the *change* was her act [changing the Sabbath to Sunday]. It could not have been otherwise, as none in those days would have dreamed of doing anything in matters spiritual and ecclesiastical and religious without her. And the act is a *mark* of ecclesiastical power and authority in religious matters.[118]

> But you may read the Bible from Genesis to Revelation, and you will not find a single line authorizing the sanctification of Sunday.

---

116 Peter Geiermann, *The Convert's Catechism of Catholic Doctrine* (St. Louis, MI: B. Herder Book Co., 1949), 50, emphasis mine.

117 *The Catholic Record*, London, Ontario, Canada, 1 Sept 1923, Volume XLV, emphasis mine.

118 A letter from James Cardinal Gibbons to J.F. Snyder of Bloomington, Illinois, signed by H.F. Thomas, dated 11 Nov 1895, emphasis mine, quoted in Kevin Morgan, *Sabbath Rest* (Brushton, New York: Teach Services, 2002), 57.

The Scriptures enforce the religious observance of Saturday, a day which we never sanctify.[119]

Perhaps the *boldest thing*, the *most revolutionary change* the Church ever did, happened in the first century. The holy day, the *Sabbath*, was *changed* from *Saturday* to *Sunday*. 'The Day of the Lord' was chosen, *not* from any directions noted in the *Scriptures*, but from the Church's sense of its own power. … People who think that the Scriptures should be the sole authority, should logically become 7th Day Adventists, and keep Saturday holy.[120]

Prove to me from the Bible that I am bound to keep Sunday holy. —There is no such law in the Bible! It is a law of the *Holy Catholic Church alone*. The Bible says, 'Remember the Sabbath day to keep it holy.' The Catholic Church says, No. By my divine power I *abolish* the *Sabbath day* and *command* you to keep holy *the first day of the week.*—And lo! The entire civilized world bows down in reverent obedience to the command of the Holy Catholic Church.[121]

Let's piece this puzzle together: the "seal" of God in the final conflict will be the faithful observance of the seventh-day Sabbath, and the "mark" of the beast will be the observance of papal Rome's counterfeit to the true seventh-day Sabbath, i.e., the institution of Sunday sacredness when enforced by law. Some have wondered as to whether or not the "mark" of the beast is being received at the present time. In answering this vital question, we should remember that the "image to the beast" will be formed when Protestant America appeals to the civil power of the United States to enforce the worship of papal Rome. In other words, when Protestant America successfully influences the civil power of the United States to legislate and enforce the papal institution of Sunday worship, at that point in time the "image to the beast" will then be fully formed, thus fully healing the "deadly wound" of the papacy. At this point in time and not before, the "mark" of the beast and the "seal" of God will be received.

---

119 James Cardinal Gibbons, *The Faith of Our Fathers* (New York: P.J. Kennedy & Sons, 1917), 72–73.

120 *Saint Catherine Catholic Church Sentinel*, Algonac, Michigan, Volume 50, Number 22, 21 May 1995, emphasis mine.

121 Thomas Enright, *The American Sentinel* (June 1893), 173, emphasis mine, quoted in Morgan, 56–57.

We should also be aware of the fact that the United States has a history of Sunday legislation, and several individual states at this present time still continue to maintain Sunday "blue laws," despite the fact that they are not fully enforced due to our First Amendment privileges. Yet, the Bible reveals that in the very near future we will see Protestant America appeal to the civil power of the U.S. government to enact legislation that will enforce Sunday sacredness on a national scale.[122]

And, when a national Sunday law is enacted, a coalition between papal Rome and the United States will then move Sunday sacredness to the global level; economic pressure will bring the nations of the world into unity on this issue, and, at that point, the test will come to every human being. Those who believe that Sunday is the real Sabbath will receive the "mark" in the "forehead," while those who believe that Sunday is not the real Sabbath, and yet still capitulate from the pressure of economic sanctions, will receive the "mark" in the "hand." Conversely, notwithstanding the economic pressures from a global union of church and state that will eventually result in a global death decree, those who remain faithful to God's true seventh-day Sabbath will receive the "seal" of God in their foreheads.[123]

Therefore, the Sabbath–Sunday issue will be the central focus of the end-time conflict between Christ and Satan on Planet Earth. Once Sunday legislation has been made a reality, its enforcement will begin with the requirement of refraining from all work on Sunday; eventually, however, it will move to the level of forcing people to desecrate the Sabbath, a tactic that Rome had used during the Dark Ages:

> The churches that were under the rule of the papacy were early compelled to honor the Sunday as a holy day. Amid the prevailing error and superstition, many, even of the true people of God, became so bewildered that while they observed the Sabbath, they refrained from labor also on the Sunday. But this did not satisfy the papal leaders. They demanded not only that Sunday be hallowed, but that the Sabbath be profaned; and they denounced in the strongest language those who dared to show it honor.[124]

---

122 G. Edward Reid, *Sunday's Coming*, 2nd Edition (Hagerstown, MD: Review and Herald, 2005), 13–32. This particular source goes into detail by mentioning several examples of past Sunday laws that were enacted by particular states before the ratification of the Bill of Rights.

123 White, *Great Controversy*, 603–612.

124 Ibid, 65.

Thus, the "time will come when men will not only forbid Sunday work, but they will try to force men to labor on the Sabbath. And men will be asked to renounce the Sabbath and to subscribe to Sunday observance or forfeit their freedom and their lives."[125] Therefore, as we contemplate the crisis before us, we should consider the observation of James Cardinal Gibbons, who stated that "Reason and sense demand the acceptance of one or the other of these alternatives: either Protestantism and the keeping holy of Saturday, or Catholicity and the keeping holy of Sunday. Compromise is impossible."[126]

> Here is wisdom. Let him that hath understanding count the number of the beast: for it is the number of a man; and his number is Six hundred threescore and six. (Revelation 13:18)

Here is wisdom. Let him that hath understanding count the number of the beast: for it is the number of a man; and his number is Six hundred threescore and six. A Catholic source, *Our Sunday Visitor*, even confirms that the number 666 refers to the number of the name of the Papacy:

> Is it true that the words of the Apocalypse in the 13th chapter, 18th verse, refer to the Pope? The title of the pope of Rome is *Vicarius Filii Dei* … and if you take the letters of his title which represent Latin numerals and add them together, they come to 666.[127]

"Vicar of the Son of God" (Latin)—"Vicarivs Filii Dei"

V (5)	F (0)	D (500)
I (1)	I (1)	E (0)
C (100)	L (50)	I (1) = 666
A (0)	I (1)	
R (0)	I (1)	
I (1)		
V (5)		
S (0)		

---

125 Ellen G. White, *The Southern Work* (Legacy of Light, 2000), 69.
126 James Cardinal Gibbons, *The Catholic Mirror*, 23 Dec 1893.
127 *Our Sunday Visitor*, 15 Nov 1914.

The above title is not the only one that adds up to 666; there are several other titles, not just in Latin, but also in the Greek and Hebrew languages, that add up to the number 666 as well:

"Captain of the Clergy" (Latin)—"Dvx Cleri"

D	V	X		C	L	E	R	I	
(500)	(5)	(10)		(100)	(50)	(0)	(0)	(1)	= 666

"Chief Vicar of the Court of Rome" (Latin)—"Lvdo Vicvs"

L	V	D	O		V	I	C	V	S	
(50)	(5)	(500)	(0)		(5)	(1)	(100)	(5)	(0)	= 666

"Latin Man" (Latin)—"Lateinos"

L	A	T	E	I	N	O	S	
(30)	(1)	(300)	(5)	(10)	(50)	(70)	(200)	= 666

"The Latin Kingdom" (Greek)—"He Latine Basileia"

H	(0)	L	(30)	B	(2)
E	(8)	A	(0)	A	(0)
		T	(300)	S	(200)
		I	(10)	I	(10)
		N	(50)	L	(30)
		E	(8)	E	(8)
				I	(10)
				A	(0) = 666

"Italian Church" (Greek)—"Italika Ekklesia"

I	(10)	E	(8)
T	(300)	K	(20)
A	(0)	K	(20)
L	(30)	L	(30)
I	(10)	E	(8)
K	(20)	S	(200)
A	(0)	I	(10)
		A	(0) = 666

"Romiith" (Hebrew)—"Roman Kingdom"

R	O	M	I	I	[TH]	
(200)	(6)	(40)	(10)	(10)	(400)	= 666

The preceding titles confirm that the number of both the papal hierarchy and the Roman Church clearly add up to 666.[128] Joseph F. Berg, a 19th century Reformed pastor, in his work entitled *The Great Apostasy*, stated that it would be quite difficult to find another power in history other than papal Rome that would have all of the above names add up to 666 and fit the same description: "Now we challenge the world to find another name in these languages, Greek, Hebrew, and Latin, which shall designate the same number."[129]

The Reformation teaching which identifies both the papal system and the Roman Catholic Church as the antichrist-beast power is a position that many famous Protestant reformers clearly held in their understanding of Bible prophecy. Michael de Semlyen, in his powerful work entitled *All Roads Lead to Rome*, confirmed this assertion:

> Wycliffe, Tyndale, Luther, Calvin, Cranmer; in the seventeenth century, Bunyan, the translators of the King James Bible and the men who published the Westminster and Baptist confessions of faith; Sir Isaac Newton, Wesley, Whitfield, Jonathan Edwards; and more recently Spurgeon, Bishop J.C. Ryle and Dr. Martin Lloyd-Jones; these men, among countless others, all saw the office of the Papacy as the antichrist.[130]

Symbol of Revelation 13	Interpretation
"Sea Beast"	Papal Rome
"Seven Heads"	City of Rome (seven hills) Seven kingdoms: Egypt, Assyria, Babylon, Media-Persia, Greece, pagan Rome, papal Rome
"Ten Horns"	Divided Europe (A.D. 476), and an end-time global alliance

128 See both Joseph F. Berg, *The Great Apostasy* (Philadelphia, PA: J.B. Lippincott & Co., 1842), 156–158, and the internet source http://www.tagnet.org/cb-south/leo/leo4.html.

129 Berg, 158.

130 Michael de Semlyen, *All Roads Lead to Rome* (Bucks, England: Dorchester House Publishers, 1993), 197–198.

"Earth Beast"	The United States of America
"Two Horns"	Civil and religious liberty
"Image to the Beast"	Sunday legislation pressured by apostate Protestant America (future)
"Mark of the Beast"	National and global Sunday legislation (still future)
"Seal of God"	Faithful Sabbath observance
"666"	Numerical value of papal names

SIX

A Review of Revelation 17
"The Mystery of Babylon the Great"

Having established a basic understanding of Daniel 2, Daniel 7, Daniel 8, and also Revelation 13, we will now establish a basic understanding of Revelation 17. We will discover later that the chronology of these five chapters all find their final culmination and complete fulfillment in Daniel 11. We will also see that Revelation 17 describes the same seven-headed, ten-horned beast that we had examined in Revelation 13; yet, there are some added details that are delineated by some very powerful prophetic symbols which will serve to repeat, expand, and confirm our understanding of what we have discovered already.

> And there came one of the seven angels which had the seven vials, and talked with me, saying unto me, Come hither; I will shew unto thee the judgment of the great whore that sitteth upon many waters: With whom the kings of the earth have committed fornication, and the inhabitants of the earth have been made drunk with the wine of her fornication. So he carried me away in the spirit into the wilderness: and I saw a woman sit upon a scarlet coloured beast, full of names of blasphemy, having seven heads and ten horns. (Revelation 17:1–3)

I will shew unto thee the judgment of the great whore that sitteth upon many waters: With whom the kings of the earth have committed fornication. To begin the vision of Revelation 17, John was shown a "great whore" that sat on "many waters." Now, as we strive to ascertain the meaning of what this "great whore" symbolizes, we must first understand that a "woman" in Bible prophecy is symbolic of a church.[131] Furthermore, a

---

131 See Ephesians 5:25–32, 2 Corinthians 11:2, Isaiah 51:16, 52:1–2, Jeremiah 6:2, Revelation 12:17, 19:6–9. See also Isaiah 1:8–21, 2 Kings 19:21, Isaiah 16:1, Isaiah 62:11–12, Lamentations 1:4–6, 2:1–13, Zephaniah 3:14 and Zechariah

pure "woman" would symbolize a pure, faithful church, while a "whore" would symbolize the opposite, namely a corrupt, unfaithful, apostate church. We have also established that "waters," which are also referred to as "seas," symbolize both the nations of the earth and highly populated areas (Revelation 17:15). Thus, this vision describes the rise of a corrupt, apostate church from a highly populated area which will ultimately gain the support of the nations of the earth.

John is also told that the "kings of the earth" have "committed fornication" with this apostate religious system. Now, the phrase "kings of the earth" is a prophetic symbol that equates to the leaders of the nations of this world; furthermore, the concept of "fornication" implies that the "kings of the earth" come together in an illegal, unholy alliance with the "great whore" to form a global union of church and state at the end of time.[132] Given this future scenario, we should remember that Jesus taught that church and state should be separate, saying, "Render therefore unto Caesar the things which are Caesar's; and unto God the things that are God's" (Matthew 22:21). Thus, the "great whore" and the "kings of the earth" will ignore Christ's mandate that church and state should not be "married," and come together in a "fornicating" relationship to enforce antichrist-beast worship on the people of the earth.

And the inhabitants of the earth have been made drunk with the wine of her fornication. John is also told that the "inhabitants of the earth" are made "drunk" with the "wine" that comes from this global union of church and state. The phrase "inhabitants of the earth" is actually synonymous with the phrase "many waters" and symbolizes the nations of the world that give their support to this corrupt, apostate church. Through this global union of church and state, a majority of the world will become spiritually "drunk" through the "wine" of the sin and false doctrine promoted by this "great whore." We should remember that both "sin" and intoxicating "wine" deaden the moral perceptions; thus, as the nations of the world follow this apostate church by participating in her sins and advocating her false doctrines, they become spiritually "drunk" with the "wine" of her "fornication," and therefore cannot discern truth from error. [133]

2:1–13, 9:9 are some biblical examples of this concept.

132 See C. Mervyn Maxwell, *God Cares*, 2 vols. (Boise, ID: Pacific Press, 1985), 2:458–459, *SDA Bible Commentary*, 12 vols. (Hagerstown, MD: Review and Herald, 1955–2000), 7:849–850, and Uriah Smith, *Daniel and the Revelation* (Nashville, TN: Southern, 1944), 707.

133 *SDA Bible Commentary*, 7:850.

So he carried me away in the spirit into the wilderness: and I saw a woman sit upon a scarlet coloured beast. John sees that this "great whore" rides on the back of a scarlet-colored "beast." We will find that this "beast" of Revelation 17 is the very same beast that we saw in Revelation 13, and ultimately symbolizes the papal Roman power. The additional detail of the "great whore" riding the back of this "beast" is an expanded description of the papal office as it gives its political support to the Roman Catholic Church. Revelation 13 describes both the political and religious side of papal Rome with a single prophetic symbol (a composite beast), while God uses two distinct and yet related prophetic symbols here in Revelation 17 to describe both the religious and political side of the papal power. The "great whore" would actually symbolize the religious side, i.e., the Roman Catholic Church,[134] while the "beast" symbolizes its political side, the actual papal hierarchy. Thus, this "great whore," the Church of Rome, would "ride" the back of the "beast," i.e., receive the support of the political power and influence of the papal office, in conjunction with the "kings of the earth."

Overall, as we blend these concepts together, it becomes clear that the unification of Rome and the United States, with the support of the nations of the world, will result in the promulgation of the Catholic version of Christianity on a global scale through the exaltation of Sunday worship. This principle was confirmed by the late Jesuit scholar Malachi Martin, who, in his popular book *The Keys of This Blood*, observed that "we are all involved in an all-out, no-holds-barred, three-way global competition" between Roman Catholicism [the papacy], Marxist Communism [the Soviet Union], and Western Capitalism [the United States] to "establish the first one-world system of government that has ever existed in the society of nations."[135]

Dr. Martin also noted that the late Pope John Paul II insisted "that men have no reliable hope of creating a viable geopolitical system unless it is on the basis of Roman Catholic Christianity."[136] Interestingly, even though Marxist Communism has all but ceased to be a major global force with a few exceptions, it is no coincidence that the other two competitors, Rome

---

134 See "Scarlet Woman," in *Webster's New World Dictionary*, College Edition (Cleveland, OH: World Publishing Company, 1957), 1302. This dictionary edition identifies this "great whore" with the Roman Catholic Church, and actually refers to Revelation 17:1–6.

135 Malachi Martin, *The Keys of This Blood: Pope John Paul II Versus Russia and the West for Control of the New World Order* (New York: Simon & Schuster, 1990), 15.

136 Ibid, 492.

and the United States, are still the dominant figures in the global political arena. While Daniel 2 confirms that a one-world government will never become a reality, the Bible does describe a unification of world governments implied by the phrase "kings of the earth," which will ultimately be led by Rome and the United States. Thus, in coalition together, Rome, the United States, and the nations of the world will unify to secure the global worship of the papacy through the promotion of Sunday sacredness.[137]

Full of names of blasphemy. This "scarlet-coloured beast" would also have "names of blasphemy," a detail that actually confirms our identity of the "great whore" as the Roman Catholic Church. To review once again, the Bible defines "blasphemy" as (1) the claim to be equal with God, and (2) the claim to have the authority to forgive sins.[138] There are several Catholic sources that promote the claim of the equality of the papacy with God; still others purport that the papacy, the Catholic Church, and its corresponding clergy all have alleged infallibility and the power to forgive sins.

So he carried me away in the spirit into the wilderness. Now, when the Bible speaks of the "wilderness" in this particular context, it is in reference to the persecuting nature of papal Rome during its Dark Age reign (A.D. 538–1798). Once again, the record of history will demonstrate that the papacy has a past resume of persecution. We can confirm this particular principle by cross-referencing the actual word "wilderness" with another passage in Revelation that describes a pure "woman," i.e., God's faithful church, who would flee into the "wilderness" to escape papal persecution:

> And the woman fled into the wilderness, where she hath a place prepared of God, that they should feed her there a thousand two hundred and threescore days. ... And to the woman were given two wings of a great eagle, that she might fly into the wilderness, into her place, where she is nourished for a time, and times, and half a time, from the face of the serpent. (Revelation 12:6, 14)

The above passage contains two of seven references to the 1,260-year Dark Age rule of papal Rome (A.D. 538–1798),[139] clearly equating "a thousand two hundred and threescore days" with "a time, and times, and half a time." During this era, God's faithful church had fled into the "wilderness,"

---

137 Ellen G. White, *The Great Controversy* (Mountain View, CA: Pacific Press, 1950), 563–581, 603–612. See also Revelation 13:11–17, and an explanation of this passage on pages 56–67.

138 See John 10:27–33, 2 Thessalonians 2:3–4, and Mark 2:1–7, and pages 26–28.

139 See Daniel 7:25, 12:7, Revelation 11:3–4, 12:6, 14, 13:5.

i.e., into hiding, to escape the persecuting wrath of the "serpent" (Satan) working through the popish persecutors of the Roman Church.[140] The unwritten history of groups like the Waldensians and the origin of papal offices such as the Catholic Inquisition clearly testify to the fact that God's true church had been forced to flee into solitary places in order to worship God according to the dictates of conscience.[141] Even so, many so-called "heretics" yielded up their lives through martyrdom in defense of Bible truth.

Having seven heads and ten horns. We offered a brief discussion in our last chapter on the identity of the seven heads and ten horns of this Roman beast.[142] To review, using John's current day as the actual pivotal point,[143] we identified these "seven heads" as a description of both the city of Rome itself (which contains seven "mountains, or "hills"), and the seven major powers in human history that have persecuted the people of God, i.e., (1) Egypt, (2) Assyria, (3) Babylon, (4) Media-Persia, (5) Greece, (6) pagan Rome, and (7) papal Rome. Also, a resurrected papal Rome would actually constitute the seven-headed beast in its entirety as the eighth power.[144]

Now, concerning the "ten horns," we have also demonstrated that, similar to the "seven heads," these also have a dual meaning. First, they symbolize the ten European nations that formed after the fall of pagan Rome in A.D. 476. History will show that the Alemanni (Germany), the Franks (France), the Suevi (Portugal), the Visigoths (Spain), the Burgundians (Switzerland), the Saxons (England), the Lombards (Italy), the Heruli (overthrown, A.D. 493), the Vandals (overthrown, A.D. 534), and the Ostrogoths (overthrown, A.D. 538) were the ten tribal nations that emerged after the demise of pagan Rome. Later, the three Arian rivals to Catholicism, the

---

140 White, *Great Controversy*, 55.

141 Ibid, 61–78. See also Benjamin G. Wilkinson, *Truth Triumphant* (Mountain View, CA: Pacific Press, 1944).

142 See pages 48–52.

143 Daniel's visions give us a precedent for this position; the chronology of both Daniel 2 and 7 began with Babylon because that was the power in control in Daniel's current day. The visions of Daniel 8 and 9 began their chronology with Media-Persia because in Daniel 8, Daniel was under the last king of Babylon, and by the time the angel came to explain Daniel 8 through the vision of Daniel 9, Daniel had been living under Media-Persian rule. Daniel 11 sees this also, beginning its chronology with Media-Persia, as again, Daniel lived under the rule of this power. Thus, prophets have their visions explained from the context of their current day.

144 See Louis F. Were, *The Woman and the Beast in the Book of Revelation* (Sarasota, FL: H.K. LaRondelle, 1993), 189–214.

Heruli, Vandals, and Ostrogoths, were uprooted and subdued by papal Rome on its way to European supremacy.[145] Second, Ellen White confirms that these "ten horns" also symbolize an end-time church-state confederacy that will unify to eradicate all non-compliant people who refuse to receive the mark of the beast.[146]

> And the woman was arrayed in purple and scarlet colour, and decked with gold and precious stones and pearls, having a golden cup in her hand full of abominations and filthiness of her fornication: And upon her forehead was a name written, MYSTERY, BABYLON THE GREAT, THE MOTHER OF HARLOTS AND ABOMINATIONS OF THE EARTH. And I saw the woman drunken with the blood of the saints, and with the blood of the martyrs of Jesus: and when I saw her, I wondered with great admiration. (Revelation 17:4–6)

And the woman was arrayed in purple and scarlet colour. This "great whore" is described as being arrayed in "purple" and "scarlet." Now, when "purple" and "scarlet" are used in the Bible, the color "blue" is usually present also.[147] And, the fact these three colors are used in triplicate signifies something very important; "blue" actually symbolizes the law of God,[148] while "scarlet" symbolizes the cleansing of sin through the atoning blood of Christ.[149] Now, "purple" is actually a combination of both "blue" and "scarlet," and ultimately symbolizes the cooperation of "law" and "grace" in the work of redemption. When the sinner experiences repentance, the blood of Jesus cleanses the individual from sin ("scarlet"); the Holy Spirit then begins the process of writing God's Law into the heart and mind ("blue"), and, if the convert ultimately prevails as an overcomer of sin, the end result will ultimately be redemption ("purple"). Thus, these three colors are used in conjunction with each other as an actual object lesson of the redemptive process through Jesus Christ.

---

145 See pages 22–25 for a review of the destruction of the Heruli, Vandals, and Ostrogoths.

146 Ellen G. White, *Selected Messages from the Writings of Ellen G. White*, 3 vols. (Hagerstown, MD: Review and Herald, 1980–1986), 3:392.

147 See Exodus 26:1, 31–33, 36, 27:16, 28:4–6, 8, 15, 33, and Exodus 35, 38, 39.

148 See Exodus 24:10, Ezekiel 1:26, and Ezekiel 10:1.

149 See Leviticus 17:11, Isaiah 1:16–18, 1 Peter 1:18–23, Matthew 26:28, Hebrews 9:22, 1 John 3:4, and Romans 4:15.

Aside from the fact that two liturgical colors of the Catholic clergy are "purple" and "scarlet,"[150] it is also worth our notice that "blue" is not mentioned with the attire of this "woman." Since "blue" symbolizes the law of God, its omission here is a confirmation of Rome's desire to "think to change times and laws" of God (Daniel 7:25). As mentioned earlier, Catholic sources will clearly demonstrate an alteration of God's Ten Commandments, removing the second commandment that forbids the worship of idols and the dividing of the tenth commandment into two parts (changing God's "laws"), and a transference of the Sabbath day from the seventh day to the first day of the week (changing God's "times").[151]

Decked with gold and precious stones and pearls. This "great whore" is also decked with "gold and precious stones and pearls." Interestingly, the Bible observes that before his fall from grace, Satan was adorned with many precious gems and jewels (Ezekiel 28:13–15); yet, since he had later become prideful on his power and appearance, he was eventually cast out of the "mountain of God" (Ezekiel 28:16). The Bible also reveals that the wearing of jewelry in general can also be associated with worldly affluence, prostitution, and spiritual infidelity to God; therefore, faithful Christians should seek to practice modesty in appearance and avoid the wearing of all types of jewelry.[152] Overall, these specific details are all appropriate prophetic symbols to describe the power, arrogance, and spiritual infidelity of the Roman Church.

---

150 See *Our Sunday Visitor's Catholic Encyclopedia* (Our Sunday Visitor Publishing Division, 1991), 175, 178, quoted in Dave Hunt, *A Woman Rides the Beast* (Eugene, OR: Harvest House Publishers, 1994), 74.

151 See *Catechism of the Catholic Church*, 2nd Edition (Washington, DC: United States Catholic Conference, 1997), 498–611, and Geiermann, 48–55, 99–100. For a good synopsis on Rome's claim of the Sabbath change, see Samuele Bacchiocchi, *From Sabbath to Sunday: A Historical Investigation of the Rise of Sunday Observance in Early Christianity* (Rome: Pontifical Gregorian University Press, 1977), Samuele Bacchiocchi, *The Sabbath in the New Testament* (Berrien Springs, MI: University Printers, 1985), Kevin Morgan, *Sabbath Rest* (Brushton, NY: Teach Services, 2002), 55–60, and *Rome's Challenge: Why Protestants Keep Sunday* (ISBN 0-8280-0378-5). See also pages 30–31, and Lucius Ferraris, "Papa," in *Prompta Bibliotheca*, Volume 6 (1772), article 2, page 29, quoted in Morgan, 63. These sources all describe the papal claim to change God's "times" and "laws" found in the Ten Commandment Law.

152 See Genesis 35:1–4, Exodus 33:4–6, Isaiah 3:16–24, Ezekiel 23:40–44, Hosea 2:13 for verses that associate the of wearing jewelry with spiritual infidelity. See also 1 Timothy 2:8–10 and 1 Peter 3:1–4.

Having a golden cup in her hand full of abominations and filthiness of her fornication. This "great whore" also has a "golden cup" which contains her "abominations" and the "filthiness of her fornication." In the Bible, a "cup" can symbolize several different concepts: (1) the bitter experience of martyrdom (Matthew 20:22–23); (2) the communion cup containing non-alcoholic wine (Matthew 26:27–28); (3) Christ's shed blood for the forgiveness of sin (Matthew 26:39, 42); and (4) God's wrath against apostasy (Revelation 14:10). We can apply all of these circumstances to Rome in a spiritual sense: (1) it has martyred many so-called "heretics;" (2) it actually uses the "golden cup" of alcoholic wine in the Catholic Mass of communion; (3) instead of promoting Christ's shed blood for sin, it promotes "sin" and "false doctrine;" and (4) it will eventually receive God's wrath for apostasy (Revelation 18:1–24). Overall, this "golden cup" symbolizes the spiritual, alcoholic "wine" of sin and false doctrine that "intoxicates," i.e., deceives Rome's followers.[153]

And upon her forehead was a name written, MYSTERY, BABYLON THE GREAT. This "great whore" also has the name of "Babylon" written on "her forehead." The example of Jacob demonstrates that names in the Bible are usually descriptive of one's character. The name "Jacob" actually means "supplanter," because of the fact that he grabbed the heel of his brother Esau at birth, used manipulation to obtain Esau's birthright, and practiced deception to steal Esau's blessing.

Yet, after a long, repentant pilgrimage, where he himself would encounter manipulation and deception at the hands of his uncle Laban, Jacob would eventually experience a supernatural character transformation; in this process, he would be renamed "Israel" (prince) because he had overcome this character defect of being a "supplanter."[154] In like manner, God's people will also have His name in their foreheads as they live the life of an overcomer.[155] Now, when considering the name "Babylon," we must understand that it does not describe a resurgent Babylonian Empire at the end of time; after its subjugation by Media-Persia, God had decreed that a literal Babylon will never again achieve superpower status (Isaiah 13:19–22). Rather, this term describes the actual spiritual character of the "great whore." Originating from the Hebrew word "Babel," the word "Babylon" symbolizes religious confusion (Genesis 11:9), and refers to the various forms of

153 White, *Great Controversy*, 388.

154 See Genesis 25:24–26, 29–34, 27:1–36, 32:24–30.

155 See Revelation 2:7, 11, 17, 26, 3:5, 12, 21, 12:11, 21:7 (overcoming); Revelation 7:1–3, 14:1, 22:4 (God's name in the forehead).

apostate, confusing, non-biblical religions which would ultimately be led by Roman Catholicism.[156]

THE MOTHER OF HARLOTS AND ABOMINATIONS OF THE EARTH. Papal Rome is labeled as the "mother of harlots and abominations of the earth," meaning that she is the "mother church," and has apostate daughter churches that follow her false doctrines.[157] John A. O'Brien, in his work entitled *The Faith of Millions*, confirmed this principle by identifying the "mother church" as the Church of Rome:

> They [Protestants] have continued the custom [Sunday observance], even though it rests upon the authority of the Catholic Church and not upon an explicit text in the Bible. That observance remains as a reminder of the Mother Church from which non-Catholic sects broke away—like a boy running away from home but still carrying in his pocket a picture of his mother or a lock of her hair.[158]

Michael de Semlyen, in his work entitled *All Roads Lead to Rome*, articulated that several Protestant reformers identified this mother harlot called Mystery Babylon as the system of Roman Catholicism:

> 'The Reformers saw the whole Catholic system as antichristian. Luther and Calvin went so far as to identify the papacy as the antichrist and they like Wycliffe, Tyndale, Matthew Henry, Spurgeon, Lloyd-Jones and many others saw the Roman Catholic Institution as Mystery Babylon, the Mother of Harlots, vividly described in Revelation chapter 17.'[159]

Furthermore, this "mother church" has apostate daughter churches, called "harlots and abominations," which are "offspring" religious systems that advocate her false doctrines. Thus, any religious system that believes and promotes any false doctrine of the Roman Church would constitute a "harlot" daughter. The Bible actually describes spiritual Babylon as consisting of three general parts. John wrote that "the great city was divided into

---

156 *SDA Bible Commentary*, 7:851–852, Smith, 643, and White, *Great Controversy*, 383.

157 Ibid, 7:852 and White, *Great Controversy*, 381–383.

158 John A. O'Brien, *The Faith of Millions* (Huntington, IN: Our Sunday Visitor, 1938), 400–401.

159 Michael de Semlyen, *All Roads Lead to Rome* (Bucks, England: Dorchester House Publications, 1993), 33.

three parts, and the cities of the nations fell: and great Babylon came in re-
membrance before God, to give unto her the cup of the wine of the fierce-
ness of his wrath" (Revelation 16:19). We should remember that Revelation
has a truth-counterfeit motif, and one set of these truth-counterfeit pairs
would be the three angels' messages (Revelation 14:6–13) vs. The Three
Unclean Spirits (Revelation 16:13–14).[160] These Three Unclean Spirits
make up spiritual Babylon:

> And I saw three unclean spirits like frogs come out of the mouth
> of the dragon, and out of the mouth of the beast, and out of the
> mouth of the false prophet. For they are the spirits of devils, work-
> ing miracles, which go forth unto the kings of the earth and of the
> whole world, to gather them to the battle of that great day of God
> Almighty. (Revelation 16:13–14)

Now, we should notice that these "three unclean spirits" go to the "kings
of the earth," and we also saw that spiritual Babylon would "commit fornication" with the "kings of the earth." Since both the "three unclean spirits"
and spiritual Babylon go to the "kings of the earth," we must conclude that
these two concepts are synonymous; as a city with "three parts," spiritual
Babylon would therefore consist of these "three unclean spirits." Going a
step further, the passage above states that the "three unclean spirits" consist
of the "dragon," the "beast," and the "false prophet." We have already identified the "beast" as the system of papal Roman Catholicism. The book of
Revelation also reveals that the "dragon" is primarily a symbol of Satan:

> And the great dragon was cast out, that old serpent, called the
> Devil, and Satan, which deceiveth the whole world: he was cast out
> into the earth, and his angels were cast out with him. … And he
> laid hold on the dragon, that old serpent, which is the Devil, and
> Satan, and bound him a thousand years. (Revelation 12:9, 20:2).

Given the fact that the "dragon" is a symbol of Satan, we must also understand that Satan is behind all three of these powers. Therefore, we must
conclude that the "dragon" also symbolizes something much deeper than
just Satan himself. It must refer to a specific religious deception that has
been especially perpetrated by Satan. Please notice that in the two references above, Satan is referred to as "that old serpent;" we see from the Bible
that the book of Genesis outlines the activity of the "serpent," which Satan

---

160 See pages 60–61 for a review of the truth-counterfeit motif.

used as a medium to cause the fall of man. In that famous Bible account, Eve told the "serpent" that she would die if she either touched or ate the forbidden fruit from the tree of knowledge; yet "the serpent said unto the woman, Ye shall not surely die: For God doth know that in the day ye eat thereof, then your eyes shall be opened, and ye shall be as gods, knowing good and evil" (Genesis 3:4–5).

In essence, the "serpent" had convinced Eve to believe that, upon eating the forbidden fruit, she would be a "god;" in other words, Satan had told Eve the lie that even in disobedience she would have immortality. Yet, the Bible teaches that man is mortal, not immortal, and lapses into a dreamless, unconscious sleep at the point of death; this would consist of a kind of "soul-sleep," where a person would "rest" in the grave until the final resurrection at the end of the world.[161]

Thus, in his first lie to the human race, Satan basically began the spiritualistic teaching of the immortality of the soul; this false teaching essentially holds that there is a "soul" or "spirit" within a human being that possesses immortality and will live on after the death of the physical body. Some versions of this philosophy also believe in supposed contact with the dead, a practice that God clearly condemns.[162] Because nearly all Christian and non-Christian religions believe in some form of "spiritualism" or "immortality of the soul," Satan has been quite successful in promoting this specific belief that had its deceptive origin in the Garden of Eden. Ellen White confirmed this conclusion:

[The] declaration of the serpent to Eve in Eden—'Ye shall not surely die'—was the first sermon ever preached upon the immortality of the soul. Yet this declaration, resting solely upon the authority of Satan, is echoed from the pulpits of Christendom and is received by the majority of mankind as readily as it was received by our first parents. The divine sentence, 'The soul that sinneth, it shall die' (Ezekiel 18:20), is made to mean: The soul that sinneth, it shall not die, but live eternally.[163]

---

161 See the following texts that associate death with a dreamless, unconscious sleep: Psalm 13:3, Acts 7:59–60, Daniel 12:1–2, 1 Corinthians 15:51–54, 1 Thessalonians 4:15–18, Matthew 27:50–53, 1 Corinthians 15:3–6, 20–25, Ecclesiastes 9:5–6, 10, Acts 2:29, 34. This is not an exhaustive list; there are actually 66 references to death being equated with sleep in the Bible.

162 See 1 Samuel 28:7–19, Leviticus 20:6, 27, Deuteronomy 18:10–12, and Isaiah 47:13–14.

163 White, *Great Controversy*, 533.

Given the above explanation, we can conclude that the "dragon" power, while in one sense symbolizing Satan himself, is also a powerful symbol of "spiritualism." Our next task will be to identify the spiritual power known as the "false prophet." In our quest to find the identity of this particular power, we should compare two powerful scriptures:

> And the beast was taken, and with him the false prophet that wrought miracles before him, with which he deceived them that had received the mark of the beast, and them that worshipped his image. These both were cast alive into a lake of fire burning with brimstone. (Revelation 19:20)

> And I beheld another beast coming up out of the earth; and he had two horns like a lamb, and he spake as a dragon. … And deceiveth them that dwell on the earth by the means of those miracles which he had power to do in the sight of the beast; saying to them that dwell on the earth, that they should make an image to the beast, which had the wound by a sword, and did live. (Revelation 13:11, 14)

In the first reference above, we find that the "false prophet" uses miracles to deceive the world into receiving the mark of the beast. In the second reference, we see that the "earth beast," the United States of America, also possesses this very same quality, which means that these two symbols basically describe the same power. We have already discussed that the "great whore" and the "beast" of Revelation 17 are descriptive of the dual-nature of the papal power; the "great whore" would symbolize the religious side of this power, while the "beast" would symbolize the political side. This same principle also applies to the "earth beast" and the "false prophet;" the "earth beast" would be descriptive of the political side of the United States, while the "false prophet" would be descriptive of the religious side. The word "prophet" deals with the realm of religion, and must therefore be symbolic of the religious majority found within the United States.

History will certainly demonstrate that "Protestantism" is one of the foundational principles of American society, and, even though religious freedom has allowed the entrance of a large variety of different religions, statistics will demonstrate that "Protestantism" is still the major religious force in America today.[164] Thus, this "prophet," i.e., the religious majority

---

164 See http://www.religionstatistics.net/statamer1.htm. Updated on June 12, 2005, this specific source indicates that approximately 40–56% of the America

within America, is actually "Protestantism;" and, the idea of the "false prophet" must then be "false Protestantism," more succinctly labeled as "apostate Protestantism."

In our last chapter we discovered that the Protestant majority in America will appeal to the civil power for the sanctification of Sunday, thus forming the "image to the beast." Just as the Church of Rome has appealed to the civil power in the past to enforce her decrees, so will Protestantism follow in this exact same course in America and thus become an "image" to the papacy. In essence, the promotion of Sunday sacredness on a global scale will make apostate Protestant America both the "image to the beast" and the "false prophet." [165]

Overall, spiritual Babylon consists of three deceptive religious ideologies: (1) Roman Catholicism ("beast"); (2) Spiritualism ("dragon"); and (3) Apostate Protestantism ("false prophet"). Since spiritual Babylon is led by Roman Catholicism, we must conclude that her harlot "daughters" consist of the other two powers, apostate Protestantism and spiritualism. Given this three-fold union, it must follow that every false, apostate religion on earth will fall into one of these three deceptive ideologies. Apostate Protestantism would essentially include any professed Protestant churches that advocate the false doctrines of papal Rome, which would especially include Sunday sacredness and the immortality of the soul. Spiritualism in turn would claim all the non-Christian religions, including Buddhism, Islam, Hinduism, and any other religious ideology that advocates either an immediate afterlife at death or attempted contact with the dead.

Therefore, spiritual Babylon, led by papal Roman Catholicism, also includes her harlot daughters, i.e., any false, apostate Protestant and spiritualistic religious ideologies that advocate the false doctrines of Catholicism.[166] This three-fold union will form a spiritual alliance to enforce the institution of Sunday sacredness at the end of time:

> By the decree of enforcing the institution of the Papacy in violation of the law of God [Sunday sacredness], our nation will disconnect herself fully from righteousness. When Protestantism shall stretch her hand across the gulf to grasp the hand of the Roman power, when she shall reach over the abyss to clasp hands with

---

population professes some form of Protestantism, while Catholicism claims 22–26%.

165 White, *Great Controversy*, 439–445.

166 See both Smith, 643–663 and White, *Great Controversy*, 384–390, 445, 571, for a description of spiritual Babylon and her harlot daughter churches.

Spiritualism, when, under the influence of this threefold union, our country shall repudiate every principle of its Constitution as a Protestant and Republican government, and shall make provision for the propagation of papal falsehoods and delusions, then we may know that the time has come for the marvelous working of Satan, and that the end is near.[167]

And I saw the woman drunken with the blood of the saints, and with the blood of the martyrs of Jesus: and when I saw her, I wondered with great admiration. Here we see another reference to the persecuting nature of papal Rome, which had been especially manifested during the Dark Age period of 1,260 years. This same persecuting spirit will be resurrected once again at the end of time after the papacy regains the backing of the civil power through the concerted effort of apostate Protestant America.[168] Looking at this power with "great admiration," the apostle John felt amazed at how successful the papacy would become in deceiving the world with her deceptions.

And the angel said unto me, Wherefore didst thou marvel? I will tell thee the mystery of the woman, and of the beast that carrieth her, which hath the seven heads and ten horns. The beast that thou sawest was, and is not; and shall ascend out of the bottomless pit, and go into perdition: and they that dwell on the earth shall wonder, whose names were not written in the book of life from the foundation of the world, when they behold the beast that was, and is not, and yet is. (Revelation 17:7–8)

The beast that thou sawest was, and is not; and shall ascend out of the bottomless pit, and go into perdition. To review, this beast (1) "was," ruling from A.D. 538 to 1798; (2) "is not," having received a deadly wound in A.D. 1798; (3) "shall ascend out of the bottomless pit," having been resurrected back into existence as a global religio-political power through the Lateran Treaty of 1929; and (4) will "go into perdition," as the "man of sin" and the "son of perdition" (2 Thessalonians 2:3–4), committing fornication with the "kings of the earth" to enforce the mark of the beast. The phrase "bottomless pit" is a symbol of the gross darkness of satanic deceptions (Revelation 9:1–2, 11), and her "ascendancy" from the "bottomless pit"

---

167 Ellen G. White, *Testimonies for the Church*, 9 vols. (Mountain View, CA: Pacific Press, 1948), 5:451.

168 White, *Great Controversy*, 571–581, 607–608.

describes her release from death or captivity (Revelation 13:10, 20:1, 3). Thus, as papal Rome heals from her deadly wound, she will be released from spiritual captivity to exercise her dark, satanic deceptions once again on the inhabitants of the world.

They that dwell on the earth shall wonder, whose names were not written in the book of life from the foundation of the world, when they behold the beast that was, and is not, and yet is. As the people of the world behold the resiliency of spiritual Babylon, they will rally behind, support, and worship this power (Revelation 13:3–4). Those who finally end up giving their allegiance to her are those whose names are not written in the Lamb's book of life (Revelation 13:8).

> And here is the mind which hath wisdom. The seven heads are seven mountains, on which the woman sitteth. And there are seven kings: five are fallen, and one is, and the other is not yet come; and when he cometh, he must continue a short space. And the beast that was, and is not, even he is the eighth, and is of the seven, and goeth into perdition. (Revelation 17:9–11)

And here is the mind which hath wisdom. The seven heads are seven mountains, on which the woman sitteth. And there are seven kings: five are fallen, and one is, and the other is not yet come; and when he cometh, he must continue a short space. We have already commented quite extensively on the "seven heads;" to briefly review, the actual passage itself conveys that these symbols have a dual meaning. First, these "seven heads" symbolize the seven-hilled city of Rome; second, they describe a series of "seven kingdoms" throughout human history that have persecuted and oppressed the people of God. Because pagan Rome was the ruling power in John's day, this empire would be the "one" who "is," and we can use this kingdom as the pivotal point to determine the other six kings.

Therefore, going back in history, the empires of Greece, Media-Persia, Babylon, Assyria, and Egypt all had a history of oppressing the faithful people of God. The seventh king would naturally be the power that had followed pagan Rome, i.e., papal Rome. Thus, the sequence of the "seven kings" would be (1) Egypt, (2) Assyria, (3) Babylon, (4) Media-Persia, (5) Greece, (6) pagan Rome, and (7) papal Rome.[169]

And the beast that was, and is not, even he is the eighth, and is of the seven, and goeth into perdition. We have also already established that the "beast" power in its entirety is a symbol of papal Rome; as the "seventh

169 See pages 48–50 for a review of the "seven heads."

king" in a series of seven, it would be the only power of the "seven kings" that would be resurrected back to superpower status. This power (1) "was" (ruled from A.D. 538–1798), (2) "is not" (received a deadly wound in 1798), (3) will be the "eighth" (come back to life as its deadly wound was healed in 1929), and (4) will go "into perdition" (commit "fornication" with the "kings of the earth").[170]

> And the ten horns which thou sawest are ten kings, which have received no kingdom as yet; but receive power as kings one hour with the beast. These have one mind, and shall give their power and strength unto the beast. These shall make war with the Lamb, and the Lamb shall overcome them: for he is Lord of lords, and King of kings: and they that are with him are called, and chosen, and faithful. And he saith unto me, The waters which thou sawest, where the whore sitteth, are peoples, and multitudes, and nations, and tongues. (Revelation 17:12–15)

And the ten horns which thou sawest are ten kings, which have received no kingdom as yet; but receive power as kings one hour with the beast. These have one mind, and shall give their power and strength unto the beast. These shall make war with the Lamb, and the Lamb shall overcome them: for he is Lord of lords, and King of kings. To review once again, these "ten horns" would have a dual meaning just as the "seven kings" would. First, in reference to John's day, the "ten horns" would symbolize a divided Europe in the future that had not yet received a kingdom while pagan Rome was still in power. Second, they also symbolize a future end-time global coalition that will form an alliance with a resurrected, resurgent papacy.

In both applications, these "ten kings" would rule "one hour," i.e., simultaneously, with papal Rome. During the Dark Ages, these "ten kings" were contemporaneous with the papacy and gave her their political strength and military power so that she could exercise control over European affairs. These "ten" future "kings" will also follow in a similar pattern by once again lending their political and military power to the "beast" in a global alliance to enforce Sunday worship. Yet, even though this alliance will "make war with the Lamb," the "Lamb shall overcome them" as the "King of kings" and "Lord of lords." [171]

---

170 *SDA Bible Commentary*, 7:817.
171 See pages 50–52 for a review of the ten horns.

And the ten horns which thou sawest upon the beast, these shall hate the whore, and shall make her desolate and naked, and shall eat her flesh, and burn her with fire. For God hath put in their hearts to fulfil his will, and to agree, and give their kingdom unto the beast, until the words of God shall be fulfilled. And the woman which thou sawest is that great city, which reigneth over the kings of the earth. (Revelation 17:16–18)

And the ten horns which thou sawest upon the beast, these shall hate the whore, and shall make her desolate and naked, and shall eat her flesh, and burn her with fire. After realizing that the deceptions of the "great whore" have caused them to be eternally lost, the "ten horns" will withdraw their support. As the forces of the world had once placed their support on the side of Babylon with great zeal, they then turn on her with the same zealousness. As a result, she will be destroyed with great violence; they will "make her desolate and naked, and shall eat her flesh, and burn her with fire." She will receive "double" (Revelation 18:6), meeting with destruction from both her own former supporters and the soon-coming Lamb of God. Prior to her impending doom, God will issue a final call for all people to exit Babylon while probation still lingers, saying, "Come out of her, my people, that ye be not partakers of her sins, and that ye receive not of her plagues" (Revelation 18:4).

For God hath put in their hearts to fulfil his will, and to agree, and give their kingdom unto the beast, until the words of God shall be fulfilled. Upon first glance, it would appear that this passage is inferring that God will manipulate the nations in order to "predestine" certain events and select certain people for eternal damnation. While it is true that God has ordained that certain events are to transpire within the context of redemptive history, these events do not override the free will of human beings to choose their eternal destiny. Redemptive history is a delicate combination of free human will exercised within the larger context of God's sovereign purposes. Therefore, "predestination" is essentially God's divine foreknowledge of every person's choice in advance and the resulting consequences of those specific choices (Romans 8:29). God will use all the events of human history that come as a result of man's free choice (whether good or evil) to further a larger, eternal purpose that will ultimately accomplish His sovereign will in the cosmic plan of redemption.

Furthermore, if people persistently choose to reject the light of Bible truth and follow the path of disobedience in spiritual matters, God will eventually allow those individuals to fall under the influence of Satan and suffer the consequences of their own choices.[172] Commenting on those who were destroyed by the flood in Noah's day, the apostle Paul related this principle, saying that "God also gave them up to uncleanness through the lusts of their own hearts" (Romans 1:24). He also articulated this same principle to the Thessalonian church:

> And then shall that Wicked be revealed, whom the Lord shall consume with the spirit of his mouth, and shall destroy with the brightness of his coming: Even him, whose coming is after the working of Satan with all power and signs and lying wonders, And with all deceivableness of unrighteousness in them that perish; because they received not the love of the truth, that they might be saved. And for this cause God shall send them strong delusion, that they should believe a lie: That they all might be damned who believed not the truth, but had pleasure in unrighteousness. (2 Thessalonians 2:8–12)

The above passage has actually been used to support the claim that God causes people to be deceived; yet, in reality, Paul is actually saying that if people love error more than the truth, then God will allow them to receive a strong satanic delusion because they have not desired nor loved the truth as it is in Jesus. God will not force people to love Him and follow the truth; He will give all people the freedom to choose whom they will serve. Yet, when people choose to love and believe a lie, that specific lie will eventually be perceived as the truth, and thus the delusion becomes a reality. And, as the strong delusion gains complete control of the individual who has chosen to reject the truth, God will withdraw and allow that person to reap the consequences of his or her own choices. In essence, God doesn't directly send this strong delusion, but simply allows the individual to fall

---

172 See Hosea 4:17, 1 Samuel 16:13, and Judges 16:20 for examples on how God will depart from those who persistently and consistently resist His will. In the reference from 1 Samuel 16:13, when the passage says that an evil spirit "from the Lord" troubled Saul, it happened from the perspective that God gave His divine permission, allowing a satanic spirit to take possession of Saul. See Job chapters 1 and 2 and 2 Chronicles 18:17–22 for evidence on God giving divine permission to evil spirits to work their deceptions. There are times when God will allow demonic forces to perform certain things. Please see the next footnote also.

under the power of his or her own deluded ideas as he or she chooses to believe error and be controlled by evil spiritual forces.[173]

In these specific cases, demonic forces actually appear as messengers of light (2 Corinthians 11:13–14), and will make sin appear as righteousness and righteousness appear as sin (Isaiah 5:20–24). We saw in our last chapter that some will receive the mark of the beast in the "forehead" and still others in the "hand." Those who receive the mark in the "hand" will know and believe the truth, but because of economic pressure they will capitulate and choose to disobey the truth; thus, through their actions, they will receive the mark of the beast in the actual "hand," as opposed to the forehead.

Those who receive the mark of the beast in the "forehead" will be in the class represented in Romans 1:24 and 2 Thessalonians 2:8–12. Paul mentions that these people specifically actually love error to such an extent that they will perceive this error to be the truth, and follow it while thinking that they are actually doing the right thing. Yet, overall, because "all things work together for good" (Romans 8:28), God will ultimately override these wrong choices in His eternal plan. This does not mean that God will save those who choose to be deceived, but that He will ultimately accomplish His eternal purposes and eventually complete the plan of redemption, regardless of the free-will choice of each person.

And the woman which thou sawest is that great city, which reigneth over the kings of the earth. This "great whore," accurately named "Babylon," is called the "great city" that reigns over the "kings of the earth." Once again, this is a direct reference to the city of Rome, the central location where the papacy exercises its global influence over both the religious and political affairs of the entire world. Yet, there will come a day very soon when Jesus will usher in the eternal world, and, in that sinless society, the New Jerusalem will be the great city that reigns over the kings of the earth; furthermore, this wonderful city will not only govern the affairs of this planet, but govern the affairs of every planet in the sinless universe of God.[174]

---

173 We find examples of God giving permission for evil spirits to work their deceptions, while not actually doing this work Himself. Some biblical examples would include 2 Chronicles 18:17–22, Job 1:6–16, and 2:1–7. The Bible writers perceived that it may have been God directly causing evil, as 1 Samuel 16:13, 16, 19:9 demonstrate; yet, when we blend these several passages, we see that He simply allows evil forces to have influence upon divine permission.

174 Ellen G. White, *The Desire of Ages* (Nampa, ID: Pacific Press, 1940), 26.

Symbol of Revelation 17	Interpretation
"Great Whore"	Religious Side of Papacy, Roman Church
"Beast"	Political Side of Papal Hierarchy
"Kings of the Earth"	Leaders of the Nations of the Earth
"Fornication"	Global Union of Church and State
"Babylon"	Confusion, 3-fold Union led by Catholicism
"Harlot Daughters"	Religious Groups who Follow Rome
"Golden Cup of Wine"	Sin and False Doctrines of Rome

— SEVEN —
Identifying Transitional Points
The Historical Transitions
of Daniel 11

When we survey Daniel 11 overall, we will find that there are certain transitional texts that give a general idea of where we are in the stream of prophetic history. This specific chapter will outline seven transitional texts that we can associate to a particular historical trend. The first transitional text states that,

> Behold, there shall stand up yet three kings in Persia; and the fourth shall be far richer than they all: and by his strength through his riches he shall stir up all against the realm of Grecia. And a mighty king shall stand up, that shall rule with great dominion, and do according to his will. (Daniel 11:2–3)

This passage presents a clear reference to two ancient empires, Media-Persia (539–331 B.C.) and Greece (331–168 B.C.). The "mighty king" mentioned is a direct reference to Alexander the Great (356–323 B.C.), who conquered Media-Persia in 331 B.C. and assembled the greatest empire that had ever been seen up to that point in history. This leads us to our next transitional text:

> And when he shall stand up, his kingdom shall be broken, and shall be divided toward the four winds of heaven; and not to his posterity, nor according to his dominion which he ruled: for his kingdom shall be plucked up, even for others beside those. (Daniel 11:4)

This passage shows that after the death of Alexander, his empire would be divided into four distinct kingdoms. Again, the historical record will show that, after the Battle of Ipsus (301 B.C.), four former generals of Alexander would divide his empire. As related earlier, these four generals would consist of Ptolemy (Egypt, Palestine), Seleucus (Syria, Eastern

Territories), Cassander (Greece, Macedonia), and Lysimachus (Thrace, Asia Minor). Building on these trends, the next two transitional texts outline specific events in the history of the pagan Roman Empire:

> Then shall stand up in his estate a raiser of taxes in the glory of the kingdom: but within few days he shall be destroyed, neither in anger, nor in battle. (Daniel 11:20)

> And in his estate shall stand up a vile person, to whom they shall not give the honour of the kingdom: but he shall come in peaceably, and obtain the kingdom by flatteries. And with the arms of a flood shall they be overflown from before him, and shall be broken; yea, also the prince of the covenant. (Daniel 11:21–22)

As we assess the first passage above, the physician Luke stated that this "raiser of taxes" would be the pagan Roman emperor Caesar Augustus (reign, 27 B.C.–A.D. 14); he stated that "it came to pass in those days, that there went out a decree from Caesar Augustus, that all the world should be taxed" (Luke 2:1). Caesar Augustus would not die "in anger, nor in battle," but would die a natural death and be succeeded by Tiberius Caesar (reign, A.D. 14–37). Tiberius is the subject of the second transitional text above, who was the emperor in power when Christ, the "prince of the covenant," was "broken," or crucified.[175] Thus, these two passages clearly place us in the history of pagan Rome (168 B.C.–A.D. 476). Our next transitional text will take us into the historical phase of the papal Roman Empire (A.D. 538–1798):

> And arms shall stand on his part, and they shall pollute the sanctuary of strength, and shall take away the daily sacrifice, and they shall place the abomination that maketh desolate. (Daniel 11:31).

Our review of Daniel 8 had established the papacy as a desolating power (Daniel 8:11–12); therefore, the "abomination that maketh desolate" in the above passage relates to the papal Roman Empire, which assumed a Dark Age reign of persecution from A.D. 538–1798. This specific period can be confirmed by our next transitional passage:

> And they that understand among the people shall instruct many: yet they shall fall by the sword, and by flame, by captivity, and by

---

175 See Isaiah 9:6, Daniel 9:24–27, and Acts 5:31.

spoil, many days. … And some of them of understanding shall fall, to try them, and to purge, and to make them white, even to the time of the end: because it is yet for a time appointed. And the king shall do according to his will; and he shall exalt himself, and magnify himself above every god, and shall speak marvellous things against the God of gods, and shall prosper till the indignation be accomplished: for that that is determined shall be done. Neither shall he regard the God of his fathers, nor the desire of women, nor regard any god: for he shall magnify himself above all. (Daniel 11:33, 35–37)

These details, when compared with Daniel 7:8, 25 and Daniel 8:24–25, confirm the exaltation of the papacy and its Dark Age reign of persecution. Our final transitional text will describe a prophetic period known as the "time of the end," which would begin after the end of the Dark Age reign of the papal power in 1798:

And at the time of the end shall the king of the south push at him: and the king of the north shall come against him like a whirlwind, with chariots, and with horsemen, and with many ships; and he shall enter into the countries, and shall overflow and pass over. (Daniel 11:40)

The key phrase in the above passage would be the "time of the end." Daniel was actually told to "seal" up his prophecy until the "time of the end" (Daniel 12:4). After Daniel asked when this "end," or "time of the end," would begin, he was told that it would take place after the "time," "times," and a "half," which would correspond to the 1,260-year papal rule (Daniel 12:5–9, 7:25). Thus, the "time of the end" began in A.D. 1798 and will span to the end of time.[176]

An examination of Daniel 11:40–45, which we have divided into six separate chapters for simplification purposes, will reveal that this passage describes the career of a resurrected, "healed" papal Rome, which will actually parallel Revelation 13:1–3 and Revelation 17:1–11. The specific passage of Daniel 11:40–45 will apply directly to last-day events that relate to our time. To summarize, here is a basic list of the seven historical passages that we have identified in Daniel 11:

---

176 Please refer to chapters 14–19 for an examination of Daniel 11:40–45. See also pages 179–180, 240–241 of this book for a review of the "time of the end."

(1) Daniel 11:2–3	Media-Persian Empire (539–331 B.C.)
	Greek Empire (331–168 B.C.)
	Alexander (356–323 B.C.)
(2) Daniel 11:4	Four Hellenistic Empires (301–30 B.C.)
(3) Daniel 11:20	Pagan Rome, Augustus (27 B.C.–A.D. 14)
(4) Daniel 11:21–22	Pagan Rome, Tiberius (A.D. 14–37)
(5) Daniel 11:31	Papacy, desolating power (A.D. 538)
(6) Daniel 11:33–37	Papal Dark Ages (A.D. 538–1798)
(7) Daniel 11:40	"The Time of the End" (1798–End)

Given these historical transitions,[177] we are now prepared to engage Daniel 11 on a verse-by-verse basis in order to confirm and solidify the prophetic chronology that we have established up to this point. And, hopefully, as we go through and discuss each historical transition, the overall chronology of Daniel 11 will become much clearer and easier to understand.

---

177 Gerhard Pfandl, *Daniel: The Seer of Babylon* (Hagerstown, MD: Review and Herald, 2004), 108–109.

EIGHT

An Examination of Daniel 11:1–4 "Media-Persia, Greece, and Four Hellenistic Empires"

H aving laid a solid foundation from our review of Daniel chapters 2, 7, 8, and Revelation 13 and 17, we are now prepared to begin our examination of Daniel 11. We will remember that in Daniel 2 and 7, the prophetic chronology began with the Babylonian Empire. Daniel 8, on the other hand, actually began its prophetic chronology with the Media-Persian Empire, omitting the Babylonian Empire altogether; similarly, Daniel 11 also begins its prophetic chronology with the Media-Persian Empire, and then traces the rise of the Greek Empire and the Hellenistic Kingdoms that emerged after the death of Alexander the Great.

> Also I in the first year of Darius the Mede, even I, stood to confirm and to strengthen him. And now will I show thee the truth. Behold, there shall stand up yet three kings in Persia; and the fourth shall be far richer than they all: and by his strength through his riches he shall stir up all against the realm of Grecia. (Daniel 11:1, 2)

Behold, there shall stand up yet three kings in Persia; and the fourth shall be far richer than they all: and by his strength through his riches he shall stir up all against the realm of Grecia. In the first year of the reign of King Darius the Mede, during the third year of the reign of King Cyrus the Persian (535–534 B.C.),[178] Gabriel gave Daniel a revelation of four future kings to emerge in Media-Persia that would be a prelude to the rise

---

178 Edwin R. Thiele, *The Mysterious Numbers of the Hebrew Kings* (Grand Rapids, MI: Kregel Publications, 1983), 227. This source reveals that Cyrus ruled from approximately 538–530 B.C. Thus, his third year would be in the years 535–534 B.C. See also Jacques Doukhan, *Secrets of Daniel: Wisdom and Dreams of a Jewish Prince in Exile* (Hagerstown, MD: Review and Herald, 2000), 167.

of "Grecia," or Greece. He stated that three of the four kings would emerge successively, and then a fourth king would arise and become more wealthy and powerful than the prior three kings, and ultimately wage war against the rising Greek Empire.

Several historical sources advocate that the chronology of these four Persian kings who had ruled after the co-regency of Darius and Cyrus would consist of (1) Cambyses (529–522 B.C.), (2) False Smerdis the Usurper (522 B.C.), (3) Darius I (521–486 B.C.), and (4) Xerxes (485–465), the king of the book of Esther.[179] This fourth king, Xerxes, would be quite rich and powerful, and would constitute the last Persian king to invade and wage war with Greece. He fought the Greek army at the Battle of Thermopylae (480 B.C.), and later in the same year suffered a disastrous defeat during a naval campaign at Salamis; by the next year, the armies of Greece drove the Persians from Greek soil forever after winning the Battle of Plataea (479 B.C.).[180] Yet, nearly 150 years later, after liberating the Greek settlements of Asia Minor (called "Ionia" by the Greeks) from Persian rule (334–333 B.C.) and winning the Battle of Gaugamela near Arbela (331 B.C.), Alexander the Great would finally conquer Media-Persia on its own soil and end its monarchy.

Interestingly enough, Adventist theologian Jacques Doukhan presents an alternate view on the chronology of the four remaining Persian kings. He suggests that the chronology of these four kings should omit the second king, False Smerdis the Usurper, and include the successor of Xerxes, i.e., Artaxerxes, for the following reasons: (1) Smerdis reigned less than one year; (2) he was Median, not Persian, and the prophecy explicitly states that these kings would be from "Persia," not Media; (3) his existence may have been a rumor concocted by Darius to justify taking the throne; (4) Herodotus, an authoritative ancient Greek historian, never mentioned False Smerdis in any of his commentaries; and (5) other "numerous commentators" besides Herodotus "overlook Smerdis."[181] Edwin Thiele, in his famous work, *The Mysterious Numbers of the Hebrew*

---

179 See Stephen N. Haskell, *The Story of Daniel the Prophet* (Brushton, NY: Teach Services, 1999), 161–178, C. Mervyn Maxwell, *God Cares*, 2 vols. (Boise, ID: Pacific Press, 1981), 1:283, Gerhard Pfandl, *Daniel: The Seer of Babylon* (Hagerstown, MD: Review and Herald, 2004), 103–104, *Seventh-day Adventist Bible Commentary*, 12 vols. (Hagerstown, MD: Review and Herald, 1957–2000), 4:864–865, and Uriah Smith, *Daniel and the Revelation* (Nashville, TN: Southern Publishing, 1949), 233–234.

180 *SDA Bible Commentary*, 4:865.

181 Doukhan, *Daniel*, 167, 180.

Kings, also excluded False Smerdis the Usurper from his chronology of the Persian kings.[182]

Doukhan therefore re-adjusts the chronology of these four Persian kings to exclude Smerdis and substitute Artaxerxes, the successor of Esther's Xerxes. He also offers further justification for this inclusion of Artaxerxes because he actually completed the decree to rebuild and restore Jerusalem, providing a starting point to begin both the 70-weeks' and 2,300-day prophecies of Daniel 8:14 and Daniel 9:20–27.[183] Although Xerxes did in fact wage extensive warfare against Greece, Artaxerxes was also a very wealthy and powerful king who meddled in Greek affairs, and was seen by many as the harshest of all the Persian kings.

Thus, Doukhan's chronology of the four Persian kings would consist of (1) Cambyses (530–522 B.C.), (2) Darius (522–486 B.C.), (3) the Xerxes of Esther (486–465 B.C.), and (4) Artaxerxes (465–423 B.C.).[184] Overall, both of these positions are viable; yet, regardless of which view one chooses to espouse, the overall chronology of Daniel chapter 11 would not be affected. Either way, the Greek Empire would be the next superpower to emerge on the scene of history.

> And a mighty king shall stand up, that shall rule with great dominion, and do according to his will. And when he shall stand up, his kingdom shall be broken, and shall be divided toward the four winds of heaven; and not to his posterity, nor according to his dominion which he ruled: for his kingdom shall be plucked up, even for others beside those. (Daniel 11:3, 4)

A mighty king shall stand up, that shall rule with great dominion, and do according to his will. While most historians agree that the kingdom of Media-Persia reigned from 539–331 B.C., they would also agree that Greece, who would clearly succeed Media-Persia, would hold supremacy from 331–168 B.C.[185] This period would also include part of the rule of the "four winds," i.e., the four Hellenistic kingdoms that four of the former generals of Alexander would establish after his unexpected death in 323 B.C.

---

182 Thiele, 227–228.

183 See Ezra 6:14, Ezra 7:11–25, and pages 43–45, 180–183.

184 Doukhan, *Daniel*, 167, 180.

185 Ibid. See also Charles Freeman, *Egypt, Greece, and Rome: Civilizations of the Ancient Mediterranean* (Oxford: Oxford University Press, 1996), 262–265. For Bible references that refer to Greece succeeding Media-Persia, see Daniel 8:20–21 and Daniel 11:2–3.

Alexander the Great was certainly one of the greatest military commanders of all time. Educated at one point by the famous Greek philosopher Aristotle, the ambitious young general inherited the Macedonian kingdom in 336 B.C. at the age of twenty after the murder of his father King Philip. By the end of his first year as king, he had moved quickly to squelch all contestants to his ascendancy by efficiently bringing all the independent Greek city states directly under Macedonian control, either through alliance or military conquest.[186] Rebellion-free security on the home front would then enable him to raise a large army and leave a politically stable homeland in order to do what his heart desired—launch an all-out invasion of the Greek archrival of Persia.

After crossing the Greek Hellespont from Macedonia into the territory of Asia Minor in 334 B.C., Alexander immediately won two decisive military engagements against Media-Persia, at the River Granicus (334 B.C.) and Issus (333 B.C.), which drove the Persian presence from the coastline of Asia Minor. He then proceeded south to conquer the entire Mediterranean coastline to Egypt, where he would build the famous city of Alexandria.

Thus, by having control of nearly all the major ports along the coastline of Asia Minor and the eastern Mediterranean, Alexander had essentially neutralized the powerful Persian naval presence by eliminating their ability to resupply land forces. The young general then moved eastward to invade the Mesopotamian region, the very heart of the Persian Empire, engaging his arch nemesis Darius III (reign, 335–331 B.C.) in a third and final battle on the plain of Gaugamela near the town of Arbela (331 B.C.).[187]

Forced to withdraw from the battle after having been outmaneuvered by the superior Greek army, Darius would eventually be murdered in cold blood by his own officers during a frantic retreat, thus signifying the end of the Media-Persian monarchy (331 B.C.).[188] Alexander would eventually

---

186 See Edwyn R. Bevan, *The House of Ptolemy: A History of Egypt under the Ptolemaic Dynasty* (Chicago: Ares Publishers, 1985), 1–17, George Willis Botsford and Charles Alexander Robinson, *Hellenic History* (New York: MacMillan Company, 1950), 298–308, Will Durant, *The Life of Greece* (New York: Simon and Schuster, 1966), 542–544, and F.W. Walbank, *The Hellenistic World* (Cambridge, MA: Harvard, 1992), 29–45.

187 See Durrant, 544–547, Freeman, 260–267, 569, Smith, 52–53, 108, 152–153, Thiele, 227–228, and Walbank, 30–33.

188 See Botsford and Robinson, 287–345, Doukhan, *Daniel*, 31–32, Durant, 538–554, Freeman, 258–267, Haskell, *Daniel the Prophet*, 35, Maxwell, 36, Pfandl, 26–27, *SDA Bible Commentary*, 4:773–774, Smith, 52–54, Thiele, 71, 227–228,

conquer an empire that would extend from the Greek Hellespont to the shores of India.[189] He had also annexed and occupied Babylon, making this wonder of the ancient world his personal capital; yet, while still only in his early thirties, after drunken reveling, he caught a fever and died unexpectedly (323 B.C.). Just before his death, when asked by his generals to whom his kingdom should go, Alexander stated the famous phrase, "To the strongest."[190]

And when he shall stand up, his kingdom shall be broken, and shall be divided toward the four winds of heaven; and not to his posterity, nor according to his dominion which he ruled: for his kingdom shall be plucked up, even for others beside those. Parallel to both the "four heads" (Daniel 7:6) and the "four notable horns" (Daniel 8:8), this passage also confirms that Alexander's kingdom would be divided toward the "four winds of heaven." His unexpected death at the near-age of 33 in 323 B.C. would cause his vast empire to go through several years of political instability because of the fact that he never had an opportunity to arrange a successor; the resulting power vacuum had produced a considerable amount of internal conflict for control between his immediate family, the Macedonian nobility, and several of his former generals. Eventually, a four-fold coalition of generals would emerge as successors to divide this vast empire.

On his deathbed, Alexander gave his royal signet ring to Perdiccas, his chief cavalry officer, who then summoned the other chief officers of the army to determine the fate of the empire. It was decided by this group that Alexander's mentally challenged half brother Arrhidaeus would be crowned king and duly renamed Philip III of Macedonia; since Alexander's wife Roxanne was pregnant at the time of the king's death, it was also decided that, if the child were a boy, he would be crowned as co-regent with Arrhidaeus. The officers decided to divide the empire into regions (satrapies) and appoint respective rulers (satraps) over these territories, which would consist of Alexander's former officers.

Incidentally, these ambitious officers could not keep the peace for long. A power struggle resulted from this complicated political situation, which eventually led to the assassination of both of Alexander's appointed heirs; Philip III was murdered by Olympias, the mother of Alexander (317 B.C.),

and Walbank, 29–45. Edwin Thiele, in his chronology of the Media-Persian kings, uses the year 332 B.C. as their last year of rule (Darius III).

189 See Botsford and Robinson, 298–341, Durant, 545–552, Freeman, 257–273, and Walbank, 32–37.

190 *SDA Bible Commentary*, 4:821–822, 865. See Freeman, 272, and Durant, 551.

and the former general Cassander murdered Alexander IV, the son of Roxanne (311–310 B.C.).

As it turned out, a powerful Macedonian noble named Antigonus the One-Eyed, the "satrap" of the region of Phrygia (i.e., Asia Minor, modern-day Turkey), emerged as the dominant military figure, and, from 316 to 301 B.C., sought to bring the entire empire under his control. He would eventually face a growing threat from a powerful four-fold military coalition between Cassander, Lysimachus, Seleucus, and Ptolemy. These four men would unite their resources and conspire to defeat and kill Antigonus in the famous Battle of Ipsus (301 B.C.).[191]

This decisive victory over Antigonus at Ipsus served as a tremendous turning point, because it had allowed these four generals to divide Alexander's former empire into four distinct kingdoms and declare themselves kings of their respective territories.[192] Thus, these "four winds" would basically consist of the four kingdoms of these former generals: (1) Ptolemy would govern Egypt, Palestine, and a portion of southern Syria; (2) Cassander would proclaim himself king of Greece and Macedonia; (3) Lysimachus would rule in Thrace and have a huge portion of Asia Minor; and (4) Seleucus would have control of northern Syria, Mesopotamia, and the eastern territories.[193]

Eventually, these four kingdoms would be reduced to three kingdoms twenty years later; Seleucus would defeat and kill Lysimachus in the Battle of Corupedium (281 B.C.), thus expanding his vast Syrian-Seleucid realm and restructuring Alexander's former empire into three remaining territories. After the death of Cassander (298 B.C.), Antigonus II Gonatus, the son of Demetrius and grandson of Antigonus the One-Eyed, would bring stability to the turbulent anarchy that had plagued

191 See the following sources about the Battle of Ipsus in 301 B.C.: Doukhan, *Daniel*, 123, Haskell, *Daniel the Prophet*, 104–109, Maxwell, 1:155–159, Pfandl, 77–79, *SDA Bible Commentary*, 4:824–825, 840–841, and Smith, 151–155. For a history on the events that took place after Alexander's death, see Bevan, *Ptolemy*, 27, Edwyn R. Bevan, *The House of Seleucus: A History of the Hellenistic Near East Under the Seleucid Dynasty*, 2 vols. (Chicago, IL: Ares, 1985), 28–39, Botsford and Robinson, 370–377, Freeman, 272–273, and Walbank, 46–59.

192 *SDA Bible Commentary*, 4:822–823. See Freeman, 272–273, Maxwell, 1:109–111, 284, and Smith 108, 109, 155, 234, 235.

193 Ibid. See also Botsford and Robinson, 381 and *SDA Bible Commentary*, 4:822–825. See the following sources on the emergence of Alexander's four generals: Haskell, *Daniel the Prophet*, 92, Maxwell, 1:109–111, 284, Pfandl, 63, *SDA Bible Commentary*, 4:821–823, and Smith, 108–109, 155, 234, and 235.

Greco-Macedonia after Cassander's death. He defeated the Gauls at Lysimacheia (277 B.C.) and would establish the Antigonid Dynasty in Macedonia (276 B.C.). Thus, by 276 B.C., three Hellenistic monarchies would stabilize, Antigonid Macedonia, Seleucid Syria, and Ptolemaic Egypt, and would dominate the Hellenistic Era, i.e., the interim of history between the death of Alexander the Great and the rise of the pagan Roman Empire.[194]

By 168 B.C., the expanding, growing pagan Roman Empire would involve themselves on a permanent basis in Greco-Macedonian affairs; led by the Roman consul and general Lucius Aemilius Paullus, the armies of Rome would deal a crushing defeat to King Perseus and the Greco-Macedonian army in the Battle of Pydna (168 B.C.). This convincing victory ended the Antigonid dynasty once and for all, and this region would later be reorganized into the Roman province of Achaea. Pagan Rome would therefore begin its reign in the year 168 B.C.[195]

Daniel 11	**Interpretation**
Verse 2	Four Persian Kings:
	(1) Cambyses,
	(2) False Smerdis,
	(3) Darius I, and
	(4) Xerxes;
	OR
	(1) Cambyses,
	(2) Darius I,
	(3) Xerxes, and
	(4) Artaxerxes
Verses 2–3	Greek Empire (331–168 B.C.)
	Alexander the Great (356–323 B.C.)

---

194 See Bevan, *Ptolemy*, 18–74, Bevan, *Seleucus*, 1:40–145, Botsford and Robinson, 368–396, Durant, 555–599, Freeman, 272–273, and Walbank, 46–59.

195 See Botsford and Robinson, 451–455, Durrant, 659–666, Freeman, 326–329, and Michael Grant, *History of Rome* (New York: Book-of-the-Month Club, 1997), 138–140.

Verse 4   Four Hellenistic Kingdoms (301 B.C.):
                        (1) Cassander (Greece, Macedonia)
                        (2) Lysimachus (Thrace, Asia Minor)
                        (3) Seleucus (Syria, Eastern regions)
                        (4) Ptolemy (Egypt, Palestine)

— NINE —
An Examination of Daniel 11:5–15 "The King of the North vs. the King of the South—Part 1"

As we examine the passage of Daniel 11:5–15, we will discover an outline of how two Hellenistic monarchies, Syria and Egypt, had fought no less than five wars in a heated border dispute over the region of Judeo-Palestine (also called Coele Syria), until their eventual overthrow by pagan Rome. In essence, God has taken the time to discuss these wars because of the fact that His people Israel dwelt in the area of contention. Furthermore, in this set of passages, Hellenistic Syria is called the "king of the north," as this power would be located "north" of Israel; in a similar fashion, Hellenistic Egypt is called the "king of the south," as this power would be located "south" of Israel.[196]

Also, it is important to note that, as this prophecy outlines the history of the relationship between Hellenistic Egypt and Hellenistic Syria, it will traverse over the history of several kings from both powers and their interaction with one another and with Israel, and yet still refer to each power as the "king of the north" and the "king of the south." We will offer a general survey of the conflict between Hellenistic Egypt and Hellenistic Syria, and discover that this section will cover each of the "Five Syrian Wars" fought between these two powers over the region of Coele-Syria, i.e., Judeo-Palestine, where the Jewish people resided.

> And the king of the south shall be strong, and one of his princes; and he shall be strong above him, and have dominion; his dominion shall be a great dominion. And in the end of years they shall join themselves together; for the king's daughter of the south shall come to the king of the north to make an agreement: but she shall not retain the power of the arm; neither shall he stand,

---

196 See *Seventh-day Adventist Bible Commentary*, 12 vols. (Hagerstown, MD: Review and Herald, 1955–2000), 4:866, and Uriah Smith, *Daniel and the Revelation* (Nashville, TN: Southern, 1949), 235–236.

nor his arm: but she shall be given up, and they that brought her, and he that begat her, and he that strengthened her in these times. (Daniel 11:5, 6)

And the king of the south shall be strong, and one of his princes; and he shall be strong above him, and have dominion; his dominion shall be a great dominion. Using Judeo-Palestine as the point of directional reference, Hellenistic Egypt would be symbolized as the "king of the south." Its first king, Ptolemy I Soter (reign, 323–282 B.C.), won distinction in the Persian campaign under Alexander the Great. Having served as one of Alexander's seven bodyguards and his personal historian, Ptolemy was one of the ablest and wisest generals in the entire Greco-Macedonian army; he foresaw that Egypt could have great possibilities because of its isolated location from the potential hostilities that could arise between the other rival generals.

At his request, he was appointed "satrap" of Egypt by Perdiccas, Alexander's former chief cavalry officer, and Philip III Arrhidaeus, one of Alexander's successors, who both oversaw the division of the empire after Alexander's death. Having established his reign without opposition, Ptolemy found that Egypt was easy to protect from invasion and possessed excellent natural defenses. He would easily consolidate his rule in this country of the Nile, becoming "strong" from the beginning of his appointment as satrap; this particular dynasty would survive the longest out of all the Hellenistic monarchies (323–30 B.C.).

Ptolemy had initially desired to greatly enhance Egyptian prestige by seizing the body of Alexander. Perdiccas had actually planned to have Alexander's body laid to rest with the house of the royal nobility in Macedonia; he had entrusted its transport to Philip III, who would take it from Babylon to Macedonia. Ptolemy, however, had other plans, and would meet the young regent at Damascus, Syria, where he would convince Philip to allow Alexander's body to be transported first to Memphis in Egypt, to await a permanent burial later at Alexandria. Perdiccas was enraged at this event, and responded by declaring war on Ptolemy; as it turned out, Perdiccas was brutally murdered in a conspiracy after attempting three separate invasions of Egypt that proved unsuccessful (320 B.C.). His own officers were among the conspirators, and the murderous entourage would be led by an ambitious former general of Alexander named Seleucus, who would later become the first Seleucid-Syrian king, Seleucus I Nicator (reign, 312–280 B.C.).

During the original breakup of Alexander's empire in 323 B.C., Seleucus was not given a territorial appointment, but would later become the "satrap" of Babylon (321 B.C.); yet, the growing power of Antigonus the One-Eyed and his son Demetrius would force him to flee to Ptolemy for protection (316 B.C.). Placing himself under Ptolemy's command, Seleucus became one of Ptolemy's "princes," receiving a commission as the commander of the Egyptian naval forces. They would later defeat Demetrius at Gaza (312 B.C.), which would allow Seleucus to return to Babylon. He eventually joined a military coalition with Cassander, Lysimachus, and Ptolemy against Antigonus and Demetrius, and would make a substantial contribution to the defeat and death of Antigonus in the Battle of Ipsus (301 B.C.).

Seleucus and Lysimachus had actually gained the most territory after the Battle of Ipsus, which later led to a showdown between these two former generals in the Battle of Corupedium (281 B.C.). After Lysimachus was defeated and killed, Seleucus emerged as the most powerful king with the largest territory of all the former generals of Alexander. He would become more powerful than his former ally Ptolemy ("strong above him"), having "great dominion" as the greatest king of all of Alexander's successors.

The contention that Ptolemy I and Seleucus I would have over Coele Syria had its origin shortly after the death of Alexander. Ptolemy was originally awarded this region and would occupy it during the defeat of Demetrius at Gaza (312 B.C.). Yet, as Seleucus I would grow more powerful, this coveted region became a strong source of contention because of its location and natural resources. Following Antigonus' defeat at Ipsus by the four generals (301 B.C.), Ptolemy I occupied Coele Syria once again, but Seleucus objected, contending that, during the Battle of Ipsus, his Egyptian colleague had withdrawn his army after hearing a false rumor that Lysimachus had been defeated; as a result, Ptolemy had provided no military support for the operation.

When the battle was over, Ptolemy I once again claimed rights over the region, but the other three generals had felt that his withdrawal from the war effort had made him unworthy of any territorial gain, and decided in favor of giving Coele Syria to Seleucus. Remaining firm, Ptolemy I refused to surrender the region to his Syrian colleague, and, because he realized that he owed his own rise to power in part to Ptolemy I for his past protection from Antigonus and Demetrius, Seleucus I was obliged to stand down in the dispute. Yet, this contention over Coele Syria would eventually resurface and result in the "Five Syrian Wars."[197]

---

197 See Edwyn R. Bevan, *The House of Ptolemy: A History of Egypt under the*

And in the end of years they shall join themselves together. This passage states that "in the end of years" Egypt and Syria would reconcile their differences and "join themselves together." This became a necessity because of the fact that the two powers had engaged in both the "First" and "Second" Syrian Wars. Ptolemy II Philadelphus (reign, 282–245 B.C.) had succeeded Ptolemy I to the throne of Egypt, and felt increasingly insecure about the growing power of Seleucus I. Yet, Seleucus I was unexpectedly assassinated in 280 B.C. by Ptolemy Keraunos, the half brother of Ptolemy II, and was succeeded by Antiochus I Soter (reign, 280–261 B.C.).

Already in occupation of Coele Syria, Ptolemy II started the "First Syrian War" (276–271 B.C.) with a first-strike invasion against Antiochus I, with the intent of preventing the new king from seeking revenge on the Egyptian family for his father's assassination. The two kings eventually concluded peace by 271 B.C., which allowed Ptolemy to retain control of Coele Syria. Antiochus I was later killed in the war against Eumenes I of Pergamos (261 B.C.), and was succeeded next by Antiochus II Theos (reign, 261–246 B.C.).[198]

For the king's daughter of the south shall come to the king of the north to make an agreement. Launching the "Second Syrian War" (261–252 B.C.), Antiochus II sought to recover the territories lost during the "First Syrian War," and met with some success. Yet, growing weary of continual conflict, the two kings would eventually "join themselves together" in peace (252 B.C.); in this treaty, "the king's daughter of the south" came "to the king of the north to make an agreement." To secure peace, Ptolemy II would offer his daughter Berenice in marriage to Antiochus II (which would include a lucrative dowry); the Seleucid king agreed to these terms, and exiled his current wife, queen Laodice, and their two sons in the process.[199]

Ptolemaic Dynasty (Chicago, IL: Ares, 1985), 21–37, Edwyn R. Bevan, *The House of Seleucus: A History of the Hellenistic Near East under the Seleucid Dynasty*, 2 vols. (Chicago, IL: Ares, 1985), 1:28–73, George W. Botsford and Charles Alexander Robinson, *Hellenic History* (New York: MacMillan, 1950), 370–384, Will Durant, *History of Greece* (New York: Simon and Schuster, 1966), 572, 579, 585, Charles Freeman, *Egypt, Greece, and Rome: Civilizations of the Ancient Mediterranean* (Oxford: Oxford Press, 1996), 272–273, C. Mervyn Maxwell, *God Cares*, 2 vols. (Boise, ID: Pacific Press, 1981), 1:277, 284–285, *SDA Bible Commentary*, 4:866, Smith, 236, and F.W. Walbank, *The Hellenistic World* (Cambridge, MA: Harvard, 1992), 101.

198 See Bevan, *Ptolemy*, 61–63, Bevan, *Seleucus*, 1:127–170, 206–237, Botsford and Robinson, 392, Maxwell, 1:284–291, *SDA Bible Commentary*, 4:866–869, and Smith, 235–255.

199 See Bevan, *Ptolemy*, 69–70, 189–204, Bevan, *Seleucus*, 1:171–237, Botsford

But she shall not retain the power of the arm; neither shall he stand, nor his arm: but she shall be given up, and they that brought her, and he that begat her, and he that strengthened her in these times. Humiliated by her former husband, Laodice exacted revenge by assassinating Antiochus II through poisoning (246 B.C.); thus, the one "who strengthened" Berenice in those "times" did not "stand." Having no protection, Berenice and her infant son were also eventually executed by Laodice, who would then have her own son proclaimed king, Seleucus II Callinicus (reign, 246–226 B.C.). Therefore, having been "given up" and murdered with "they that brought her" (her attendants), Berenice would "not retain the power of the arm," and her infant son, "he that begat her," literally "whom she brought forth," would also meet with the same fate, falling victim to the avenging wrath of the former queen Laodice.[200]

> But out of a branch of her roots shall one stand up in his estate, which shall come with an army, and shall enter into the fortress of the king of the north, and shall deal against them, and shall prevail: And shall also carry captives into Egypt their gods, with their princes, and with their precious vessels of silver and of gold; and he shall continue more years than the king of the north. So the king of the south shall come into his kingdom, and shall return into his own land. (Daniel 11:7–9)

But out of a branch of her roots shall one stand up in his estate, which shall come with an army, and shall enter into the fortress of the king of the north, and shall deal against them, and shall prevail. Hearing that his sister was besieged by Laodice, Ptolemy III Euergetes (reign, 247–221 B.C.), the son of Ptolemy II, a "branch" of Berenice's "roots," launched the "Third Syrian War" (246–240 B.C., also called the "Laodicean War"), marching against Syria while his sister was still alive. Having arrived too late to save the life of Berenice, Ptolemy III then desired to "deal against them" by coming "with an army;" he would ultimately "prevail," as this invasion "into the fortress of the king of the north" had led to the greatest military victory over Seleucid Syria ever achieved by the Ptolemaic dynasty. He conquered many Syrian cities, and would have completed the total conquest of the Syrian Empire altogether had he not been forced to withdraw to Egypt because of

---

and Robinson, 393–394, Maxwell, 1:284–291, *SDA Bible Commentary*, 4:866–869, and Smith, 235–255.

200 Ibid, and Walbank, 123–140.

a homeland rebellion. Even so, Ptolemy III still returned to the land of the Nile as a conquering king sporting the spoils of victory.[201]

And shall also carry captives into Egypt their gods, with their princes, and with their precious vessels of silver and of gold; and he shall continue more years than the king of the north. So the king of the south shall come into his kingdom, and shall return into his own land. Despite having to return home in the face of an uprising, Ptolemy III would return to Egypt in triumph, carrying "captives into Egypt their gods" and the "precious vessels of silver and gold," thus recovering pagan idols that had been taken from Egypt by the Persians in former conquests. In the face of Ptolemy's return to Egypt, a resurgent Seleucus II would regain much of his former territory (242–241 B.C.), and would even attempt an invasion of Coele Syria. This would result in a disastrous defeat for Seleucus II, and the two powers would eventually reach another peace agreement in 240 B.C. that would end the "Third Syrian War." Overall, Ptolemy III would come "into his kingdom," returning to "his own land," and continue "more years than the king of the north," living until 221 B.C.; the worn-down Seleucus II would die an unexpected death after falling from his horse during a Parthian military campaign in 226 B.C.[202]

> But his sons shall be stirred up, and shall assemble a multitude of great forces: and one shall certainly come, and overflow, and pass through: then shall he return, and be stirred up, even to his fortress. And the king of the south shall be moved with choler, and shall come forth and fight with him, even with the king of the north: and he shall set forth a great multitude; but the multitude shall be given into his hand. And when he hath taken away the multitude, his heart shall be lifted up; and he shall cast down many ten thousands: but he shall not be strengthened by it. For the king of the north shall return, and shall set forth a multitude greater than the former, and shall certainly come after certain years with a great army and with much riches. (Daniel 11:10–13)

---

201 See Bevan, *Ptolemy*, 69–70, 189–204, Bevan, *Seleucus*, 1:171–237, 328, Botsford and Robinson, 393–394, Maxwell, 1:284–291, *SDA Bible Commentary*, 4:866–869, and Smith, 235–255.

202 See Bevan, *Ptolemy*, 69–70, 189–204, Bevan, *Seleucus*, 1:171–237, 328, Botsford and Robinson, 393–394, Durrant, 587, Maxwell, 1:284–291, *SDA Bible Commentary*, 4:866–869, and Smith, 235–255.

But his sons shall be stirred up, and shall assemble a multitude of great forces: and one shall certainly come, and overflow, and pass through: then shall he return, and be stirred up, even to his fortress. Because of the unprecedented victory of Ptolemy III in the Third Syrian War, the two sons of Seleucus II were "stirred up" to avenge the humiliation of their father. The weak and short-tempered Seleucus III Ceraunus Soter (reign, 225–223 B.C.) ascended to the throne, but ruled only for a short time after being poisoned by his military officers. He was succeeded by his eighteen-year-old brother Antiochus III Magnus (reign, 223–187 B.C.), who assembled "a multitude of great forces" to launch the Fourth Syrian War (219–217 B.C.). He would "overflow," meeting with initial success, re-capturing much of the territory lost during the Third Syrian War, which would also include the prize of Coele Syria.

These victories by Antiochus III were so decisive that the Egyptian naval presence in the Mediterranean had been neutralized and its army demoralized, thus leaving Egypt open to invasion; yet, despite the vulnerability of his rival, Antiochus III delayed to capitalize on this opportunity. This costly hesitation on his part, coupled with the distraction of an internal rebellion in the east by a disloyal satrap in Babylon, would delay Antiochus' attention on Egypt long enough to give the successor of Ptolemy III, Ptolemy IV Philopater (reign, 221–203 B.C.), the necessary time needed to regroup and assemble a powerful army. Later, by the time Antiochus III had returned from his eastern distraction in Babylon to resume his warfare against Egypt, Ptolemy IV had rebuilt a large enough military force to contend with his Seleucid rival and attempt to recapture Coele Syria.[203]

And the king of the south shall be moved with choler, and shall come forth and fight with him, even with the king of the north: and he shall set forth a great multitude; but the multitude shall be given into his hand. And when he hath taken away the multitude, his heart shall be lifted up; and he shall cast down many ten thousands: but he shall not be strengthened by it. Having secured enough time to assemble and train a large invasion force, described in this passage as a "great multitude," Ptolemy IV would thus "be moved with choler" to continue the "Fourth Syrian War" against the "king of the north." He would march his army into Palestine once again, taking up a position south of Gaza near Raphia (217 B.C.); on June 22 the two armies met in battle, and Antiochus III would

---

203 See Bevan, *Ptolemy*, 222–230, Bevan, *Seleucus*, 1:181–237, 300–320, 2:14–38, Botsford and Robinson, 395–396, Maxwell, 1:284–291, *SDA Bible Commentary*, 4:866–869, and Smith, 235–255.

initially taste success; but after the cavalry on both sides had neutralized each other, the infantry would be left to decide the outcome.

As it turned out, the superior wisdom of his Greek commanders and the well-disciplined condition of his army would allow Ptolemy IV to triumph. In the end, the "multitude" of the Seleucid army was "given" into his "hand." His victory at Raphia would present a similar opportunity to that of Antiochus III two years earlier, as Syria would then lay open to invasion. Yet, consistent with the cautious attitude characteristic of the Ptolemaic dynasty, Ptolemy IV would be content with only regaining Coele Syria and did not complete the conquest of Syria in its entirety. Thus, while having "taken away the multitude," Ptolemy IV would "not be strengthened by" this victory and would return to his homeland, fully content with the status quo.[204]

For the king of the north shall return, and shall set forth a multitude greater than the former, and shall certainly come after certain years with a great army and with much riches. Once again, the "king of the north" would "return" with "a multitude greater than the former," coming "after certain years with a great army and with much riches." In other words, Antiochus III would regroup militarily from the years 212–204 B.C., and attempt to renew his warfare with Egypt; he would also seek to capitalize on the death of Ptolemy IV, who would be succeeded by a five-year-old boy-king named Ptolemy V Epiphanes (reign, 203–181 B.C.).

Antiochus III felt that the youth of Ptolemy V presented an ample opportunity to seek revenge for his defeat at Raphia (217 B.C.). By starting the "Fifth Syrian War" (202–200 B.C.) through an invasion of southern Syria, the seizure of Gaza, and the occupation of Palestine, Antiochus III desired to press south to pulverize the young Egyptian monarch with an outright invasion of Egypt itself.[205] The young boy-king would respond by dispatching his army under the leadership of an Aetolian commander named Scopas, who would initially meet with success in recapturing southern Syria, Gaza, and Palestine, driving the forces of Antiochus III back into the region of Lebanon (202–201 B.C.).[206]

---

204 Ibid.

205 See Bevan, *Ptolemy*, 189–216, Bevan, *Seleucus*, 1:171, 205, 328, Botsford and Robinson, 391–396, Durant, 587, Maxwell, 1:287, *SDA Bible Commentary*, 4:867, and Smith, 238–242.

206 See Bevan, *Ptolemy*, 252–258, Bevan, *Seleucus*, 1:181–237, 2:14–38, Botsford and Robinson, 451, Maxwell, 1:284–291, *SDA Bible Commentary*, 4:866–869, Smith, 235–255, and Walbank, 101.

Yet, even in the face of Scopas' initial success during the re-invasion of Coele Syria, Antiochus III would not be deterred and launched another attack on the region; he would eventually meet Scopas in battle near a mouth of the Jordan River at a place called "the Panium" (201–200 B.C.), later renamed Caesarea Philippi. This battle would serve as the major turning point in the history of the Syrian wars, because Antiochus III would rout Scopas and the Egyptian armies so decisively that Ptolemaic control of Coele Syria would end once and for all. With the eventual besiegement of the remaining Egyptian forces at Sidon, Scopas had no choice but to surrender unconditionally. Thus, the Battle of the Panium eventually concluded the "Fifth Syrian War" and Egypt would never have control over Coele Syria again.[207]

> And in those times there shall many stand up against the king of the south: also the robbers of thy people shall exalt themselves to establish the vision; but they shall fall. So the king of the north shall come, and cast up a mount, and take the most fenced cities: and the arms of the south shall not withstand, neither his chosen people, neither shall there be any strength to withstand. (Daniel 11:14–15)

And in those times there shall many stand up against the king of the south: also the robbers of thy people shall exalt themselves to establish the vision; but they shall fall. So the king of the north shall come, and cast up a mount, and take the most fenced cities: and the arms of the south shall not withstand, neither his chosen people, neither shall there be any strength to withstand. The Battle of the Panium (201–200 B.C.) resulted in the expulsion of Egypt from Coele Syria once and for all, while at the same time seriously weakening its status as a Mediterranean power. Having become vulnerable to foreign invasion, this defeat had marked the beginning of the end for Ptolemaic Egypt. Many "in those times" would "stand up against the king of the south," and this would be especially true in the career of Antiochus IV Epiphanes (reign, 175–163 B.C.). He had launched a successful invasion of Egypt that would later bring pagan Rome directly into Middle Eastern affairs and eventually lead to the demise of both the Seleucid and Ptolemaic dynasties.

After the death of Ptolemy V Epiphanes (181 B.C.), another young boy-king, Ptolemy VI Philometor (reign, 181–145 B.C.), would ascend to the throne at a very young age. This young king would be under the guardianship

---

207 Ibid.

of two ministers of state, Eulaeus and Lenaeus, who began to plan another invasion of Coele Syria (170 B.C.) in revenge for the Egyptian defeat at the Battle of the Panium. Despite a recent warning from Rome, Antiochus IV purposed to defeat the plans of Eulaeus and Lenaeus by launching a "first-strike" invasion of Egypt. As it turned out, Rome was still involved in the affairs of Greece in dealing with King Perseus of Macedonia, and could not involve itself in this particular conflict; furthermore, Antiochus IV moved with such speed that he actually met the Egyptian army before they even crossed the desert area into southern Syria.

Because the "arms of the south" would not have "any strength to withstand" him, Antiochus IV crushed the Egyptian army so convincingly that he marched unopposed into Egypt and occupied the city of Memphis. Meanwhile, at Alexandria, Eulaeus and Lenaeus had been overthrown and replaced by two new ministers of state, Comanus and Cineas, who proclaimed the younger brother of Ptolemy VI as king, Ptolemy VII Euergetes II (reign, 145–116 B.C.). Satisfied that Egypt was divided in an internal conflict between two rival brother-kings, Antiochus IV withdrew and returned home to Syria (169 B.C.).

Yet, interestingly enough, Ptolemy VI and Ptolemy VII formed an alliance and agreed to share the throne of Egypt; this alarming development moved Antiochus IV to rethink his position and re-invade the "king of the south" in the next year (168 B.C.). Once again, he met with no resistance, marching into both Memphis and Alexandria. Meanwhile, having defeated King Perseus of Macedonia with a victory at Pydna (168 B.C.), Rome was now in a position to intervene in behalf of Egypt; the Roman embassy, headed by Gaius Popillius Laenas, met Antiochus IV at Alexandria in the same year. As the two men greeted, Popillius promptly took his staff and drew a circle on the ground around the feet of the Seleucid king, ordering him to evacuate Egypt at once. He was not allowed to step outside the circle until he had acquiesced to Rome's demands. Thus, under the threat of Roman intimidation, Antiochus IV agreed to withdraw, and the Roman ambassadors escorted both him and his army safely out of Egypt.

In addition to being one of the many Seleucid kings that would "stand up" against the "king of the south," Antiochus IV would also be one of the "robbers of thy people," namely Daniel's people Israel. While occupying Egypt the second time (168 B.C.), Antiochus IV had heard that Jerusalem had rebelled against Seleucid rule and declared for Ptolemy; still upset from his humiliation at the hands of Rome and in desperate need of financial resources, Antiochus IV viewed this defection as treason and sought to exact revenge by plundering the city and the temple. Because Daniel's "chosen people" could "not withstand" him, Antiochus IV would successfully invade Jerusalem (168–167 B.C.) and "rob" the people of Daniel. He would strip the sanctuary of all its treasures, plunder the resources of the city, and murder thousands of people, selling many more thousands into slavery.

Antiochus would also eventually pass a royal edict to ban Judaism and implement a policy of forced Hellenism, erecting pagan altars and instituting sacrifices in the process (167 B.C.). In essence, he desired the total eradication of the Jewish culture and religion, but this desire would ultimately backfire. By sending his army back into Judea with the intention of committing genocide, Antiochus had actually provoked a Jewish revolt that would arise under the leadership of Judas Maccabeus. This revolt would eventually result in the complete removal of the Seleucid presence from Judea altogether (141 B.C.). Thus, Antiochus IV, who attempted to "exalt" himself by "robbing" the people of Daniel, would ultimately "fall" and fail "to establish the vision."[208]

Overall, as we blend Bible prophecy with the record of history, we can see that the passage of Daniel 11:5–15 describes a very interesting historical period consisting of the "Five Syrian Wars" between Hellenistic Seleucid-Syria, the "king of the north" (north of Palestine), and Hellenistic Ptolemaic-Egypt, the "king of the south" (south of Palestine) over the region of Judeo-Palestine (Coele Syria). In this interim period of history that spanned from the death of Alexander the Great (323 B.C.) to the rise of pagan Rome (168 B.C.), Syria and Egypt fought these "Five Syrian Wars" at different times, spanning the reigns of several different kings from each of these two powers. In conclusion, God has included this era of history in the Bible because these "Five Syrian Wars" had a direct effect on His chosen people at that time, namely the Jewish people who were located in the region of Coele Syria, i.e., Judeo-Palestine.

Daniel 11	Interpretation
Verse 5	*King of South*—Ptolemaic Egypt Ptolemy I Soter (323–282 B.C.)
	King of North—Seleucid Syria Seleucus I Nicator (312–280 B.C.)

---

208 Bevan, *Ptolemy*, 282–286, Bevan, *Seleucus*, 2:134–145, 162–177, 267, Botsford and Robinson, 451–455, Freeman, 292–293, 326–329, 349, Grant, 131–145, 196, and *SDA Bible Commentary*, 4:868–869.

Verses 6–9	*First Syrian War* (276–271 B.C.) Ptolemy II Philadelphus vs. Antiochus I Soter
	Second Syrian War (261–252 B.C.) Antiochus II Theos vs. Ptolemy II Philadelphus
	Third Syrian War (246–240 B.C.) Ptolemy III Euergetes vs. Seleucus II Callinicus
Verses 10–13	*Fourth Syrian War* (219–217 B.C.) Antiochus III Magnus vs. Ptolemy IV Philopater
Verses 14–15	*Fifth Syrian War* (202–199 B.C.) Antiochus III Magnus vs. Ptolemy V Epiphanes
	Robbers of people—Seleucid plunder of Jerusalem and the temple under Antiochus IV Epiphanes (reign, 175–163 B.C.)

— TEN —
An Examination of Daniel 11:16–22
"The Rise of Pagan Rome and the Crucifixion of Christ"

I n this particular chapter, we will discuss the main historical transitions of Daniel 11:16–22, which highlight certain trends in the career of pagan Rome. These particular trends can be divided into four basic categories: (1) the conquest of Seleucid-Syria and Judeo-Palestine by Pompey the Great (verse 16); (2) the involvement of Gaius Julius Caesar in Egyptian affairs (verses 17–19); (3) the rise and peaceful death of Caesar Augustus, the grandnephew of Julius Caesar (verse 20); and (4) the emergence of the "vile" Tiberius Caesar, Augustus' successor, who reigned as emperor when Christ was crucified (verses 21–22).

> But he that cometh against him shall do according to his own will, and none shall stand before him: and he shall stand in the glorious land, which by his hand shall be consumed. (Daniel 11:16)

But he that cometh against him shall do according to his own will, and none shall stand before him. In essence, this passage is speaking of the time when pagan Rome would subjugate the Seleucid-Syrian kingdom. We could state the above passage like this: "But he [pagan Rome] that cometh against him [Seleucid-Syria, the "king of the north"] shall do according to his own will, and none shall stand before him [pagan Rome]." Furthermore, because pagan Rome would come from the "north" to conquer Syria, it would "replace" this empire as the "king of the north."[209] And, as this new "king of the north" would expand in influence throughout the entire Mediterranean world, thus doing "according to his own will," each of the kingdoms of Alexander's former empire would eventually fall under Roman authority.

At the end of our last chapter, we had discussed that the passage of Daniel 11:14–15 offers a description of the conquest of Egypt and

---

209 See pages 37–38 concerning the "replacement principle."

Judeo-Palestine by the Seleucid-Syrian king Antiochus IV Epiphanes. After the Roman general and consul Lucius Aemilius Paullus defeated King Perseus of Greco-Macedonia in the Battle of Pydna (168 B.C.), which would bring Greece under Roman authority, Rome would then come "against" Antiochus IV, who had by that time occupied Egypt (169–168 B.C.). As stated in our last chapter, a Roman ambassador, Gaius Popillius Laenas, went to Alexandria with the express purpose of forcing Antiochus IV to withdraw from Egypt. After greeting him, Popillius promptly drew a circle around the feet of the Seleucid king with his staff, demanding that he not step outside of the circle until he had decided in favor of a complete Syrian withdrawal. Thus, Rome would "do according to" its "own will," as Antiochus IV would acquiesce to Rome's demands under the threat of military force and withdraw from Egypt.

And he shall stand in the glorious land, which by his hand shall be consumed. This phrase actually describes that pagan Rome would further involve itself in Syrian affairs by ending the Seleucid monarchy and intervening in the affairs of Judeo-Palestine. Thus, we could rephrase the above passage by stating that "he [pagan Rome, the new "king of the north"] shall stand in the glorious land [Judeo-Palestine, Israel], which by his hand shall be consumed." History will demonstrate that the end of the Seleucid-Syrian Empire and the subsequent subjugation of Judeo-Palestine would become a reality in the career of Gnaeus Pompeius Magnus, also known as "Pompey the Great."

The son of a former Roman consul, Pompey would make his entry into public life by winning acclamation as a powerful military commander serving under the Roman dictator Lucius Cornelius Sulla. In fact, his exceptional ability as a general made him so successful that he would earn the surname "the Great" by the young age of twenty-five (83 B.C.). His suppression of rebellions in both Italy (77 B.C.) and Spain (72 B.C.), and his military contribution in the defeat of the famous Thracian slave-gladiator Spartacus (73–72 B.C.) would enable Pompey to win a consulship without going through the traditional political channels of the Roman republican system (70 B.C.).[210]

After retiring to private life in 69 B.C., he would soon be called back to active duty. The rise in Mediterranean piracy had brought significant instability to Roman shipping and had even threatened Rome's corn supply.

---

210 See Charles Freeman, *Egypt, Greece, and Rome: Civilizations of the Ancient Mediterranean* (Oxford: Oxford University Press, 1996), 347–348, and Michael Grant, *The History of Rome* (New York: Book-of-the-Month Club, 1978), 192–194.

After Rome experienced the sack of specific Greek shrines and the capture of two Roman politicians during a pirate raid on Italy, the Roman senate ratified a three-year command for Pompey, granting him the power to clear the Mediterranean sea of all piracy (67 B.C.). Amazingly, Pompey had brought complete stability to the seas within the space of only three months; this swift success against Mediterranean piracy would earn him an "eastern command" the very next year to handle Roman affairs in the Middle East (66 B.C.).

This "eastern command" would bring the Roman presence directly into Judeo-Syrian affairs. The question of Syria would be one of several issues that would require the immediate attention of Pompey. Antiochus XIII Asiaticus, the rightful heir to the Syrian throne, had requested that Pompey help to establish his rule over Syria; as it turned out, Pompey had rejected this request and decided instead to end the Seleucid dynasty and reorganize Syria into a Roman province (64–63 B.C.).[211] This conquest would allow pagan Rome to "replace" Syria as the "king of the north," leaving Hellenistic Egypt as the sole survivor of the legacy of Alexander the Great.

Soon after settling the Syrian question, Pompey would next involve himself in Judeo-Palestinian affairs. He would learn that two rival brothers, Hyrcanus and Aristobulus, were engaged in a struggle for the throne of Judea, and both had appealed to him for support. After hearing the case of each brother, Pompey had been inclined to decide in favor of the oldest brother, Hyrcanus, but decided to postpone a settlement of the conflict until after his completion of a prospective Arabian campaign. Pompey informed both Hyrcanus and Aristobulus to stand down in their conflict with each other until he returned from Arabia to settle the dispute.

Incidentally, Aristobulus, who had seized rulership from his older brother by force, became greatly disaffected at Pompey's favoritism of Hyrcanus, and returned to Judea with the intention of preparing for war with the Romans. Pompey would eventually hear of this activity, and moved on Judea to deal with Aristobulus. He came to a place called Coreae, near the entrance of Judea, and found that Aristobulus and his supporters had fled to a fortification in Coreae called Alexandrium; coming to his senses, Aristobulus eventually decided to meet with Pompey and attempt to make peace with him. He offered large amounts of tribute and the submission of Judea to Roman authority in exchange for peace; Pompey agreed to these

---

211 Edwyn R. Bevan, *The House of Seleucus: A History of the Hellenistic Near East under the Seleucid Dynasty*, 2 vols. (Chicago: Ares Publishers, 1985), 2:267, Freeman, 348–350, and Grant, *History of Rome*, 195–197.

terms and also ordered Aristobulus to compel his regional governors to submit unconditionally to Roman authority.

Yet, once again, Aristobulus became greatly disaffected at the thought of submission to Rome; he promptly returned to Jerusalem with the intent of raising another army, and again made immediate preparations for war. This second disaffection by Aristobulus would compel Pompey to march directly on Jerusalem itself. Interestingly, Aristobulus would have another change of heart; he met Pompey outside of the city, promising to pay the allotted tribute and surrender Jerusalem to Roman control. Holding Aristobulus in custody, Pompey again agreed to these terms, and sent a commander named Gabinius to the city with a detachment of soldiers to receive the tribute and accept the terms of surrender. Unfortunately, Gabinius was spurned by the supporters of Aristobulus, and he returned to Pompey empty-handed.

This blatant act of contempt moved Pompey to place Aristobulus under arrest and make immediate plans to besiege Jerusalem. After the followers of Hyrcanus had opened the city gates to the Roman armies, the supporters of Aristobulus fled to the temple fortification with the intention of offering a bold resistance. Yet, after a lengthy three-month siege, Pompey would finally overrun the temple stronghold and capture the temple itself. Surprisingly, he would leave the temple furniture and its treasury intact; he did, however, demolish the walls of the city during the siege, and ended up slaughtering 12,000 Jewish rebels who had fought against him in the resistance. When Jerusalem was finally pacified, Hyrcanus was rightfully restored to power, while Aristobulus and his family were taken to Rome in chains. Thus, by 63 B.C., through the military might of Pompey the Great, pagan Rome would "stand in" and "consume" the "glorious land" of Israel, as both Syria and Judeo-Palestine would become pagan Roman provinces.[212]

> He shall also set his face to enter with the strength of his whole kingdom, and upright ones with him; thus shall he do: and he shall give him the daughter of women, corrupting her: but she shall not stand on his side, neither be for him. After this shall he turn his face unto the isles, and shall take many: but a prince for his own

---

212 See *The Complete Works of Josephus*, translated by William Whiston (Lynn, MA: Hendrickson Publishers, 1981), 291–293, 434–436, *Seventh-day Adventist Bible Commentary*, 12 vols. (Hagerstown, MD: Review and Herald, 1957–2000), 4:869, and Uriah Smith, *Daniel and the Revelation* (Nashville, TN: Southern Publishing, 1949), 246–247.

behalf shall cause the reproach offered by him to cease; without his own reproach he shall cause it to turn upon him. Then he shall turn his face toward the fort of his own land: but he shall stumble and fall, and not be found. (Daniel 11:17–19)

He shall also set his face to enter with the strength of his whole kingdom, and upright ones with him; thus shall he do. The "He" mentioned above is still pagan Rome in a general sense, but transitions from the career of Pompey the Great and his involvement in Judeo-Syrian affairs to that of Gaius Julius Caesar, the most famous general in Roman history, and his specific involvement in Egyptian affairs. We should remember that, after both Greco-Macedonia and Syria had fallen into Roman hands (168 B.C. and 63 B.C. respectively), only Egypt would remain as the sole surviving kingdom of the Hellenistic era. Yet, Egyptian independence would not last for very long, as Julius Caesar would accelerate the process of Egypt's submission to Rome.[213]

Having ascended from a wealthy patrician family with ties to famous Romans such as Gaius Marius and Lucius Cornelius Cinna, Caesar emerged in a time when the disintegration of the Roman republic proved to be the perfect opportunity for a man with his exceptional abilities. As the empire would expand in influence and territory, it became increasingly apparent that the Roman senate alone was not capable of governing such a vast empire. The provincial commands that controlled the Roman military machine proved to be quite tempting to those who were ambitious for power. Such was the status of the Roman world out of which Caesar would grow to unprecedented greatness.

As it turned out, the Roman senate would alienate three of the most powerful men in Rome. It had refused to offer Caesar a military triumph for his brilliant campaigns in the province of Spain. It had also refused to ratify the territorial acquisitions secured by Pompey during his eastern command, and would not grant him the land necessary to settle his military veterans. Marcus Licinius Crassus, the richest man in Rome, had also been denied a rebate on certain contracts dealing with tax collection in Asia. Thus, with the senate as a common enemy, Caesar, Pompey, and Crassus would form an alliance, the "first triumvirate," to divide and govern the empire among themselves (60 B.C.).[214]

---

213 See both *SDA Bible Commentary*, 4:869–870, and Smith, 247–252.

214 See Freeman, 353–357, Grant, *History of Rome*, 201–209, Michael Grant, *The Twelve Caesars* (New York: Barnes & Noble, 1975), 29–51, and Alonzo T. Jones, *The Two Republics* (Ithaca, MI: A.B. Publishing, n.d.), 42–56.

Yet, after the death of Crassus at the hands of Parthia in the Battle of Carrhae (53 B.C.), the relations between Caesar and Pompey would eventually deteriorate to the point of civil war. Pompey's wife Julia, the daughter of Caesar, had already died unexpectedly while giving birth (54 B.C.), and, to make matters worse, the Roman senate, fearing the ever-increasing popularity of Caesar, begrudgingly committed themselves to the complete support of Pompey. Eventually the two generals would meet off the Greek coast in the Battle of Pharsalus (48 B.C.), which proved to be a disastrous defeat for Pompey; he was later brutally murdered by the Egyptian authorities after fleeing to Egypt.

The pursuance of Pompey after his victory at Pharsalus would bring Caesar directly into Egyptian affairs. Having landed there shortly after Pompey's assassination, Caesar would then "set his face to enter with the strength" of the "whole kingdom" by beginning the process of bringing this last remaining Hellenistic kingdom under Roman control, which would actually be finalized later under the authority of Octavian, Caesar's grandnephew. Nevertheless, after the elimination of Pompey and his supporters, Caesar would stand unrivaled as the sole ruler of the Roman world (48–47 B.C.).[215]

And he shall give him the daughter of women, corrupting her: but she shall not stand on his side, neither be for him. After this shall he turn his face unto the isles, and shall take many. This sub-passage describes the association of Caesar with the famous Egyptian queen Cleopatra, labeled here as the "daughter of women." After landing in Egypt (48 B.C.), Caesar would learn that Cleopatra had been involved in a "dynastic war" with her husband and brother, Ptolemy XII Theos Philopater. Taking up residence in the royal palace at Alexandria, he would decree that Cleopatra and Ptolemy should reign jointly. Ironically, after bringing about a public reconciliation between the king and queen, Caesar would make Cleopatra his mistress as a show of power, taking "the daughter of women" and "corrupting her."

Later, Caesar would "turn his face to the isles" and "take many" through the pacification of Egypt; he would also eliminate all remaining Pompeian and senatorial military forces scattered throughout the Mediterranean basin that had fought against him in the civil war. After his success in the "Alexandrine War" (47 B.C.), Caesar would win military victories at Zela (47 B.C.), Thapsus (46 B.C.), and Munda (45 B.C.), thus removing all opposition to his authority, standing unrivaled as the greatest military

---

215 See Freeman, 362–368, Grant, *History of Rome*, 225–231, Grant, *Twelve Caesars*, 29–51, and Jones, 56–63.

commander of his age. Eventually, however, Cleopatra would "not stand on his side, neither be for him;" she would be virtually powerless to stop his untimely assassination in March of 44 B.C.[216]

But a prince for his own behalf shall cause the reproach offered by him to cease; without his own reproach he shall cause it to turn upon him. Then he shall turn his face toward the fort of his own land: but he shall stumble and fall, and not be found. Because he will be discussed again in our examination of Daniel 11:25–28, this passage introduces a "prince" for Caesar's "own behalf," Marcus Antonius (Mark Antony), who would protect Caesar's political interests in Rome while he was away on provincial commands. Serving as tribune (49 B.C.), Antony had vetoed several legislative proposals designed to weaken Caesar's political ambitions. Because Caesar was not present in Rome personally, Antony would often be the target of criticisms aimed at Caesar during senatorial debates because of his personal loyalty to the famous general. In one specific instance, Caesar was issued a senatorial ultimatum to either disband his troops and return to Rome as a private citizen, or be declared an outlaw of the state. Antony promptly vetoed this decree, which then led the senate to illegally suspend his tribunal power and take legal action against him. He would later flee to Caesar and serve under him in the civil war. Thus, Antony would "cause" Caesar's "reproach" to fall upon himself, similar to the way that Christ would take our reproaches on Himself (Psalm 69:9, Romans 15:3).

Eventually the Roman senate would grow weary of Caesar and conspire to kill him just before he was to leave for a major eastern military campaign. Led by Gaius Cassius Longinus, Marcus Junius Brutus, and Decimus Brutus Albinus, a crowd of senators would fatally stab Caesar, assassinating him during a government meeting in Pompey's Theatre. Thus, on March 15, 44 B.C., the dictator would "stumble and fall, and not be found," bleeding to death at the feet of a statue of Pompey.

Later, however, with unfailing loyalty to his deceased friend, Antony would exact revenge for Caesar, causing his "reproach to cease" by hunting down his assassins. He would eventually win two decisive battles against Brutus and Cassius at Philippi in Macedonia, which later led both of these men to commit suicide in the year 42 B.C.[217]

---

216 See Edwyn R. Bevan, *The House of Ptolemy: A History of Egypt under the Ptolemaic Dynasty* (Chicago, IL: Ares Publishers, 1985), 345–369, Freeman, 365–368, Grant, *History of Rome*, 231–232, Grant, *Twelve Caesars*, 29–57, Jones, 63–67, *SDA Bible Commentary*, 4:870, and Smith, 247–251.

217 See Freeman, 371–373, Grant, *History of Rome*, 240–243, Grant, *Twelve*

Then shall stand up in his estate a raiser of taxes in the glory of the kingdom: but within few days he shall be destroyed, neither in anger, nor in battle. And in his estate shall stand up a vile person, to whom they shall not give the honour of the kingdom: but he shall come in peaceably, and obtain the kingdom by flatteries. And with the arms of a flood shall they be overflown from before him, and shall be broken; yea, also the prince of the covenant. (Daniel 11:20–22)

Then shall stand up in his estate a raiser of taxes in the glory of the kingdom: but within few days he shall be destroyed, neither in anger, nor in battle. As we continue in our study of pagan Rome, we will see that this passage transitions to a survey of the successor of Julius Caesar, Gaius Octavian, who was later renamed Caesar Augustus (reign, 27 B.C.—A.D. 14). This transference can be easily demonstrated by an understanding of the phrase "raiser of taxes." In his gospel rendition, Luke actually referred to Augustus in this manner:

And it came to pass in those days, that there went out a decree from Caesar Augustus, that all the world should be taxed. And this taxing was first made when Cyrenius was governor of Syria.) And all went to be taxed, every one into his own city. (Luke 2:1–3)

Thus, the sub-passage under examination can be rephrased "Then shall stand up [come to power] in his [Caesar's] estate a raiser of taxes [Caesar Augustus] in the glory of the kingdom [pagan Rome]: but within few days he [Augustus] shall be destroyed, neither in anger, nor in battle [die a natural death]."

With his decisive naval victory over Mark Antony in the famous Battle of Actium (31 B.C.), Octavian would "stand up" in the "glory of the kingdom" by completing the conquest of Hellenistic Egypt that had been initiated by Caesar. Later renamed Caesar Augustus, Octavian would emerge as the undisputed ruler of the Roman world, and became the first official emperor recognized by the Roman senate (A.D. 27).[218] The rise of Octavian and his crucial naval victory in the Battle of Actium will be discussed in

---

Caesars, 29–51, Jones, 67–77, SDA Bible Commentary, 4:870, and Smith, 252.

218 See Bevan, Ptolemy, 372–384, Freeman, 371–395, Grant, History of Rome, 242–273, Grant, Twelve Caesars, 52–80, Jones, 67–85, C. Mervyn Maxwell, God Cares, 2 vols. (Boise, ID: Pacific Press, 1981), 1:293, SDA Bible Commentary, 4:870, and Smith, 252–253.

greater detail when we examine the specific passage of Daniel 11:25–28 in our next chapter.

And in his estate shall stand up a vile person, to whom they shall not give the honour of the kingdom: but he shall come in peaceably, and obtain the kingdom by flatteries. After the peaceful death of Augustus (A.D. 14), Tiberius Caesar would become the second official Roman emperor (reign, A.D. 14–37). Stemming from a noble patrician family, the "Claudian" clan (one of the oldest and most reputable families in Rome), Tiberius Claudius Nero would grow to earn great distinction as a military commander on the Roman frontier. Initially, Augustus had believed that, as the child of his wife Livia from a previous marriage, his stepson Tiberius was "too vile" to become emperor;[219] yet, after the death of several successors, he would eventually adopt Tiberius as his own son (A.D. 4), and designate him to be the sole heir to the Roman throne.

Tiberius would eventually ascend to the emperorship "peacefully" in a natural succession after the death of Augustus (A.D. 14), and "obtain the kingdom by flatteries," receiving a fabricated and albeit artificial flattery from the Roman senate. Yet, because he was a soldier at heart and preferred the army camp over the palace, Tiberius detested dealing with the senatorial hierarchy and never could fully adjust to political life. He did possess exceptional administrative skills that were developed through his experience as a military commander, but he didn't have the proper temperament needed to command the respect of the senate or his subordinates in government. Thus, he would have the reputation of a "vile person" who would not receive the respect and "honour of the kingdom" as did his predecessor Augustus. The two quotations below will confirm this observation:

> Tiberius … was a proud member of the ancient Claudian clan who had a splendid record of military and administrative achievement. But he was also grim, caustic, and suspicious, and lacked Augustus' talent for public relations. … he found it difficult to get on with senators, both individually and *en masse*.[220]

> Domestically, the reign of Tiberius was at first beneficent. … Gradually, however, a change took place, and the latter part of his reign was marked by a series of conspiracies and consequent executions. … Tiberius' coldness and reserve and his desire for economy in government rendered him unpopular with the people

---

219 Smith, 255.
220 Grant, *History of Rome*, 277.

and, together with his supposed depravity, gave him a bad name in legend and history.[221]

To further develop an accurate character sketch of the "vile" attributes of Tiberius, we should understand that history portrays him as greatly deficient in self-confidence and slow to make decisions; he was not naturally amiable toward people and had trouble communicating effectively. His self-esteem would suffer further damage after he contracted a debilitating, disfiguring skin disease. And, because Tiberius was also naturally sensitive to criticism, the constant worry of conspiracy, coupled with his low self-esteem, eventually drove him into a state of paranoia. This would lead him to commit unspeakable acts of cruelty toward alleged seditionists. He would eventually grow weary of Roman politics and decide to leave Rome permanently, retiring to the island of Capreae (A.D. 26), where he would finish out his remaining years and die of natural causes.[222]

And with the arms of a flood shall they be overflown from before him, and shall be broken; yea, also the prince of the covenant. The phrase above would describe and confirm Tiberius' ruthless executions of many suspected conspirators. This sub-passage could read "And with the arms of a flood [swift exacting judgment] shall they [conspirators against Tiberius] be overflown [removed] from before him [Tiberius], and shall be broken [executed]." The execution of the praetorian prefect Sejanus, seen by some historians as somewhat justifiable, is one particular example of the swift judgment and merciless brutality of Tiberius toward those he suspected of sedition.

As a leader of the Praetorian Guard and protector of the emperor, Lucius Aelius Sejanus grew to become a close personal friend of Tiberius. Having the social status of a mere knight, he would boldly request a marriage alliance with the niece of Tiberius, Julia Livilla, an aristocrat; yet, the fear of senatorial reprisal from a marriage alliance between two distinct social classes moved Tiberius to reject this request. Even so, Sejanus would continue to consolidate his power by manipulating Tiberius' constant fear of sedition; he would use his influence with the emperor to eliminate most of his political opponents.

---

221 "Tiberius," *Microsoft® Encarta® Encyclopedia 2000.* © 1993–1999. Microsoft Corporation.

222 See the following sources on Tiberius: Freeman, 397–402, Grant, *History of Rome*, 277–280, Grant, *Twelve Caesars*, 83–107, Jones, 85–91, *SDA Bible Commentary*, 4:870, Smith, 255–258, and "Tiberius," *Microsoft Encarta Encyclopedia*.

After holding the consulate in concert with Tiberius in A.D. 31, Sejanus would later receive, from the emperor himself, both supreme authority over the military and permission to enter into the marriage alliance with Julia Livilla that he had formerly requested. Yet, because he was but a mere knight in social status, these specific appointments provoked the senate to action against Sejanus, as they would not tolerate being governed by one of a lesser social class. Accusing Sejanus of an actual plot against the emperor himself, several powerful people warned Tiberius that he must be eliminated immediately.

Convinced that Sejanus was plotting against his throne, Tiberius secretly transferred control of the Praetorian Guard to Quintus Marco so that the Praetorian Guard could not be used by Sejanus to defend himself. The emperor dictated an urgent letter condemning Sejanus, which was read to the senate body without delay. After hearing the letter, the senate rallied behind the emperor's accusations, conducting the efficient and merciless execution of Sejanus and his family without a trial. Many of his friends and former associates were also brutally executed.

Thus, while history will show that Tiberius possessed excellent administrative skills and demonstrated efficient management of the empire, it will also show that his specific character qualities proved to be downright contemptible when compared to the more popular Augustus. Therefore, as Adventist theologian Uriah Smith accurately observed, "Tyranny, hypocrisy, debauchery, and uninterrupted intoxication characterized the reign of Tiberius," and, "if these traits and practices show a man to be vile, Tiberius exhibited that character to perfection."[223]

Having established the context of his severity toward alleged conspirators, we can see that Tiberius would even cause the "prince of the covenant" to be "broken." The Bible will clearly demonstrate that the "prince of the covenant" is none other than Jesus Christ (Isaiah 9:6, Acts 5:31); and, since Tiberius had served as emperor from A.D. 14 to 37, we can easily demonstrate through the 70-weeks' prophecy of Daniel 9 that Christ was crucified during the reign of Tiberius:

> Know therefore and understand, that from the going forth of the commandment to restore and to build Jerusalem unto the Messiah the Prince shall be seven weeks, and threescore and two weeks ... (Daniel 9:25)

---

223 Smith, 256. See Freeman, 397–402, Grant, *History of Rome*, 277–280, Grant, *Twelve Caesars*, 83–107, and Jones, 85–91.

In the passage above, Daniel was told that 69 prophetic weeks would span from the time of the decree to rebuild Jerusalem to the appearance of the Messiah. Since seven days are in a week, the 69 prophetic weeks would equal 483 prophetic days; and, since a prophetic day translates into a literal year, the 483 prophetic days can be accounted as 483 literal years. Thus, 483 literal years would span from the commandment to restore Jerusalem to the appearance of Christ. This commandment would be issued by King Artaxerxes in 457 B.C. (Ezra 6:14, 7:11–25), and, counting 483 prophetic years from 457 B.C., we arrive at the year A.D. 27 (See chart on page 45).

Both John the Baptist and Jesus began their public ministries in the 15th year of Tiberius' reign (Luke 3:1–3). Again, Tiberius actually began his reign in A.D. 14, but had also reigned jointly with Augustus for two years (A.D. 12–13); so, if we go 15 years from the date of A.D. 12, we arrive at the year A.D. 27. Just as Daniel 9:25 had foretold, A.D. 27 is the exact year that the "Messiah the Prince" began His public ministry, and He would be crucified 3½ years later in A.D. 31 (Daniel 9:26–27). Since Tiberius reigned until A.D. 37, he would be the emperor in power in A.D. 31 when "the prince of the covenant" was "broken."[224] Incidentally, Christ was also wrongly accused of alleged sedition against Caesar (Luke 23:2, John 19:12–15), and was thus crucified by the Roman governor of Judea, Pontius Pilate, as a result. Therefore, Tiberius was the actual emperor in power when Christ was crucified on the cross in A.D. 31.

Daniel 11	Interpretation
"he that cometh against him"	Pagan Rome subjugates Syria, becoming the new "king of the north"
"stand in glorious land"	Pompey the Great, 63 B.C.
"enter whole kingdom"	Julius Caesar in Egypt
"daughter of women"	Caesar's Cleopatra
"stumble and fall"	Caesar's assassination
"raiser of taxes"	Caesar Augustus
"vile person"	Tiberius Caesar
"Prince of covenant broken"	Crucifixion of Christ

224 See *SDA Bible Commentary*, 4:870, and Smith, 257.

— ELEVEN —
An Examination of Daniel 11:23–28
"The King of the North vs.
the King of the South—Part 2"

I n this specific chapter we will continue with the second part of our examination on the career of pagan Rome as outlined in Daniel 11:23–28. Now, there are a variety of interpretations on this specific passage; yet, regardless of what conclusions one may draw, we should realize that, (1) this passage is a definite description from pagan Roman history, and (2) irrespective of what specific historical events in pagan Roman history one ascribes to this passage, it will not affect the overall prophetic chronology of Daniel 11. We will discover that verse 31 describes a transition into the history of the papal Roman Empire, thus maintaining consistency with the earlier chapters of Daniel.

Now, I personally believe that verses 23–28 offer a survey of three general historical trends in the history of pagan Rome as the new "king of the north:" (1) the history of a Judeo-Roman "league" (verse 23); (2) the Roman subjugation of Syria, Judea, and Egypt, which would include the destruction of Jerusalem in A.D. 70 (verse 24); and (3) the resumption of the warfare between the "king of the north" (pagan Rome) and the "king of the south" (Egypt) in two different conflicts, Caesar vs. Pompey, and Octavian vs. Antony (verses 25–28).

> And after the league made with him he shall work deceitfully: for he shall come up, and shall become strong with a small people. (Daniel 11:23)

And after the league made with him he shall work deceitfully: for he shall come up, and shall become strong with a small people. Having ended verse 22 with the crucifixion of Christ under the reign of the "vile" Tiberius Caesar (reign, A.D. 14–37), verse 23 shows a shift to a time when the Jewish nation would enter into an alliance, or "league," with pagan Rome. This Jewish-Roman "league" was first initiated by Judas Maccabaeus, who had appealed to Rome for assistance during the Jewish struggle against the forced Hellenization of Judea by Seleucid-Syrian oppressors (161 B.C.). He had hoped that Roman assistance would intimidate the Seleucid dynasty to free its grip on Judea and help the Jewish people to eventually establish an independent nation that would be completely free of all foreign control.

The Seleucid oppression of Judea would reach its climax under the era of the Syrian king Antiochus IV Epiphanes (reign, 175–163 B.C.). Still fuming from his expulsion from Egypt under the threat of Roman military force in 168 B.C., Antiochus IV invaded Judea and plundered Jerusalem on his way back to Syria. Through his strict policy of "forced Hellenism," i.e., the forceful conversion of conquered peoples to Greek culture, Antiochus IV designed the total eradication of Judaism altogether. He promptly banned all Jewish religious services and dedicated the temple at Jerusalem to the Greek god Zeus (167 B.C.). This blatant act of desecration, coupled with the burden of foreign occupation, gave birth to a Jewish nationalist movement under the leadership of Judas Maccabaeus, whose family, the Hasmonaean family, had fled the city of Jerusalem during the initial invasion of Antiochus IV.

Believing that God had raised up Judas as their deliverer, Jewish nationalists rallied to support him as he organized the many fractured, scattered communities still faithful to Judaism into a powerful nationalist guerilla army. He would launch several raids against Syrian positions and areas of Hellenized Jews that had conspired with the enemy, and later won the battles of both Emmaus (166 B.C.) and Mizpah (165 B.C.) so decisively that Jerusalem fell back under Jewish control without any resistance whatsoever. Judas promptly ordered that the city be cleansed of all pagan altars and that the temple itself be rededicated to the worship of God (164 B.C.).

A few years later, after his defeat of the famous Syrian general Nicanor in the Battle of Adasa (161 B.C.), Judas appealed to the rising Roman power for assistance in their struggle against Syrian oppression. He sent two of his closest friends, Jason and Eupolemus, to Rome as ambassadors to ask the senate for both political and military aid to the Jewish nationalist movement in their struggle for political autonomy. As it turned out, the Roman senate gladly offered its assistance, decreeing a "league" of "friendship" with the Jewish nation; the famous Jewish historian Flavius Josephus quoted this specific decree as saying,

'The decree of the senate concerning a league of assistance and friendship with the nation of the Jews. It shall not be lawful for any that are subject to the Romans to make war with the nation of the

Jews, nor to assist those that do so, either by sending them corn, or ships, or money. And if any attack be made upon the Jews, the Romans shall assist them, as far as they are able; and again if any attack be made upon the Romans, the Jews shall assist them.'[225]

Unfortunately, after achieving this "league" of friendship with Rome in 161 B.C., Judas would never see the day of Jewish independence; he was eventually killed at Elasa later that same year after presumptuously charging a superior Syrian force with only a small band of faithful supporters. Yet, through the influence of Rome, Jewish independence would be achieved several years later under the leadership of his younger brother Simon (141 B.C.), who, as the high priest and head of all Jewish military forces, established the Hasmonaean dynasty.[226]

Yet, even after Jewish freedom from Seleucid-Syrian oppression had been realized, pagan Rome would use the Jewish "league" to its advantage by working "deceitfully" to "become strong" with this "small people." As we have discussed earlier, the complete subjugation of the Jewish nation would eventually take place under the authority of Pompey (64–63 B.C.). And, Rome would use this alliance to further its own political interests, not just in Judea, but in the entire coastal region of the eastern Mediterranean area. As it turned out, by the year 30 B.C., the main coastal regions of the east, namely Syria, Judea, and Egypt, were completely under Roman control.

He shall enter peaceably even upon the fattest places of the province; and he shall do that which his fathers have not done, nor his fathers' fathers; he shall scatter among them the prey, and spoil, and riches: yea, and he shall forecast his devices against the strong holds, even for a time. (Daniel 11:24)

---

225 *The Complete Works of Josephus*, translated by William Whiston (Lynn, MA: Hendrickson Publishers, 1981), 265. See also Uriah Smith, *Daniel and the Revelation* (Nashville, TN: Southern Publishing, 1949), 258–259.

226 See Edwyn R. Bevan, *The House of Seleucus: A History of the Hellenistic Near East under the Seleucid Dynasty*, 2 vols. (Chicago, IL: Ares Publishers, 1985), 2:162–233, *Complete Works of Josephus*, 265, Will Durant, *The Life of Greece* (New York: Simon & Schuster, 1966), 555, 582–584, Charles Freeman, *Egypt, Greece, and Rome: Civilizations of the Ancient Mediterranean* (Oxford: Oxford University, 1996), 292–293, *Seventh-day Adventist Bible Commentary*, 12 vols. (Hagerstown, MD: Review and Herald, 1957–2000), 4:870–871, and Smith, 258–259.

He shall enter peaceably even upon the fattest places of the province. This phrase continues to describe how pagan Rome, through the Jewish "league," would "enter peaceably upon the fattest places of the province." As stated above, pagan Rome would use this Jewish alliance to further its own political interests in the eastern Mediterranean basin, growing stronger over time to eventually assume control of the "fattest places of the province," i.e., the areas that would contain the most abundant wealth and natural resources. This would especially be true in the case of Egypt, as this region contained vast amounts of wealth. In fact, as we will discuss later, when Octavian (Caesar Augustus) finally confiscated the Ptolemaic treasure at Alexandria after his defeat of Mark Antony (31–30 B.C.), he would personally become wealthier than the entire Roman state itself.[227]

Therefore, the Jewish "league," with all of its successive renewals over time, would be a sort of "entering wedge" for pagan Rome to eventually incorporate Syria, Judea, and Egypt into its empire.[228] Josephus himself had claimed to "sufficiently" explain the "friendship and confederacy" that the Jewish nation "at those times had with the Romans,"[229] and referred to several instances where the Jewish "league" had been renewed periodically until the eastern Mediterranean had been pacified by pagan Rome. In one such instance, Josephus noted that the high priest Hyrcanus, the son of Simon Maccabaeus (Judas' brother), renewed this "league" with the Roman senate in 129–128 B.C.:

> Hyrcanus the high priest was desirous to renew the league of friendship they had with the Romans ... and when the senate had received their epistle, they made a league of friendship with them.[230]

In another example, Julius Caesar, who had a great deal of respect for the Jewish people after their support of him during the "Alexandrine War" (48–47 B.C.), also decreed that the Roman senate renew their alliance with the Jewish nation; Josephus penned that "It therefore pleased [the senate] to make a league of friendship and goodwill with them [the Jews], and to bestow upon them whatsoever they stood in need of."[231] After

227 Michael Grant, *History of Rome* (New York: Book-of-the-Month Club, 1997), 245.
228 See *SDA Bible Commentary*, 4:871, and Smith, 258–259.
229 *Complete Works of Josephus*, 302.
230 Ibid, 279. See also Bevan, *Seleucus*, 2:236–250.
231 Ibid, 296. See also Ibid, 296–300.

Caesar's assassination (44 B.C.), Josephus noted that his ally Mark Antony, along with another consul named Publius Dolabella, would also confirm the Jewish "league" with another high priest named Hyrcanus, the same person who had actually sided with Pompey in the struggle against his brother Aristobulus:

> Now after Caius [Gaius Julius Caesar] was slain, when Marcus Antonius [Mark Antony] and Publius Dolabella were consuls, they both assembled the senate, and introduced Hyrcanus' ambassadors into it … and made a league of friendship with them."[232]

Again, this historical evidence offered by Josephus concerning the Jewish "league" with Rome demonstrates that Rome would enter "peaceably" into the "fattest places of the province." In other words, Rome would use this particular alliance to exploit the natural resources that the eastern provinces contained; and, as a result of the conquest of Syria, Judea, and Egypt, vast amounts of wealth would flow into the pagan Roman treasury.[233]

And he shall do that which his fathers have not done, nor his fathers' fathers; he shall scatter among them the prey, and spoil, and riches. In this sub-passage, Daniel states that pagan Rome would eventually do what their "fathers" and "fathers' fathers" had not done, namely, destroy Jerusalem and the temple in A.D. 70. Even when Pompey had pacified Jerusalem in 63 B.C., he had not destroyed the temple itself, having left the temple treasury and its furniture untouched. Yet, under the command of Titus Flavius Vespasianus (reign, A.D. 79–81), pagan Rome would "do that which" its "fathers" had "not done," razing both Jerusalem and the temple to the ground. In fact, in Rome itself, the Arch of Titus depicts this specific victory, showing a depiction of the actual candlestick from the temple.

The doom of both Jerusalem and the temple actually started four years earlier when, in A.D. 66, a major Jewish revolt arose against Roman authority in Judea; the Roman commander Cestius Gallus responded by invading Judea to suppress the revolt, and set himself to besiege Jerusalem. After moving into an advantageous position to easily take the city, Cestius suddenly withdrew his armies for no apparent reason, retreating to the city of Antipatris. Ellen White noted that God had providentially directed this movement to give the Christians inside Jerusalem an opportunity to escape

232 Ibid, 300.
233 See *SDA Bible Commentary*, 4:871, and Smith, 259–260.

the impending destruction.[234] Sensing a chance to inflict a serious blow on the Roman army, Jewish soldiers attacked the retreating Roman troops, inflicting heavy casualties, with Cestius himself having barely escaped.

Disgusted at the performance of Cestius, the Roman emperor Lucius Germanicus Nero (reign, A.D. 54–68), would then commission a veteran military commander named Titus Flavius Vespasianus, also called Vespasian (reign, A.D. 69–79), to replace Cestius. After re-invading Judea, Vespasian had also placed himself in a perfect position to overrun Jerusalem as did Cestius; yet, after hearing that Nero had committed suicide (A.D. 68), he would leave the region and turn over command to his son Titus (reign, A.D. 79–81), also called Flavius Vespasianus. After his father was eventually proclaimed the next emperor of Rome in A.D. 69, Titus would resume the siege on Jerusalem in the very next year, A.D. 70.

As it turned out, it would take Titus five months to penetrate the thick defensive walls that surrounded the city. With great difficulty he would eventually overrun most of Jerusalem itself, with the exception of the temple fortification. As he planned an assault on this position, he gave specific orders that the temple was not to be harmed in any way. Yet, at one point, a Jewish night attack provoked an armed response from his soldiers; while defending their position, a Roman soldier had accidentally thrown a flaming torch into the temple itself, and in a short amount of time the entire structure was engulfed in flames. Despite a frantic effort to extinguish the fire, which included the personal effort of Titus himself, the temple would burn to the ground. As the Arch of Titus depicts, the Romans were able to save some of the precious vessels of the temple; yet, Titus would eventually have the smoldering ruins of the temple acreage plowed to the ground.

Later, as he observed Jerusalem lying in ruin, Titus told his Jewish captives that God had delivered their city into his hands. Overall, more than a million people were killed in the siege, while another hundred thousand were taken into captivity.[235] Thus, with the complete destruction of the temple, the razing of the city of Jerusalem, and the dispersion of the Jewish people, Titus would "do that which his fathers have not done, nor his father's fathers," scattering "among them the prey, and spoil, and riches."[236]

---

234 Ellen G. White, *The Great Controversy*, (Mountain View, CA: Pacific Press, 1950), 28–36.

235 Smith, 266. See also Ibid, 264–266.

236 See Grant, *Complete Works of Josephus*, 496–497, 502, *History of Rome*, 288–289, Michael Grant, *The Twelve Caesars* (New York: Barnes & Noble, 1976), 177–210, 211–213, 226–229, Smith, 265–266, and White, *Great Controversy*, 28–36.

Yea, and he shall forecast his devices against the strong holds. Coupled with its destruction of Jerusalem in A.D. 70, pagan Rome would also "forecast his devices against the" spiritual "strongholds" of Christ by engaging in extensive persecution against the rising Christian church. Even though Christians had enjoyed a certain degree of religious freedom during the reign of pagan Rome,[237] history will nevertheless demonstrate there were several vehement persecutions at various times, where many martyrs gave up their lives for the Gospel of Jesus Christ.

Now, an extensive commentary on the history of Christian persecution during the reign of pagan Rome is certainly beyond the scope of this specific work; yet, it should suffice to say that *Fox's Book of Martyrs* outlines ten separate Christian persecutions under the specific reigns of certain pagan Roman emperors: (1) Nero in A.D. 67, (2) Domitian in A.D. 81, (3) Trajan in A.D. 108, (4) Marcus Aurelius in A.D. 162, (5) Severus in A.D. 192, (6) Maximus in A.D. 235, (7) Decius in A.D. 249, (8) Valerian in A.D. 257, (9) Aurelian in A.D. 274, and (10) Diocletian in A.D. 303.[238]

Even for a time. It would appear that this passage also articulates that Christian persecution would last for the period of a "time," which would translate into one prophetic year.[239] Now, again, one prophetic year contains 360 prophetic days. And, since a prophetic day translates into a literal year of time, this "time" of 360 prophetic days would equal 360 literal years of actual time. Given this observation, our challenge will now be to determine a starting point as to when this 360-year period would begin. Some have suggested that it began with Octavian's victory over Mark Antony at Actium in 31 B.C. and his subsequent subjugation of Egypt, which will again be referred to as the "king of the south." This pivotal date would take us to the year A.D. 330, the very same year that the Roman emperor Constantine (reign, A.D. 312–337) would move the capital of the Roman Empire to Constantinople, which would later prove to seriously weaken pagan Rome and help to give rise to the papal Roman Empire.[240]

---

237 See Alonzo T. Jones, *The Two Republics* (Ithaca, MI: A.B. Publishing, n.d.), 109–136. Jones advocates that the so-called "Ten Persecutions" are for the most part a myth.

238 *Fox's Book of Martyrs*, William Byron Forbush, editor (Grand Rapids, MI: Zondervan, 1967), 5–33.

239 In Daniel 4:17, 23, and 34, Nebuchadnezzar of Babylon was driven from his throne for seven "times," which actually translated into "years." See also our study of Daniel 7:25 in chapter three of this work.

240 See both *SDA Bible Commentary*, 4:871, and Smith, 259–260.

Yet, this 360-year prophecy can also be understood from the point of the end of Christian persecution under pagan Rome, which had also been achieved under the reign of Constantine. He would sign the famous Edict of Milan in A.D. 313, which had granted religious freedom to all Christians throughout the Roman Empire; this decree would also eventually pave the way for Christianity to become the state religion of the empire. Thus, if we use A.D. 313 as the end of the 360-year prophecy, it would take us back to a starting point of 48 B.C., which, incidentally, was the very same year that Caesar had defeated Pompey in the Battle of Pharsalus and began to intervene in the affairs of Egypt. We will see that both of these perspectives are quite viable (48 B.C. to A.D. 313 and 31 B.C. to A.D. 330), as verses 25–28 will comment on the pagan Roman war with Hellenistic Egypt.

> And he shall stir up his power and his courage against the king of the south with a great army; and the king of the south shall be stirred up to battle with a very great and mighty army; but he shall not stand: for they shall forecast devices against him. (Daniel 11:25)

And he shall stir up his power and his courage against the king of the south with a great army. The "he" in the above sub-passage would obviously still refer to pagan Rome, the new "king of the north," and, based on our understanding of Daniel 11:5–15, the "king of the south" would still be Hellenistic Egypt. Yet, after Octavian finally subjugated Egypt in 30 B.C., this power would lose its status as the literal "king of the south." Therefore, verses 25–28 must be referring to a time when, prior to Octavian's subjugation of the region, Hellenistic Egypt would war against pagan Rome. This war did take place simultaneously with the rise of Octavian to power, and it will now prove useful to discuss a brief history of the Roman involvement in Egypt.

While Pompey was in the process of subjugating Judeo-Syria in 64–63 B.C., he was aided by the Egyptian king Ptolemy XI Auletes (reign, 80–51 B.C.), who was later driven to Rome in exile because of a revolt in Alexandria (58 B.C.). After a usurper named Archelaus was placed on the Egyptian throne, the exiled Ptolemy XI appealed to Roman senate for his restoration to power (57 B.C.). After securing senatorial support, he would recruit one Aulus Gabinius, the proconsul of Syria and protégé of Pompey, to lead an actual invasion into Egypt (55 B.C.). The military operation proved to be a success, resulting in the death of Archelaus; thus, this restoration to power left Ptolemy XI indebted to Rome.

When Ptolemy XI died in 51 B.C., his will revealed that he had bequeathed Egypt to Rome with the stipulation that his two oldest children, Cleopatra VII and Ptolemy XII Theos Philopater (reign, 51–47 B.C.), should marry and reign jointly. Caesar would eventually appear in Egypt after his defeat of Pompey at Pharsalus (48 B.C.), to settle a dynastic dispute that would eventually take place between these two co-regents. He justified his presence by stating that he was there on official Roman business to serve as an arbitrator in the conflict between the king and queen; yet, in reality Caesar coveted the wealth and resources of the rich land of the Nile, and determined an extended stay. This would lead to an armed rebellion against the Roman presence in Egypt, which resulted in the "Alexandrine War" (48–47 B.C.).

Initially besieged in the royal capital at Alexandria, Caesar's Syrian legions, along with a Jewish force of 3,000 men led by the faithful Antipater, would come to his rescue. With this relief force, Caesar would "stir up his power and his courage against the king of the south with a great army," winning a decisive battle at the mouth of the Nile near Alexandria. At the conclusion of the battle, the royal army had been destroyed, Ptolemy had drowned, and Caesar had once again proven himself as a brilliant military commander who could improvise in a crisis to overcome tremendous odds. Honoring the will of the late Ptolemy XI, he replaced Ptolemy XII with his brother, Ptolemy XIII, also called Theos Philopater (reign, 47–44 B.C.), who would also marry his sister Cleopatra and reign with her as co-regent.[241]

And the king of the south shall be stirred up to battle with a very great and mighty army; but he shall not stand: for they shall forecast devices against him. After Caesar's death in 44 B.C., the "king of the south" would "be stirred up to battle" once again, coming "with a very great and mighty army" against the "king of the north." This would become a reality through the influence of Mark Antony, whose authority over Egyptian affairs after the death of Caesar had essentially made him the "king of the south," while pagan Rome under the authority of Octavian would constitute the "king of the north." This growing rivalry would lead to an inevitable showdown for control of the Roman world. Antony had initially formed an alliance known as the "second triumvirate" with both Octavian and Marcus Aemilius Lepidus (43 B.C.), with the express purpose

---

241 See Edwyn R. Bevan, *The House of Ptolemy: A History of Egypt under the Ptolemaic Dynasty* (Chicago, IL: Ares Publishers, 1985), 342–368, Freeman, 367–368, Grant, *History of Rome*, 231–232, Grant, *Twelve Caesars*, 30, and Smith, 247–251.

of eliminating the murderers of Caesar and removing their own political opponents. When the triumvirs divided the empire in 40 B.C., Antony assumed control of the eastern provinces, which would include Egypt, thus making him the "king of the south," while Octavian would retain portions of the north and west, which would include Rome itself, thus making him the "king of the north."

As it turned out, Antony's involvement in Egypt would expose him to the romantic suggestions of Cleopatra, who had murdered Ptolemy XIII after the death of Caesar. Despite his marriage to Octavia, the sister of Octavian, Antony would become romantically involved with the Egyptian queen, thus alienating Octavian and turning public favor against him in Rome. As a result, he would become increasingly dependent upon Cleopatra and the resources of Egypt for his own political support. He made matters worse when he held an excessive military triumph in Alexandria (not Rome) after his defeat of Armenia (34 B.C.), thus strengthening public opinion in favor of Octavian. Finally, in 32 B.C., he publicly broke with Octavian by divorcing Octavia, which then provoked Octavian to declare war on Egypt.[242]

At this point, Antony became totally committed as the "king of the south;" Octavian's declaration of war against Egypt in behalf of pagan Rome "stirred" him "up to battle" as the "king of the north" with "a very great and mighty army." Antony would challenge the authority of the young grandnephew of Caesar by crossing into Greece with Cleopatra at his side in 31 B.C., and, through their combined forces, established military strongholds along the western coast of Greece. Octavian viewed this move as an attack against the empire itself, and, forecasting "devices against" Antony, dispatched the famous Marcus Vipsanius Agrippa, his best friend and former schoolmate, to go ahead of him and attempt to check Antony's military aggression. Meeting with some initial success, Agrippa would recapture several key positions from Antony along the Greek coastline.

As it turned out, by the time Octavian had arrived in Greece to join up with Agrippa, Antony had been cornered in the Gulf of Ambracia. As he attempted to break out of this situation, the naval forces of each side would meet head-on just outside the gulf, near a place called Actium (31 B.C.). Even though Antony and Cleopatra had superior numbers in the ensuing

---

242 See Bevan, *Ptolemy*, 368–384, Freeman, 374–375, Grant *History of Rome*, 242–245, Grant, *Twelve Caesars*, 52–54, James Richard Joy, *Rome and the Making of Modern Europe* (New York: Flood and Vincent, 1893), 146–154, *SDA Bible Commentary*, 4:871–872, Smith, 260–264, and Hutton Webster, *Early European History* (Boston: D.C. Heath & Company, 1920), 188–191.

naval battle, Cleopatra would abandon her partner at the height of the conflict; coming to realize that Octavian had the upper hand, she would withdraw her naval forces and retreat to Egypt, leaving Antony to suffer a humiliating defeat. He eventually managed to escape to Egypt also, but his land forces defected to Octavian and only one-quarter of his fleet survived to return to Egypt. When the land of the Nile fell to his rival in the next year, Antony would "not stand," committing suicide with Cleopatra (30 B.C.), thus allowing Octavian to emerge as master of the Roman world.[243]

> Yea, they that feed of the portion of his meat shall destroy him, and his army shall overflow: and many shall fall down slain. (Daniel 11:26)

Yea, they that feed of the portion of his meat shall destroy him, and his army shall overflow: and many shall fall down slain. This passage reviews the fact that because Cleopatra had removed her naval support from Antony at the height of the Battle of Actium, she who had once fed "the portion his meat" would eventually "destroy him." Having stood by his side in the past as his lover, while offering both political support and necessary supplies for the development and maintenance of his army and naval forces, she would eventually leave him to be defeated by Octavian. And, as Octavian's army would later "overflow" into Egypt and conquer this last remaining Hellenistic kingdom, many would "fall down slain."[244]

> And both these kings' hearts shall be to do mischief, and they shall speak lies at one table; but it shall not prosper: for yet the end shall be at the time appointed. (Daniel 11:27)

And both these kings' hearts shall be to do mischief, and they shall speak lies at one table; but it shall not prosper: for yet the end shall be at the time appointed. This passage actually reviews a time when "both these kings," Octavian and Anthony, would set their "hearts" to "do mischief," and "speak lies at one table." Antony and Octavian had originally unified after the death of Caesar to defeat his murderers and their own political opponents; yet, as time went on, it became apparent that they would view each other as an obstacle to gaining complete control of the empire. Although they had met at various times to put away their differences, the

---

243 Ibid.
244 Smith, 263.

peace between them would be superficial at best, hidden under the garb of an imaginary friendship.

Antony's involvement with Cleopatra had also aroused tremendous suspicion in Rome; eventually Octavian, the senate, and the Roman citizenry at large grew to believe that Antony had fallen under the manipulation of the strong-willed Egyptian queen. In an attempt to curb his negative image, Antony renewed his friendship with Octavian, marrying his sister Octavia in 40 B.C., and managed to remain clear of Cleopatra for the next four years.

He would, however, renew his ties with Cleopatra while on an eastern campaign against Parthia (36 B.C.), which created major friction with Octavian, not just because of the dishonor cast upon his sister from marital infidelity, but also because of a specific ceremony conducted by Cleopatra during Antony's military triumph at Alexandria (34 B.C.). In this ceremony, Cleopatra had insulted Octavian by proclaiming Caesarion, Caesar's illegitimate son by the queen, as the rightful heir of the dead dictator. When the news of this insult had reached Rome (33 B.C.), the populace began to view Antony with great contempt, and the senate moved to give Octavian the authority to act against Egypt with the necessary military force. Thus, the artificial alliance between Antony and Octavian would "not prosper," but come to an end "at the time appointed." Through his victory at Actium and the final subjugation of Hellenistic Egypt (31–30 B.C.), Octavian would eventually stand alone as sole ruler of the pagan Roman Empire.[245]

> Then shall he return into his land with great riches; and his heart shall be against the holy covenant; and he shall do exploits, and return to his own land. (Daniel 11:28)

Then shall he return into his land with great riches. As we have discussed before, Octavian would enter Egypt with his land forces from Syria in the very next year after his victory at Actium (30 B.C.). Upon arrival, he seized Alexandria, declared Egypt a Roman province, and promptly confiscated the treasury of the Ptolemaic dynasty, which made him richer than the entire Roman state. Also, having eliminated this last surviving dynasty from the kingdom of Alexander, Octavian made Egypt his own special province. Therefore, having emerged as the undisputed ruler of

---

245 See Bevan, *Ptolemy*, 368–384, Freeman, 374–375, Grant *History of Rome*, 242–245, Grant, *Twelve Caesars*, 52–54, Joy, 146–154, *SDA Bible Commentary*, 4:871–872, Smith, 260–264, and Webster, 188–191.

the pagan Roman Empire, Octavian would "return" to "his land" of Rome "with great riches," and later be renamed Caesar Augustus, the first official pagan Roman emperor.[246]

And his heart shall be against the holy covenant; and he shall do exploits, and return to his own land. Similar to our discussion of verse 24, this passage can also be a description of the destruction of Jerusalem by Titus in A.D. 70 and the various Christian persecutions that took place under specific pagan Roman emperors. It can also apply to the brief involvement of Octavian in Judeo-Palestinian affairs after his victory at Actium (31–30 B.C.).

As he marched with his land forces through Syria on the way to Egypt after defeating Antony, Octavian confirmed the subservience of each region that he passed through. Josephus commented on how he had stopped in Judea specifically to settle certain territorial questions that had arisen between rival kings.[247] Prior to the first advent of Christ the Jews were still God's chosen people, and had possession of the "holy covenant." Thus, because Octavian had intervened in Jewish affairs and required the submission of Judea to Rome, one could say that his "heart" was "against the holy covenant" in a sense. And, after "doing exploits" with the final conquest of Egypt, Octavian would "return to his own land" of Rome as sole master of the empire.[248]

Daniel 11	Interpretation
Verse 23	Judeo-Roman League (161 B.C.) Pagan Rome, as the new "king of the north," becomes "strong" with the Jewish nation (small people);
Verse 24	Pagan Rome enters "peaceably" upon the "fattest places of the province" (Syria, Judea, Egypt); Pagan Rome would do what "his fathers" have "not done," destroy Jerusalem (Titus, A.D. 70);

---

246 See Bevan, *Ptolemy*, 379–384, Freeman, 374–375, Grant, *History of Rome*, 242–245, and Webster, 188–191.

247 See *Complete Works of Josephus*, 332–333, 367–370, 474–475.

248 See Freeman, 381–382, and Grant, *History of Rome*, 242–273.

Pagan Rome would "forecast devices" against the Christian Church through ten periods of Christian persecution;

Even for a "time" (360 literal years); this would go from both 48 B.C. (Caesar's involvement in Egypt) to A.D. 313 (Edict of Milan ending Christian persecution) <u>AND</u> 31 B.C. (Octavian's defeat of Antony and Egypt) to A.D. 330 (dedication of Constantinople);

Verses 25–28

Pagan Rome (the "king of the north") vs. Egypt (the "king of the south"); this describes a history of warfare between pagan Rome (led by Octavian) and Egypt (led by Mark Antony and Cleopatra); Octavian would win the Battle of Actium (31 B.C.) and later seize control of Egypt (30 B.C.).

—— TWELVE ——
An Examination of Daniel 11:29–30 "The Ships of Chittim and the Triumph of Christianity"

A
s we examine Daniel 11:29–30 in this specific chapter, we will discover that this particular passage is actually a transitional text that will show transference from Rome in its pagan phase to the emergence of Rome in its papal phase through the "Christianization" of the Roman Empire. Overall, it demonstrates the following trends: (1) the rise of Constantine the Great, the end of Christian persecution, and the dedication of Constantinople (verse 29); (2) the Germanic tribal invasions ("ships of Chittim") that caused the political collapse of western Rome (first part of verse 30); and (3) the rise of Roman Catholic Christianity and the papacy, its victory over paganism, and a general outline of it's warfare against true Christianity (second part of verse 30).

> At the time appointed he shall return, and come toward the south;
> but it shall not be as the former, or as the latter. (Daniel 11:29)

At the time appointed he shall return, and come toward the south; but it shall not be as the former, or as the latter. This passage points out that the Roman Empire, "at the time appointed" (the end of 360-year prophecy), would "return" by coming "toward" (not "to") the "south" (Egypt). This "return" would not be like the "former" time (when Octavian, the "king of the north," conquered Egypt in 30 B.C.), or the "latter" time (the future conquest of "Egypt" by "the king of the north" in Daniel 11:40–45), but peacefully, without the intention of waging war. This passage actually reached its fulfillment when the emperor Constantine the Great (reign, A.D. 312–337) moved the capital of the Roman Empire from Rome to Constantinople, thus relocating the imperial capital "toward" Egypt, i.e., in the direction of Egypt, but not exactly "to" Egypt itself, having peaceful intentions.

Constantine the Great came to power under an interesting series of events. When the pagan emperor Diocletian (reign, A.D. 284–305) came to power, he sought for a way to contain the Germanic invasions along the Roman frontier borders that had caused considerable political and economic upheaval. Diocletian believed that these crises could be handled more efficiently by delegating imperial authority, so he created a system of government called the "tetrarchy." This system would divide the empire into two halves, east and west; two co-emperors, called "Augusti," would rule each half, while two "Caesars" would be appointed as "vice-emperors" and be the successors of the "Augusti." If an emperor were to die or abdicate, the "Caesar" would move up into the emperorship and appoint a new "Caesar" to take his place. This reorganization actually proved to control Germanic invasions and be quite helpful in maintaining political control of the empire.

In A.D. 305 both Diocletian and his co-emperor Maximian would abdicate their emperorships and be replaced by Constantius and Galerius. After the short-lived reign of Constantius, who died in A.D. 306, his son Constantine was declared emperor in his stead by his troops in Britain and Gaul (France). Two other rivals, Maxentius and Licinius, also became contenders for the emperorship. As it turned out, Constantine would eventually meet Maxentius in a battle that took place just north of Rome on the Tiber River at a placed called the Milvian Bridge (A.D. 312). After routing the superior forces of his rival (who drowned in the Tiber River during a hasty retreat), Constantine would emerge as the undisputed "Augustus" of the west; and, having attributed his victory to Christ's intervention, he would also profess to convert to Christianity.

Later, after the death of Galerius (A.D. 311), Licinius, an ally of Constantine, would defeat his rival Maximinus in battle near Adrianople (A.D. 313) and become the "Augustus" of the east. Having entered into a marriage alliance together, Constantine and Licinius would sign the famous "Edict of Milan," which would grant religious freedom to every citizen in the Roman Empire (A.D. 313). Christianity would be the special benefactor of this edict, because it would essentially bring an end to Christian persecution.[249] A portion of this actual edict stated that,

---

249 See Charles Freeman, *Egypt, Greece, and Rome: Civilizations of the Ancient Mediterranean* (Oxford: Oxford University, 1996), 470–482, 499–500, Edward Gibbon, *The Decline and Fall of the Roman Empire*, 6 vols. (New York: Everyman's Library, 1993), 1:385–487, 2:248–295, Michael Grant, *The History of Rome* (New York: Book-of-the-Month Club, 1997), 395–419, Alonzo T. Jones, *The Two Republics* (Ithaca, MI: A.B. Publishing, n.d.), 167–182, 245–262, *Seventh-day Adventist Bible Commentary*, 12 vols. (Hagerstown, MD: Review and Herald, 1957–2000), 4:872, Uriah Smith, *Daniel the Revelation*

'We [Constantine and Licinius] have resolved among the first things to ordain those matters by which reverence and worship to the Deity might be exhibited. That is, how we may grant likewise to the Christians, *and to all, the free choice to follow that mode of worship which they may wish.* ... Therefore, we have decreed the following ordinance as our will ... that no freedom at all shall be refused to Christians. ... But that *to each one power be granted to devote his mind to that worship which he may think adapted to himself.*[250]

Constantine would eventually become estranged from Licinius to the point of war because of specific border disputes, and would later defeat him in three successive battles (A.D. 323–324); he dissolved the "tetrarchy" for a time, ruling as the sole emperor until his death in A.D. 337. By holding this position, he was able to elevate and promote Christianity to where it would later become the state religion of the empire. In this process, he would also empower the bishop of Rome with both religious and political authority in the west.

As stated earlier, Constantine would also seek to relocate the imperial capital of the empire after realizing that Rome was not a practical location for effective governance. He selected the site of Byzantium (located at modern-day Istanbul, Turkey), and built a new imperial capital there called Constantinople. Dedicated in A.D. 330, at the end of the 360-year prophecy (31 B.C. to A.D. 330),[251] this new imperial city would eventually become the future metropolis of the empire. Thus, with the emperor now reigning primarily from the east, Roman political authority in the west would eventually transition into the hands of the bishop of Rome (the papacy), who would later be left free to exercise religious and political authority over Western Europe. As stated before, this authority would continue to strengthen over time until papal ascendancy would become a reality by March of A.D. 538.[252]

(Nashville, TN: Southern Publishing, 1949), 266, and Williston Walker, *A History of the Christian Church* (New York: Charles Scribner's Sons, 1918), 108–119.

250 *Eusebius' Ecclesiastical History*, Book 10, Chapter 5, quoted in Jones, 181. Italics are exactly as found in Jones' work.

251 See pages 133–134 for a review of the 360-year prophecy.

252 See Freeman, 470–482, 499–500, Gibbon, 1:385–487, 2:248–295, Grant, *History of Rome*, 395–419, Jones, 167–182, 245–262, *SDA Bible Commentary*, 4:872, Smith, 266, and Walker, 108–119.

For the ships of Chittim shall come against him: therefore he shall be grieved, and return, and have indignation against the holy covenant: so shall he do; he shall even return, and have intelligence with them that forsake the holy covenant. (Daniel 11:30)

For the ships of Chittim shall come against him. As a symbol of foreign oppression, the phrase "ships of Chittim" can symbolize "invaders and destroyers from any quarter," and, as we apply this phrase to Rome in the context of Daniel 11:30, it offers a perfect description of the "the barbarian hordes" that "invaded and broke up the western Roman Empire."[253] History will clearly demonstrate that four tribal groups, the Visigoths, the Huns, the Vandals, and the Heruli, each made significant contributions to the final collapse of the political infrastructure of western Rome.[254]

The Visigoths ("west" Goths) had originally settled just north of the Danube River on the Roman frontier; yet, by A.D. 376, they would appeal to Rome for permission to cross the Danube into Roman territory because of a series of devastating raids from the migrating Asian Huns. Having been converted to Arian Christianity by Bishop Ulfilas in A.D. 340–341,[255] they were granted entrance into the empire by the emperor Valens (reign, A.D. 364–378), and would later rise in rebellion against Roman authority under their chieftain Fritigern because of certain injustices perpetrated by Roman officials. Valens moved to suppress this revolt, but met

253 *SDA Bible Commentary*, 4:872–873.

254 Please consider the following sources on the barbarian contribution to the collapse of the western Roman Empire: J.B. Bury, *History of the Later Roman Empire: From the Death of Theodosius I to the Death of Justinian*, 2 vols. (New York: Dover Publications, 1958), J.B. Bury, *The Invasion of Europe by the Barbarians* (New York: W.W. Norton & Company, 1967), Will Durant, *The Age of Faith* (New York: Simon & Schuster, 1950), 22–43, Peter Heather, *The Fall of the Roman Empire: A New History of Rome and the Barbarians* (New York: Oxford, 2006), Peter Heather, *The Goths* (Oxford: Blackwell Publishers, 1997), Warren Treadgold, *A History of the Byzantine State and Society* (Stanford, CA: Stanford University Press, 1997), Herwig Wolfram, *History of the Goths* (Berkeley, CA: University of California Press, 1979), and Herwig Wolfram, *The Roman Empire and Its Germanic Peoples* (Berkeley, CA: University of California Press, 1990).

255 See Treadgold, 54. See also Philip Schaff, *History of the Christian Church*, 8 vols. (Peabody, MA: Hendrickson, 2006), 3:641. See also Richard Fletcher, *The Barbarian Conversion to Christianity* (Berkeley, CA: University of California Press, 1977) for an excellent source on the conversion of the barbarians to Christianity.

with a violent death after his army was crushed by the Visigothic army at Adrianople on August 9, A.D. 378. The "friend of the Goths," Theodosius (reign, A.D. 378–395), would succeed Valens and make peace with the Visigoths in A.D. 382; he also granted them land for settlement in exchange for service in the imperial army.

After Theodosius died in A.D. 395, he was succeeded by his two sons, Arcadius in the east (reign, A.D. 395–408) and Honorius in the west (reign, A.D. 395–423). A formidable warrior named Alaric had also emerged as the leader of the Visigoths in that same year; he decided to invade Italy when Honorius denied him a military command, but was eventually repelled by the famous general Flavius Stilicho at Pollentia, Italy (A.D. 403). As it turned out, Stilicho would enter into a peace treaty with Alaric, also offering to enlist Visigothic soldiers into the imperial army. Yet, Honorius, who had fled to the city of Ravenna from Rome at the approach of Alaric, viewed this peace treaty by Stilicho as treason, and had him executed in A.D. 408.

Honorius promptly outlawed any barbarian involvement in the imperial army, which led Alaric to take military action against him; he resumed an invasion of Italy, and, on August 24, A.D. 410, Alaric sacked and plundered the city of Rome. This sacking of Rome, which had not taken place in nearly 800 years, horrified the Roman world and exposed the weakening power of the western empire. The Visigoths would later settle in Gaul and be defeated by the Frankish king Clovis at Voulon (A.D. 507–508); they would later migrate to Toledo in Spain and settle there until the arrival of the Muslim Saracens (A.D. 711).[256]

The notorious Huns were a nomadic people from central Asia who caused desolation and destruction all along the Roman frontier territories. Their famous leader Attila, who called himself the "scourge of God," would lead them on a series of devastating raids against the empire from A.D. 441–450, until he was finally stopped by the famous general Aetius at the Battle of Chalons (A.D. 451). Attila would later launch an invasion into Italy, capturing Aquileia and Milan (A.D. 453), and would have also sacked

---

256 See Charles Bemont and G. Monod, *Medieval Europe from 375–1270* (New York: Henry Holt and Company, 1906), 37–44, Freeman, 519–520, Gibbon, 3:32–73, 196–228, Michael Grant, *History of Rome*, 423–430, James Richard Joy, *Rome and the Making of Modern Europe* (New York: Flood and Vincent, 1893), 207–208, 225, John Moorhead, *The Roman Empire Divided, 400–700* (Edinburgh: Pearson Education Limited, 2001), 35–40, Smith, 476–478, Walker, 131, and Hutton Webster, *Early European History* (Boston: D.C. Heath and Company, 1920), 241–244.

Rome if it weren't for the diplomacy of Pope Leo the Great, who met the famous warrior and offered a marriage alliance with a large sum of money in exchange for a retreat. Attila accepted the offer and turned back his advance on Rome; he later died of a hemorrhage after drinking excessively at his marriage celebration. As for the Huns themselves, some retreated out of Italy altogether, while others remained and intermarried with the local populations.[257]

The Germanic Vandals, who contributed more to the collapse of the western empire than any other tribe, were able to cross the undefended Rhine frontier when the Roman armies were occupied with Alaric and the Visigoths (A.D. 406). They would eventually invade North Africa (A.D. 425–429), and, under their famous king Gaiseric (reign, A.D. 428–477), sacked the city of Carthage in A.D. 439. Having made this famous city their capital, the Vandal tribe would grow into a powerful naval empire, thus especially fulfilling the phrase "ships of Chittim." The devastation inflicted by this pirate state became so notorious that the term "vandalism" would originate from their legacy of destruction.

The Vandals would later become directly involved in Roman affairs after the murder of the emperor Valentinian III (reign, A.D. 427–455); his murderer, Petronius Maximus, had assassinated him because of his execution of the famous general Aetius (who had defeated Attila at Chalons). Eudoxia, the widow of Valentinian, appealed to Gaiseric for revenge, who responded by invading Italy with such speed that Maximus was stoned by his own people after fleeing for his life (A.D. 455). Gaiseric also sacked the city of Rome in the same year, spending two whole weeks stripping the city of all its wealth; he would even capture the treasures taken from the temple at Jerusalem that Titus had confiscated in A.D. 70. Eventually, by A.D. 474, the Vandals would make peace with the empire, but, because they were Arian in their Christian orientation, they would later become vehement persecutors of Catholics and awaken the wrath of the Catholic emperor Justinian, who would eventually send the general Belisarius to eradicate them in A.D. 533–534.[258]

---

257 See the following sources: Bemont and Monod, 37, 46–51, Freeman, 519, 522–523, Gibbon, 3:426–465, Grant, *History of Rome*, 425, 431–433, Joy, 213–215, Moorhead, 36, 41, Smith, 483–485, Walker, 132, and Webster, 247–248.

258 See Bemont and Monod, 44–46, 51–52, Freeman, 521–522, Gibbon, 3:465–472, Grant, *History of Rome*, 432–434, Joy, 211–212, Moorhead, 41, 50–55, Smith, 479–483, and Webster, 245, 248–249.

The last tribal people, the Arian Heruli, would settle in Italy and actually complete the collapse of the western empire. By the mid-fifth century, this group would be at the mercy of two notable Germanic military leaders, Ricimer and Orestes, who had controlled the throne of Rome from A.D. 455 to A.D. 476. During this period, they had placed nine different emperors on the throne of the west; eventually, in A.D. 473, Orestes would place the young Romulus Augustulus on the throne. His rule would not last long, however, because Orestes refused the distribution of land to the veteran soldiers of Italy, which led to an armed rebellion by the Heruli, under the famous Germanic military commander Odoacer (reign, A.D. 476–493). He would move against Orestes and kill him in a siege at Pavia, but would later spare the life of Romulus in a famous act of clemency after laying siege to the city of Ravenna where the emperor had fled. Romulus decided to abdicate the throne peacefully in favor of Odoacer, who then proclaimed himself king of Italy with the reluctant endorsement of the eastern emperor Zeno (A.D. 476). Thus, Odoacer's ascension to the throne as the first barbarian king of Italy would signify the complete political collapse of the west (A.D. 476).[259]

Therefore he shall be grieved, and return, and have indignation against the holy covenant: so shall he do; he shall even return, and have intelligence with them that forsake the holy covenant. We will discover that this particular passage has two specific applications that apply to both pagan Rome and papal Rome. The actual collapse of paganism began under the reign of Constantine the Great (A.D. 312–337). This ancient ideology would actually go through several failed attempts to revive itself as the Roman state religion, until its eventual destruction at the hands of the rising power of Christianity. Even so, its legacy would be perpetuated in the Christian context, as many pagan converts to the Christian faith would bring their pagan traditions into the Roman Catholic version of Christianity.

Thus, in our first application, the above passage describes the last-ditch effort of paganism to revive itself against the rising power of Christianity, and its eventual destruction and incorporation into the Catholic faith. It could be rephrased as saying, "Therefore he [pagan Rome, paganism] shall be grieved, and return [attempt to revive itself], and have indignation [war against] the holy covenant [Christianity]: so shall he do [make war against Christianity]; he [paganism] shall even return [attempt to revive itself],

---

259 See Bemont and Monod, 52–56, Freeman, 518, 524–525, 546, Gibbon, 3:472–527, Grant, *History of Rome*, 434–436, Joy, 216–217, Moorhead, 42, Walker, 132–133, and Webster, 249.

and have intelligence [gain the support] with them [professed Christians] that forsake the holy covenant [compromise paganism with Christianity]."

When the emperor Diocletian came to power (A.D. 284), he began a widespread revival of Roman patriotism based on the worship of the old pagan gods of Rome. And, because most Christians refused to participate in the state worship of these pagan gods, they were essentially viewed as subversive to the Roman state. Thus, Diocletian was faced with two options: he could either crush Christ's followers into submission through brute force, or enter into an alliance with them in an attempt to control their growth. While Constantine would later choose the second option, Diocletian opted for the first option. Beginning in February of A.D. 303, he ordered the removal of all Christians from military service and employment at the imperial palace, forbade all gatherings in places of public worship, mandated the destruction of all Christian buildings and sacred literature, and sanctioned the arrest and torture of all Christians who refused to sacrifice to the pagan state gods. Aside from the later efforts of Julian the "Apostate" (reign, A.D. 361–363), Diocletian would be the last Roman emperor to attempt the complete preservation of the ancient pagan religion of Rome.

Even though these edicts were especially enforced in Italy, North Africa, and in the eastern empire, the "Caesar" of the west, Constantius Chlorus (the father of Constantine), refused to persecute the Christians in his specific domain (Gaul, i.e., France) and would only comply with the destruction of church property. When both Diocletian and Maximian abdicated their positions as "Augusti" in A.D. 305, Constantius became "Augustus" of the west and granted open toleration to the Christians, which no doubt had an impact on his son Constantine. Even Galerius, the new "Augustus" in the east, who had initially persecuted Christians in accordance with the edicts of Diocletian, eventually saw the overall futility of this enterprise, and, together with Constantine and Licinius, signed the Edict of Serdica (A.D. 311), the first of several edicts that would grant open toleration to Christianity.[260]

Constantine would become the next western emperor after his father's death in A.D. 306, and his famous victory over Maxentius at the Milvian Bridge (A.D. 312) would lead him to promote his adherence to Christianity. As stated earlier, he would sign the Edict of Milan (A.D. 313) with the eastern emperor Licinius, which would grant complete toleration to Christianity. And, when Constantine became sole emperor by A.D. 323–324, he would

---

260 See Freeman, 480–481, Gibbon, 2:58–80, Grant, *History of Rome*, 395–405, and Walker, 108–109.

begin the process of destroying paganism by enacting a series of measures that would highly favor the growing Christian Church. These measures included the exemption of all clergy from state taxation and the subsidizing of church buildings that would later become prominent worship centers of the empire. He also lodged the bishop of Rome in the Lateran Palace, empowering this office with political jurisdiction, so that both church and state could operate together in the overall governance of the empire.

Thus, Constantine's political favoritism of Catholic Christianity specifically became a crucial step in both destroying paganism and elevating Catholicism to the state religion of the Roman Empire. He envisioned a theocratic state with one emperor and one empire, with its citizenry welded together by one common, universal ("Catholic") state religion, thus achieving both political and spiritual unity. As it turned out, Constantine's elevation of Christianity would create such spiritual momentum for the rising Christian Church that paganism would barely survive for even a century after his death in A.D. 337.[261]

Constantine bequeathed his empire to his three remaining sons, Constantine II, Constantius II, and Constans, who would continue the legacy of Christianity. After both Constantine II and Constans were killed in A.D. 340 and A.D. 350 respectively, Constantius II would eventually emerge as sole emperor by A.D. 352, having defeating a pagan usurper named Magnentius in the famous Battle of Mursa. He would initially lead a determined effort to eradicate paganism, but, after seeing its popularity in Rome during a visit in A.D. 357, he suspended this effort until his death in A.D. 361. He was succeeded by the notorious Julian (reign, A.D. 361–363), who made the last concerted attempt by a Roman emperor to reinstate paganism.

Known as "the Apostate," Julian was actually raised a devout Christian, but later became estranged from Christianity after growing tired of the endless debates by church leaders over theological issues. He had a natural affinity for classical Greek philosophy, and, having converted back to paganism, he launched a short-lived program of pagan revival. This was attempted, surprisingly enough, through an edict of universal toleration that would be used to reinstate the old pagan state religion. Julian had actually succeeded in reversing many pro-Christian policies of Constantine and Constantius, but his premature death in A.D. 363 while on a military campaign in Persia ended any hope of a revival of paganism, and no more pagan emperors were to emerge after his death. His three successors, Jovian (reign, A.D. 363–364), Valentinian I (reign, A.D. 364–375), and Valens

261 See Freeman, 499–502, Gibbon, 2:248–296, Grant, *History of Rome*, 405–416, and Walker, 112–114.

(reign, A.D. 375–378), would restore Christianity as the state religion of the empire and allow the Church to resume her ascendency to power.

Paganism was all but eliminated under the reign of Theodosius I (reign, A.D. 378–395), who would galvanize the emperor's office into the imperial defender of the Christian faith. Having ordered the complete destruction of all pagan centers and sacrificial ceremonies, he would later crush a pagan usurper named Arbogast and his puppet emperor Eugenius (a professed Christian) in the Battle of the River Frigidus near the Alps in A.D. 394,[262] thus assuring the eventual annihilation of paganism. Its final deathblow came with the nominal conversion (A.D. 496) and consulship (A.D. 508) of Clovis the Frank (reign, A.D. 486–511), and would survive only in memory through its subtle inception into Catholic Christianity. Even so, nearly three decades after the death of Theodosius, all visible relics of paganism in the Roman Empire were forever gone.[263]

Again, as stated earlier, this second part of Daniel 11:30 has a secondary application that applies to papal Rome. Ellen White actually associated this passage with the papacy; she cited that "Much of the history that has taken place in fulfillment of this prophecy will be repeated," because "In the thirtieth verse a power is spoken of that 'shall be grieved, and return, and have indignation against the holy covenant: so shall he do; he shall even return, and have intelligence with them that forsake the holy covenant.'"[264]

Thus, because Ellen White clearly used this passage in reference to the persecuting nature of the papacy, we could also rephrase it to say "Therefore he [papal Rome] shall be grieved, and return, and have indignation [war against] the holy covenant [true Christianity]: so shall he do [make war against true Christianity]; he [the papacy] shall even return, and have intelligence with them that forsake the holy covenant [use those who recant the true faith to war against true Christianity]." Thus, similar to paganism, the papacy (the pagan version of Christianity), in both its Dark Age and end-time phases, will also war against true Christianity. Papal Rome's victory over Arian Christianity and its Dark Age reign will be specifically addressed in our next chapter.

---

262 Treadgold, 75–78.

263 See Freeman, 503, 507–517, Gibbon, 2:361–364, 407–457, 517–520, 3:137–169, and Grant, *History of Rome*, 416–427, and 453–461.

264 Ellen G. White, *Manuscript Releases*, 21 vols. (Legacy of Light, 2000), 13:394.

Daniel 11	Interpretation
"At the time appointed" (verse 29)	End of 360-year prophecy (31 B.C. to A.D. 330 and 48 B.C. to A.D. 313);
"Come toward the south" (verse 29)	Constantine's removal of the Roman capital to Constantinople, "toward," not "to," Egypt (A.D. 330);
"Not as former, or latter" (verse 29)	This move "toward" Egypt would be peaceful, not like the "former," Octavian's defeat of Egypt, or like the "latter" time, Egypt's defeat by the "king of the north" in Daniel 11:40–45;
"Ships of Chittim" (verse 30)	Barbarian Tribes that caused the collapse of the western empire (Visigoths, Huns, Vandals, and Heruli);
"Against the holy covenant" (verse 30)	First, a revival of paganism in face of Christianity, and its absorption into Roman Catholicism; second, the triumph of Catholicism over both paganism and Arian Christianity, and its attempt to destroy true Christianity.

THIRTEEN

An Examination of Daniel 11:31–39 "The Abomination That Maketh Desolate"

H aving conducted a basic historical survey of the pagan Roman Empire and the development of Catholic Christianity in the last three chapters, we will now examine the "abomination that maketh desolate," i.e., the history of the papal Roman Empire, as outlined in Daniel 11:31–39. Consistent with our understanding of the "replacement principle," the succession of papal Rome after pagan Rome would allow the papacy to "replace" paganism as the new "king of the north." Overall, this specific passage can be divided into four basic trends in the history of papal Rome: (1) its eventual supremacy through the complete destruction of Arian Christianity (verse 31); (2) its 1,260-year Dark Age reign of persecution from A.D. 538 to 1798 (verses 32–35); (3) its exaltation to the level of God (verses 36–37); and (4) its exaltation of a "strange god" and the exploitation of Europe for material gain (verses 38–39).

> And arms shall stand on his part, and they shall pollute the sanctuary of strength, and shall take away the daily sacrifice, and they shall place the abomination that maketh desolate. (Daniel 11:31)

And arms shall stand on his part. We had established in our last chapter that the eventual supremacy of Christianity would deal the final deathblow to paganism in the fourth century; yet, in a subtle manner, paganism would still survive in a Christian context, as many of its practices would infiltrate Roman Catholic Christianity. Although it would cease to exist as an independent, non-Christian religion, paganism would "have indignation against the holy covenant" (Daniel 11:30) by corrupting the pure faith of Christianity through its penetration into Catholicism. As a result, a large number of former pagans were attracted to the Roman version of Christianity because of its similarity to their former pagan orientation, which in turn would strengthen the spiritual position of the Roman Catholic Church in Europe.

The position of the Roman Catholic Church would also be strengthened in the political arena through the military "arms" of Christian emperors who would "stand" on its "part." Beginning with supportive emperors like Constantine (reign, A.D. 312–337) and Theodosius (reign, A.D. 378–395), the subsequent Christian emperors who followed after them would also make their respective contributions to the elevation of the papal power.

And, as the "heresy" of Arianism would grow to have an major influence in Roman affairs after the political collapse of the western empire in A.D. 476,[265] two Catholic emperors in particular, Zeno (reign, A.D. 474–491) and Justinian I (reign, A.D. 527–565) would fulfill key roles in aiding the Catholic Church on its rise to supremacy. In fact, their political contributions were absolutely crucial in the establishment of the papal Roman Empire, because they would essentially help to eliminate the three leading Arian kingdoms who opposed papal supremacy, i.e., the Heruli (Italy), Vandals (North Africa), and Ostrogoths (Italy).

After deposing the last western Roman emperor in A.D. 476, the Herulian king Odoacer (reign, A.D. 476–493) would establish his reign in

---

265 Arianism was a sect of Christianity that denied the eternal pre-existence of Christ as fully God, and claimed that He was the first "creation" of God. This belief began with an Alexandrian priest named Arius; later, Constantine held a church council at Nicaea (A.D. 325) to discuss this issue, among others. The council decided against Arius' view, and later, under the reign of Theodosius, a council at Constantinople condemned this view as heresy (A.D. 381). Yet, prior to Theodosius, several Germanic tribes converted to Arian Christianity under the reigns of Constantius II (reign, A.D. 337–361) and Valens (reign, A.D. 364–378), who were professed Arians themselves. Thus, the Heruli, Vandals, Visigoths, and Ostrogoths were the major Germanic proponents of Arian Christianity. See Charles Bemont and G. Monod, *Medieval Europe from 395 to 1270* (New York: Henry Holt and Company, 1906), 108, Charles Freeman, *Egypt, Greece, and Rome: Civilizations of the Ancient Mediterranean* (Oxford: Oxford University Press, 1996), 502, 509, Edward Gibbon, *The Decline and Fall of the Roman Empire*, 6 vols. (New York: Everyman's Library, 1993), 2:297–357, 3:62–133, Michael Grant, *History of Rome* (New York: Book-of-the-Month Club, 1997), 452, John Moorhead, *The Roman Empire Divided, 400–700* (Harlow, England: Pearson Education Limited, 2001), 37, Philip Schaff, *History of the Christian Church*, 8 vols. (Peabody, MA: Hendrickson Publishers, 2006), volumes 2–3, Williston Walker, *A History of the Christian Church* (New York: Charles Scribner's Sons, 1918), 117–128, and Hutton Webster, *Early European History* (Boston: D.C. Heath & Company Publishers, 1920), 235–236.

Italy and eventually wage war with a Germanic tribe called the Rugii. The Arian Ostrogoths, having been driven east by the Huns, had actually received an appeal from the Rugii for military assistance against Odoacer. The Ostrogothic king Theodoric then appealed to Zeno (the eastern emperor) for permission to intervene in behalf of the Rugii; he offered to help this tribe by launching an invasion of Italy in order to crush Odoacer and establish a permanent Ostrogothic settlement.

Zeno would actually grant Theodoric his request for two reasons: (1) he desired to be free from the Arian Ostrogothic presence in the east; and (2) he desired to remove the Herulian yoke from the Italian peninsula in behalf of the bishop of Rome because of Odoacer's close involvement in matters that infringed on church authority. Therefore, by the fall of A.D. 488, Theodoric and the Ostrogothic tribe acted on their imperial commission from Zeno, and began the trek to Italy in search of both Odoacer and a permanent home.

As it turned out, Theodoric would deal Odoacer three devastating defeats in A.D. 489–490, which forced the Herulian king to take up refuge in the city of Ravenna. There the stubborn Odoacer would hold out for what would turn out to be an exhausting three-year siege (A.D. 490–493). Eventually, the two kings would end the stalemate by proposing peace; yet, Theodoric would treacherously murder Odoacer in a secret plot with the Catholic bishop of Ravenna, and soon thereafter the Herulian people were massacred (A.D. 493). Theodoric then established his position as king of Italy (reign, A.D. 493–526), and his people, who would give the Catholic Church some breathing room, created a permanent settlement on the Italian peninsula. Thus, Zeno's imperial commission to Theodoric would eliminate the Heruli, the first of the three Arian rivals who stood in the way of papal supremacy.[266]

As a staunch adherent to both the old Roman values and the orthodox Catholic faith, Justinian had also determined to fulfill his respective role in extinguishing all potential rivals to the supremacy of the papacy. In A.D. 533, he passed a decree that made the bishop of Rome supreme over all the Christian churches in Europe, thus bringing all European Christians under the authority of Rome.[267] He then sanctioned the use of military force to eliminate the Vandals and Ostrogoths, the two remaining Arian rivals of

266 See Bemont and Monod, 54–56, Freeman, 527, Gibbon, 4:128–139, Alonzo T. Jones, *The Two Republics* (Ithaca, MI: A.B. Publishing, n.d.), 531–535, James Richard Joy, *Rome and the Making of Modern Europe* (New York: Flood and Vincent, 1893), 218–219, Moorhead, 43, Walker, 133, and Webster, 298–299.

267 See page 24 for a quote by Dr. Alberto Treiyer concerning Justinian's decree. See footnote 40.

the Roman Catholic Church. Fully determined to follow through with his assertions to promote the Catholic religion, Justinian commissioned a worthy general named Belisarius to execute his decree and begin the process of liberating the Catholic Church from Arian oppression in the west.

Now, because they were vehement persecutors of Catholic Christians in both North Africa and in the Italian islands, the Vandals would be the first of the two remaining Arian kingdoms to feel the wrathful stroke of Justinian. Belisarius landed on the North African continent in September of A.D. 533, and within a few weeks he had captured the Vandal capital of Carthage. By the spring of A.D. 534, he had crushed the Vandal military machine and captured their famous king Gelimer, thus causing the complete collapse of the Vandal Empire. Much to the delight of Justinian, Belisarius had easily reduced this former pirate kingdom to a state of non-existence within a year's time, thus liberating the Catholics of North Africa from Arian control. Interestingly, he had also recovered the temple vessels that had been captured by Gaiseric in his sack of Rome in A.D. 455, which had originally been captured by Titus during his siege on Jerusalem in A.D. 70. At the end of the African campaign, Justinian would grant Belisarius a well-earned military triumph at Constantinople because of his swift and impressive victory over the Arian Vandals.[268]

Justinian's next task would be to liberate Italy from the last remaining Arian kingdom, the Ostrogoths. When they had settled in Italy under King Theodoric after their elimination of the Heruli (A.D. 493), Catholics and Arians on the Italian peninsula would initially co-exist together in peace. Yet, over time, the doctrinal differences between the two groups would once again create an unsettling situation for the bishop of Rome. Thus, in A.D. 534, Justinian would again commission Belisarius to begin the liberation of Italy from Arian Ostrogothic control. After landing successfully at Sicily (A.D. 535), he would capture the city of Rome by December of A.D. 536. And, as Belisarius and his imperial army settled in Rome for the winter of A.D. 536–537, the Ostrogothic army withdrew with the intention of regrouping to resume a siege in the spring of A.D. 537. When they returned a few months later to begin the siege on Rome, King Vitiges mobilized nearly all of the Ostrogothic military resources in the operation to recapture the city.

Yet, because the imperial army of Belisarius proved to be quite resilient, the entire Ostrogothic military machine would exhaust itself just over

---

268 See Bemont and Monod, 102–103, Freeman, 546, Gibbon, 4:242–269, Grant, *History of Rome*, 464, Jones, 548–550, Joy, 220, Moorhead, 127–128, Walker, 133, and Webster, 330.

a year later and withdraw into northern Italy (A.D. 538). Thus, Belisarius, "in 537–8," having "withstood a mighty siege,"[269] first liberated Rome from Arian control in the spring of A.D. 538, which would allow the pro-Catholic bishop of Rome, Vigilius, to fulfill his position as mandated by the decree of Justinian in A.D. 533. Thus, A.D. 538 is a pivotal date that marked the beginning of the 1,260-year period of papal supremacy in Europe.

The complete end of the Arian Ostrogothic kingdom would actually come several years later when they would revolt against Roman authority under a leader named Totila (A.D. 541). As it turned out, the general Narses, who replaced the famous general Belisarius, would crush the Ostrogothic army in two major battles during A.D. 552–553; he would defeat and kill Totila at Taginae (also called Busta Gallorum), and massacre Teias, the successor of Totila and last Ostrogothic king, at Mons Lactarius. These two victories later led to the complete destruction of the Ostrogothic kingdom by A.D. 555. Thus, by A.D. 555, the military might of Justinian had finally eradicated this last Arian rival to challenge the supremacy of the papacy, which would thus complete its ascendency as the "king of the north."[270]

And they shall pollute the sanctuary of strength, and shall take away the daily sacrifice. As the papal Roman Empire would establish its supremacy, it would "pollute the sanctuary of strength" and "take away the daily sacrifice" by destroying paganism, usurping Christ's ministry in the heavenly sanctuary, inculcating the earthly sanctuary of the church with false doctrines, and shedding the blood of countless martyrs who were executed for non-compliance.[271]

---

269 Norman Davies, *Europe: A History* (New York: HarperPerennial, 1998), 242.

270 See Bemont and Monod, 103–104, Freeman, 546–547, Gibbon, 4:269–312, Grant, *History of Rome*, 464, Jones, 550–553, Joy, 221, Moorhead, 133, Uriah Smith, *Daniel and the Revelation* (Nashville, TN: Southern Publishing, 1949), 270–278, 489–490, Walker, 133, and Webster, 299–300. See the following historical sources on the Roman war against the Ostrogothic Kingdom which led to its eventual destruction: G.P. Baker, *Justinian: The Last Roman Emperor* (New York: Cooper Square Press, 2002), Robert Browning, *Justinian and Theodora* (New York: Thames and Hudson, 1971), Thomas Burns, *A History of the Ostrogoths* (Bloomington, IN: Indiana University Press, 1984), William Gordon Holmes, *The Age of Justinian and Theodora*, 2 vols. (London: George Bell and Sons, 1907), and Procopius, *History of the Wars*, vols. 3–5, translated by H.B. Dewing (Cambridge, MA: Harvard University Press, 1919–1928). Incidentally, Procopius was a personal secretary for Belisarius, and went with him on his campaign in Italy against the Ostrogoths.

271 There are many doctrines of Catholicism that find their respective roots in paganism; a few examples include the use of relics and idols, Sunday worship,

Again, we have demonstrated that the papacy would also seek to elevate the Church, the pope, and the priesthood to the level of man's intercessor. Thus, we can rephrase the sub-passage above by stating that, "And they [papal Rome and its supporters] shall pollute [corrupt with false doctrine] the sanctuary of strength [earthly sanctuary of the church], and shall take away the daily sacrifice [destroy paganism and eventually seek to usurp Christ's intercessory ministry in the heavenly sanctuary]."

And they shall place the abomination that maketh desolate. The phrase "abomination that maketh desolate," i.e., the "abomination of desolation" (Matthew 24:15), is another phrase for the papacy. To review, the papal power would utilize the military assistance of both Zeno and Justinian in order to eliminate their three Arian rivals and be "placed" into a position of authority. It would be an "abomination" because it would incorporate many pagan, false, "abominable" doctrines into its theological infrastructure; it would also be a "desolating" power because it would persecute the faithful followers of God and remove Christ's true intercessory ministry in heaven from the minds of those under its authority, thus causing "spiritual desolation." As a result, God would remove His presence from this false system, thus making it spiritually "desolate," similar to Christ's pronounced "desolation" against Jerusalem for their rejection of Him (Matthew 23:37–38).

Now, while being "placed" into power, papal Rome would also receive the military aid of another rising kingdom from Gaul (modern-day France), which would greatly complement the support of Zeno and Justinian. This rising kingdom, the Frankish kingdom, would grow into a Catholic champion under the reign of their famous king Clovis (reign, A.D. 481–511), who, after coming to the throne at age fifteen, would pursue his desire of bringing all the tribes of Gaul under his authority. His first step toward this desired accomplishment would take place when he had defeated the Roman imperial army at Soissons and executed the local Roman governor Syagrius at Toulouse (A.D. 486–487).

Clovis would next deal with the powerful Germanic Alemanni, meeting them in battle near Strassburg in A.D. 496. When the outcome of this particular engagement was uncertain, he vowed that he would convert to Roman Catholicism (the religion of his wife Clotilda) if he emerged victorious. As it turned out, the battle would swing in his favor; the Frankish army would recover to route the Alemanni in decisive fashion. Thus, being

---

and the exaltation of Mary and the saints. Please refer to pages 28–29 for sources that demonstrate the terrible persecutions by papal Rome that resulted in countless deaths during its 1,260-year rule.

true to his promise, Clovis professed to convert to Catholicism, being baptized by the Bishop of Rheims with 3,000 of his soldiers on Christmas day of A.D. 496. Clovis' conversion transformed him from "the pillager of altars" to "the right arm of the church."[272]

As the new champion of the Roman Catholic faith, Clovis would eventually march against the Arian Visigoths in Gaul; he would seize the Visigothic stronghold of Bordeaux and meet them in battle at Voulon near Poitiers in A.D. 507–508. After crushing this Arian rival, Clovis forced their remaining bands to flee to Spain, while those who stayed in Gaul probably experienced a forced Catholic conversion. Thus, after being the first barbarian king to convert to Catholicism and having been named an honorary consul as a "son" of Rome, Clovis would unify most of Gaul under a single authority loyal to the Catholic Church; this victory by Clovis in A.D. 508 would prove to be a major step in the ascendency of the papacy.[273]

Richard Joy noted that the "fortune which made Clovis a Catholic prepared a staff for the papacy to lean upon and a sword for it to wield in the mighty effort which it was soon put forth for the sovereignty of Europe."[274] The two quotations confirm this significant trend:

> Thus, by what seems the merest accident, Catholicism, instead of Arianism, became the religion of a large part of Western Europe. More than this, the conversion of Clovis gained for the Frankish king and his successors the support of the Roman Church. The friendship between the popes and the Franks afterwards ripened into a close alliance which greatly influenced European history.[275]

---

272 Joy, 224. See also Edward James, *The Franks* (Oxford: Butler & Tanner Limited, 1988), 123, quoted in Dr. Alberto R. Treiyer, *The Seals and the Trumpets* (Dr. Alberto R. Treiyer, 2005), 98, who advocates that Clovis may have been baptized in A.D. 508. See also Richard Fletcher, *The Barbarian Conversion from Paganism to Christianity* (Berkeley, CA: University of California Press, 1997), Edward James, *The Origins of France: From Clovis to the Capetians, 500–1000* (London: MacMillan Press, 1982) and Katharine Scherman, *The Birth of France: Warriors, Bishops, and Long-Haired Kings* (New York: Paragon House, 1987) for more information on the history of Clovis.

273 Treiyer, 100. See also Bemont and Monod, 68, and Benjamin G. Wilkinson, *Truth Triumphant: The Church in the Wilderness* (Mountain View, CA: Pacific Press, 1944), 146–149.

274 Joy, 224–225.

275 Webster, 305.

His was the first Germanic tribe ... to be converted to the orthodox faith. ... That the Franks were 'Catholic' was ultimately,
though not immediately, to bring connections between them and
the papacy of most far-reaching consequences.[276]

Thus, overall, the alleged conversion of Clovis to Roman Catholicism
is significant for the following five reasons: (1) he was the first barbarian
king ever converted to Roman Catholicism; (2) he unified a majority of
Gaul under one single authority loyal to the papacy; (3) he liberated the
local Roman Catholic populations in Gaul from Arian rule; (4) he set up a
model church-state government in Paris that would have close ties to papal
Rome and serve as a model for later church-state relationships; and (5) as
a "son" of Rome and honorary consul, he would give the Roman Catholic
Church his "arm" of political and military support to further papal interests in Europe. Since all these significant events were accomplished by the
year A.D. 508, this year should be viewed as a pivotal date in the "setting up"
of the papal power; therefore, in this very year, Clovis would emerge as the
political champion of the Roman Catholic Church.[277]

And such as do wickedly against the covenant shall he corrupt by
flatteries: but the people that do know their God shall be strong,
and do exploits. And they that understand among the people shall
instruct many: yet they shall fall by the sword, and by flame, by
captivity, and by spoil, many days. (Daniel 11:32–33)

**And such as do wickedly against the covenant shall he corrupt by
flatteries: but the people that do know their God shall be strong, and
do exploits**. In this passage, the "covenant" would refer to those who were
faithful to Christ while living under the reign of papal Rome. Once again,
history will record countless examples of faithful believers who were forced
to recant either through torture or economic pressure; others were corrupted by "flatteries," i.e., were presented with flattering prospects of social,
economic, and even political advancement. As a result, many former true

---

276 Walker, 133–134.
277 See Bemont and Monod, 63–72, Freeman, 529–530, Gibbon, 4:52–70, Grant,
History of Rome, 462, 464, Joy, 223–225, Moorhead, 62–63, 73–76, *Seventh-
day Adventist Bible Commentary*, 12 vols. (Hagerstown, MD: Review and
Herald, 1957–2000), 4:881, Smith, 270–278, 324–330, Treiyer, 94–104, Walker,
133–134, 200, and Webster, 303–305.

believers in Christ would recant their faith in order to escape physical pain or secure temporal advantages.

The various leaders of the European nations would also do "wickedly against the covenant" by empowering the papacy with the necessary civil and military power to persecute those who had refused submission to Roman Catholic Church authority. Even so, there were faithful "people" who would "know their God" and would be "strong" to do "exploits." In other words, many people would remain faithful to Christ, despite the pressure to conform to Roman authority, and would "do exploits" by winning souls into the kingdom of God.[278]

And they that understand among the people shall instruct many: yet they shall fall by the sword, and by flame, by captivity, and by spoil, many days. This sub-passage offers a continuation of the same thoughts brought out in verses 32–33; those who would "understand," i.e., who were faithful to Christ and desired to uphold the truths of the Bible, would "instruct many" in the ways of righteousness. The spiritual "exploits" achieved by these faithful sentinels of God would awaken the wrath of popish persecutors and ultimately cause many to "fall by the sword" (military force), "flame" (being burned at the stake), "captivity" (prison), and "spoil" (loss of material property) during the "many days" of the papal Dark Ages (A.D. 538 to 1798).[279]

To discuss specific accounts of papal Roman persecution over the Dark Age centuries is certainly beyond the scope of this particular work; it would be an impossible task to accurately cover this 1,260-year period in an efficient manner. To speak of faithful peoples such as the Waldensians, Albigensians, and French Huguenots, and the faithful Protestant reformers, like Wycliffe, Huss, Jerome, and Luther, just to name a few, would require much intensive study. We can briefly state, however, that modern Christianity does in fact owe a tremendous debt to these faithful people who stood true to Christ and the Bible through the many centuries of papal persecution:

> Amid the gloom that settled upon the earth during the long period of papal supremacy, the light of truth could not be wholly extinguished. In every age there were witnesses for God—men who

---

278 Ellen G. White, *The Great Controversy* (Mountain View, CA: Pacific Press, 1950), 49–60.

279 See Treiyer, 119–176 for an excellent summarization of the major persecutions conducted by the Catholic Inquisition. See also "Inquisition," *Microsoft® Encarta® Encyclopedia 2000*. © 1993–1999 Microsoft Corporation. All rights reserved.

cherished faith in Christ as the only mediator between God and man, who held the Bible as the only rule of life, and who hallowed the true Sabbath. How much the world owes to these men, posterity will never know. They were branded as heretics, their motives impugned, their characters maligned, their writings suppressed. ... Yet they stood firm, and from age to age maintained their faith in its purity, as a sacred heritage for the generations to come.[280]

Thus, through the faithful legacy of our Protestant heritage, we have been blessed with the precious gift of religious liberty. Ellen White duly observed that the "banner of truth and religious liberty held aloft by the founders of the gospel church and by God's witnesses during the centuries that have passed since then, has, in this last conflict, been committed to our hands."[281] She also noted that many of the atrocities committed by the papacy would be repeated in the last great conflict against those who stand for religious freedom:

We have no time to lose. Troublous times are before us. The world is stirred with the spirit of war. Soon the scenes of trouble spoken of in the prophecies will take place. The prophecy in the eleventh of Daniel has nearly reached its complete fulfillment. Much of the history that has taken place in fulfillment of this prophecy will be repeated. In the thirtieth verse a power is spoken of that 'shall be grieved, and return, and have indignation against the holy covenant: so shall he do; he shall even return, and have intelligence with them that forsake the holy covenant.' [Verses 31–36, quoted.] ... Scenes similar to those described in these words will take place. ... Let all read and understand the prophecies of this book, for we are now entering upon the time of trouble spoken of: [Daniel 12:1–4, quoted.].[282]

Overall, only the heavenly ledger itself can produce an accurate account of both the fidelity of Christ's followers and the heinous crimes committed by popish persecutors during the 1,260-year Dark Age era. We can rest assured that this ledger contains a faithful record of the number of victims who would rather give up their lives than compromise freedom

280 White, *Great Controversy*, 61.

281 Ellen G. White, *The Acts of the Apostles* (Mountain View, CA: Pacific Press, 1911), 68–69.

282 Ellen G. White, *Manuscript Releases*, 21 vols. (Legacy of Light, 2000), 13:394.

of conscience and submit to the authority of Rome.[283] And, as we near the close of this earth's history, God is calling all Christians in this modern age to have this same spirit of courage in defending religious liberty.

> Now when they shall fall, they shall be holpen with a little help: but many shall cleave to them with flatteries. And some of them of understanding shall fall, to try them, and to purge, and to make them white, even to the time of the end: because it is yet for a time appointed. (Daniel 11:34–35)

Now when they shall fall, they shall be holpen with a little help: but many shall cleave to them with flatteries. And some of them of understanding shall fall, to try them, and to purge, and to make them white, even to the time of the end: because it is yet for a time appointed. Once again, this sub-passage emphasizes the Dark Age persecution of the faithful followers of God; some would "fall" in death, while others would recant their faith through "flatteries." This time of trial for the faithful would be part of the purification process; tribulation would purge them from the dross of sin and worldliness, and prepare them to receive the white robe of Christ's righteousness.

This sub-passage also states that this time of persecution would extend "to the time of the end." Again, we can identify the "time of the end" when we cross-reference several passages in Daniel 12. In this specific chapter, Daniel was told to "shut up the words, and seal the book, even to the time of the end" (Daniel 12:4). As he contemplated the "time of the end," Daniel heard the question, "How long shall it be to the end of these wonders?" (Daniel 12:6). He was told that it would "be for a time, times, and a half; and when he shall have accomplished to scatter the power of the holy people, all these things shall be finished" (Daniel 12:7). Thus, the "time of the end" would arrive after the "time, times, and a half," which would refer to the 1,260-year period of papal rule. We have actually covered this time

283 See John Dowling, *The History of Romanism* (Pensacola, FL: Vance, 2002), 299–322, 387–417, 541–618, and White, *Great Controversy*, 61–264. See also Christian Edwardson, *Facts of Faith* (Nashville, TN: Southern Publishing, 1943), 118–133. For excellent sources on the history of the church in the wilderness, see Benjamin G. Wilkinson, *Truth Triumphant: The Church in the Wilderness* (Mountain View, CA: Pacific Press, 1944), *Fox's Book of Martyrs*, William Byron Forbush, ed. (Grand Rapids, MI: Zondervan, 1967), and J.H. Merle D'Aubigne, *History of the Reformation*, 5 vols. (Rapidan, VA: Hartland Publications, n.d.).

period earlier in this work,[284] but it will prove useful to discuss this period once again. To review, it is mentioned a total of seven times in Bible prophecy, yet with some differing phraseology:

Daniel 7:25—"a time, times, and the dividing of a time"

Daniel 12:7—"a time, times, and a half"

Revelation 11:2—"forty and two months"

Revelation 11:3—"a thousand two hundred and threescore days"

Revelation 12:6—"a thousand two hundred and threescore days"

Revelation 12:14—"a time, times, and half a time"

Revelation 13:5—"forty and two months"

We have demonstrated that a "time" can be one year, "times" two years, and "half a time" one-half of a year; a biblical year also consists of 360 days.[285] So, 3½ prophetic years multiplied by 360 days per year would equal 1,260 total prophetic days. Furthermore, since a prophetic day equals a literal year of time in prophecy (Numbers 14:34, Ezekiel 4:6), the 1,260-day period translates into 1,260 literal years of actual time.

We should also remember that papal supremacy began in A.D. 538 when Belisarius first delivered Rome from Arian Ostrogothic control and installed the anti-Arian, pro-Catholic bishop Vigilius on the papal seat. Going forward 1,260 years from this pivotal year would take us to the year A.D. 1798; and, as the Bible has accurately predicted, this would be the very year that papal Rome would receive its "deadly wound" at the hands of revolutionary France (Revelation 13:3). Thus, after this 1,260-year period would transpire in 1798, then the "time of the end" would actually begin (Daniel 12:4–9), and continue through to the second advent of Christ.[286]

> And the king shall do according to his will; and he shall exalt himself, and magnify himself above every god, and shall speak marvellous things against the God of gods, and shall prosper till the indignation be accomplished: for that that is determined shall be done. Neither shall he regard the God of his fathers, nor the

---

284 See page 31 for a review of this concept.

285 See Daniel 4:16, 25, 32, 34 to demonstrate that a "time" can be a year; see Genesis 7:11, 24, and 8:3–4 for proof that a biblical month is equated with 30 days, and, multiplied by 12 months in a year, this would equal 360 days in a biblical year.

286 See pages 93, 179–180, 240–241.

desire of women, nor regard any god: for he shall magnify himself above all. (Daniel 11:36–37)

And the king shall do according to his will; and he shall exalt himself, and magnify himself above every god, and shall speak marvellous things against the God of gods, and shall prosper till the indignation be accomplished: for that that is determined shall be done. When the papacy had ascended to power by the year A.D. 538, it would gradually grow into a medieval institution that could dictate the affairs of the European nations, and thus "do according to his will." In this process, he would "exalt" and "magnify himself above every god," and "speak marvellous things against the God of gods." These phrases are similar to others found in Daniel 7:8, 25, Daniel 8:11, 25, and Revelation 13:4–6), which all discuss the blasphemous claims of the papal office.

We have already established that blasphemy consists of the claim to be equal with God and the claim to have the power to forgive sins; we have also established that several Catholic sources state that the papacy, the priesthood, and the Catholic Church all claim to have these two prerogatives.[287] This passage also says that this power would "prosper until the indignation" would "be accomplished," meaning that the papacy would rule for 1,260 consecutive years until its time of authority, i.e., the "times of the Gentiles," would be "fulfilled" (Luke 21:24, Revelation 11:2).

Neither shall he regard the God of his fathers, nor the desire of women, nor regard any god: for he shall magnify himself above all. As the papal power would exalt itself to the level of God, it would not "regard the God of his fathers" or "regard any god" because it "would magnify" itself "above all." This power would not regard "the desire of women," which is a clear reference to the required celibacy of the Catholic priesthood. Please notice the following two quotations from the 1997 edition of the *Catechism of the Catholic Church*:

All the ordained ministers of the Latin [Catholic] Church, with the exception of permanent deacons, are normally chosen from among men of faith who live a celibate life and who intend to remain celibate 'for the sake of the kingdom of heaven.'[288]

---

287 See pages 26–28.

288 *Catechism of the Catholic Church*, 2nd ed. (Washington, DC: United States Catholic Conference, 1997), 395.

In the Latin Church the sacrament of Holy Orders [ordination of priests to ministry] for the presbyterate is normally conferred only on candidates who are ready to embrace celibacy freely and who publicly manifest their intention of staying celibate for the love of God's kingdom and the service of men.[289]

Thus, these specific phrases offer clear evidence in identifying the papal Roman Empire as the power described in these texts.

But in his estate shall he honour the God of forces: and a god whom his fathers knew not shall he honour with gold, and silver, and with precious stones, and pleasant things. Thus shall he do in the most strong holds with a strange god, whom he shall acknowledge and increase with glory: and he shall cause them to rule over many, and shall divide the land for gain. (Daniel 11:38–39)

But in his estate shall he honour the God of forces: and a god whom his fathers knew not shall he honour with gold, and silver, and with precious stones, and pleasant things. Interestingly, this specific sub-passage states that the papacy would "honour the God of forces." As we seek to understand the meaning of this phrase, we should not let the capitalized word "God" lead us to think that this is referring to the God of heaven. The *Interlinear Hebrew-Aramaic Old Testament* renders the text to say, "he shall honor the god of forces."[290] With the smaller case word "god," we can interpret this phrase to mean that the papacy would "honor the god of forces" by using force as a means of exercising its authority; the armed forces of the European nations were used by the Catholic Church to maintain its medieval supremacy.

This passage also states that papal Rome would honor "a god whom his fathers knew not" with "gold, and silver, and precious stones, and pleasant things." This "god" not formerly known by the Catholic "fathers" can only refer to the exaltation and deification of the virgin Mary. Notice these five statements from the 1997 *Catechism of the Catholic Church* concerning the role and status of the virgin Mary:

'But while in the most Blessed Virgin the Church has already reached that perfection whereby she exists without spot or wrinkle,

---

289 Ibid, 399.

290 *The Interlinear Hebrew-Aramaic Old Testament*, 3 vols. Jay P. Green, Sr., editor (Peabody, MA: Hendrickson Publishers, 1985), 3:2072.

the faithful still strive to conquer sin and increase in holiness. And so they turn their eyes to Mary': in her, the Church is already the 'all holy.'[291]

Through the centuries the Church has become ever more aware that Mary, 'full of grace,' through God, was redeemed from the moment of her conception.[292]

The Fathers of the Eastern tradition call the Mother of God 'the All-Holy' (*Panagia*) and celebrate her as 'free from any stain of sin, as though fashioned by the Holy Spirit and formed as a new creature.' By the grace of God Mary remained free of every personal sin her whole life long.[293]

'Finally the Immaculate Virgin, preserved free from all stain of original sin, when the course of her earthly life was finished, was taken up body and soul into heavenly glory, and exalted by the Lord as Queen over all things, so that she might be the more fully conformed to her Son, the Lord of lords and conqueror of sin and death.'[294]

'Taken up to heaven she [Mary] did not lay aside this saving office [the supposed mother of God] but by her manifold intercession continues to bring us the gifts of eternal salvation. ... Therefore the Blessed Virgin is invoked in the Church under the titles of Advocate, Helper, Benefactress, and Mediatrix.'[295]

Interestingly enough, recent trends in the Christian Church at large give a strong indication that many Protestant pastors, scholars, and lay people are also showing a certain level of interest and devotion to Mary. In a recent article entitled "Hail, Mary" in *Time* magazine, David Van Biema observed that, "In a shift whose ideological breadth is unusual in the fragmented Protestant world, a long-standing wall around Mary appears to be eroding."[296] He also noted, "Mary is also gaining popularity at Protestant divinity schools, where her icons adorn future pastors' walls.

291 *Catechism of the Catholic Church*, 220.
292 Ibid, 123.
293 Ibid, 124.
294 Ibid, 252.
295 Ibid.
296 David Van Biema, "Hail, Mary," *Time* (21 March 2005), 62.

Even evangelical publishing is interested."[297] He confirmed this modern evangelical interest, stating that,

> Arguments on the virgin's behalf have appeared in a flurry of scholarly essays and popular articles, on the covers of the usually conservative *Christianity Today* (headline: THE BLESSED EVANGELICAL MARY) and the usually liberal *Christian Century* (ST. MARY FOR PROTESTANTS). They are being preached, if not yet in many churches then in a denominational cross section ... like at Chicago's Fourth Presbyterian Church, where longtime senior pastor John Buchanan recently delivered a major message on the virgin ending with the words 'Hail Mary ... Blessed are you among us all.'[298]

This elevation of Mary by some modern Protestant pastors and scholars is actually quite appalling, because of the fact that, while professing to uphold the Bible, they seem to omit the passage below where Jesus redirected the thinking of an individual in His day who tried to exalt His earthly mother:

> And it came to pass, as he spake these things, a certain woman of the company lifted up her voice, and said unto him, Blessed is the womb that bare thee, and the paps which thou hast sucked. But he said, Yea rather, blessed are they that hear the word of God, and keep it." (Luke 11:27–28)

Therefore, the evidence is overwhelmingly clear that, while honoring the "god of forces" (having used force in the past to push its dogmas), the papal Roman Empire has also clearly elevated the virgin Mary, i.e., a "god" that their "fathers knew not." This is just another piece of evidence to confirm the blasphemous nature of the Catholic Church.

Thus shall he do in the most strong holds with a strange god, whom he shall acknowledge and increase with glory: and he shall cause them to rule over many, and shall divide the land for gain. This passage reconfirms the exaltation of Mary, the "strange god," not only in Catholic Churches around the world, but also in the "strongholds" of the Protestant realm as well. Those who exalt Mary "acknowledge" her alleged authority, and thus "increase" her "with glory."

---

297 Ibid, 68.
298 Ibid, 63.

The next phrase of this sub-passage also states that "he shall cause them to rule over many;" the "them" mentioned here is in reference to both the virgin Mary and the deceased saints that have allegedly been elevated to "sainthood." Catholic theology does in fact assign both Mary and the saints to an intercessory role. Having already referred to Mary's alleged intercessory role,[299] the next two quotations will confirm the alleged intercessory role of the saints in Catholic doctrine:

> *The intercession of the saints.* 'Being more closely united to Christ, those who dwell in heaven fix the whole Church more firmly in holiness. … [T]hey do not cease to intercede with the Father for us, as they proffer the merits which they acquired on earth. … So by their fraternal concern is our weakness greatly helped.'[300]

> The witnesses who have preceded us into the kingdom, especially those whom the Church recognizes as saints, share in the living tradition of prayer by the example of their lives. … Their intercession is their most exalted service to God's plan. We can and should ask them to intercede for us and for the whole world.[301]

This sub-passage also states that the papacy "would divide the land for gain." Interestingly, when the pagan emperor Diocletian instituted his system of government known as the "tetrarchy" (from A.D. 286–293), he divided the empire and its corresponding territories and provinces into "dioceses," and appointed rulers in those respective areas.[302] When the papal Roman power replaced pagan Rome, the Roman Catholic Church would also maintain regional dioceses by appointing bishops over each divided area.[303]

Furthermore, many areas had "patron saints" who were supposedly in charge of these specific territories (which quite possibly included different professions as well), and they allegedly would watch over all faithful inhabitants. Catholic believers in these areas would often pay homage to their patron saints, which would prove to be a large source of income for the church.[304] Truly, as the power who had actually "replaced" pagan Rome

299 See footnote 295 on page 167.

300 *Catechism of the Catholic Church*, 249.

301 Ibid, 645.

302 Grant, *History of Rome*, 397, and pages 158, 164–165.

303 *Catechism of the Catholic Church*, 221.

304 In one example, Martin Luther, before his conversion, paid homage to the patron saint called St. Anne; since his family owned a mine, this patron saint was

as the "king of the north," the papal Roman system had divided "the land for gain" during its Dark Age period of supremacy. Overall, we can see an abundance of historical information to confirm the papal Roman Empire as the subject of Daniel 11:31–39:

Daniel 11	Interpretation
Verse 31	"arms shall stand on his part" (Force used by papacy to end arianism)
	"the abomination that maketh desolate" (the papal power, who "replaced pagan Rome as the new "king of the north")
Verse 33	"sword, flame, captivity, and spoil" (Description of Dark Age persecution) "many days" (1,260-year papal reign, A.D. 538–1798)
Verse 35	"even to the time of the end" (Beginning of "time of end" in A.D. 1798)
Verse 36	"speak marvellous things" (Description of papal blasphemy)
Verse 37	"nor the desire of women" (Celibacy of Catholic priesthood)
Verse 38	"honor a god his fathers knew not" (Exaltation, deification of virgin Mary)
Verse 39	"cause them to rule over many" (Exaltation of Mary and the saints) "divide the land for gain" (Exploit dioceses for financial gain)

---

allegedly the patron saint for miners and the people of the area in which he lived. He would later repudiate this "cult of the saints." Also, during papal inquisitions, Catholic authorities would often seek to persecute the upper classes to seize the wealth and divide it with the ruling authorities that provided the force to perform the persecutions. See both Roland H. Bainton, *Here I Stand: A Life of Martin Luther* (Nashville, TN: Abingdon Press, 1978), 15, and Treiyer, 133.

—— FOURTEEN ——
Re-identifying the King of the North
"The King of the North in the Time of the End"

B efore we embark on the journey of understanding Daniel 11:40–45, we must first re-identify the "king of the north" in Daniel 11:40. The "king of the north" was first mentioned in verses 5–15, and consisted of Seleucid-Syria, a kingdom located "north" of Judeo-Palestine (Israel). We had also discovered that when pagan Rome conquered Syria, it "replaced" Syria as the new "king of the north." A similar transition also took place when papal Rome arose in the place of pagan Rome—it would also "replace" paganism as the new "king of the north."[305] Now, as we seek to re-identify the "king of the north" in Daniel 11:40, we should understand that it must also be representative of an end-time spiritual power who would have a crucial role in final events after the pivotal year of 1798.

We will discover that the "king of the north" of Daniel 11:40 is actually a description of the papacy in its resurrected phase during the "time of the end," as described in both Revelation 13:1–3 and Revelation 17:7–11. To review, we have understood that the year 1798 would see the papal power receive its "deadly wound" at the hands of revolutionary France; the quotation below emphasizes this very significant event:

> Pius VI (1717–99), pope (1775–99), whose reign, ending in captivity by the French, marked the low point of the modern papacy. … In 1798 French armies under General Louis Alexandre Berthier marched on Rome … and demanded that Pius renounce his temporal sovereignty. At his refusal the pope was taken prisoner and held first at Siena and ultimately at Valence, France, where he died.[306]

---

305 See pages 37–38, 115–116 for examples of the "replacement principle."

306 "Pius VI," *Microsoft® Encarta® Encyclopedia 2000.* © 1993–1999 Microsoft Corporation. All rights reserved. See also William Barry, *The Papacy and Modern Times: A Political Sketch, 1303–1870* (New York: Henry Holt and Company, 1911), 196.

In confirmation, Nicholas Cheetham observed that "General Berthier, Napoleon's future Chief of Staff, was ordered to occupy the city [Rome], to remove the Pope and to set up a Republic. On 15 February [1798], the twenty-third anniversary of Pius' election, the French marched in and installed their puppet government."[307] Frank Coppa also added that "On 10 February 1798 the French entered Rome without opposition," and "Shortly thereafter, on 15 February, the anniversary of the pope's election, Berthier encouraged the deposition of the pope as head of state and the proclamation of a Roman republic."[308]

As we consider when this "deadly wound" would be "healed," history will demonstrate that the Lateran Treaty of 1929 between papal Rome and Mussolini restored the papacy as a sovereign political power. Norman Davies wrote that the "Vatican State ... was created in 1929 in pursuance of the Lateran Treaty signed by Mussolini's Italy and Pope Pius XI," and "Its creation ended ... the Pope's 'captivity.'"[309] Frank Coppa confirmed that this treaty of "11 February 1929" had "established the Holy See as a sovereign state."[310] Thus, through this agreement, papal Rome had "re-entered the ranks of independent sovereign rulers." In essence, the "papacy was back on the map of Europe and the world."[311]

These sources clearly demonstrate that the Lateran Treaty of 1929 had clearly initiated the "healing" of the papal "wound" of 1798, and would begin the return of a resurrected, resurgent papal Rome. As the Bible has predicted, this "healed wound" would bring the papacy back into a position where it will grow to play a major role in end-time prophecy. We will now supplement this assertion by presenting five valid reasons as to why the "king of the north" is in fact this resurrected, resurgent papal Roman power.

First, we should remember that all of the prior prophetic chronologies from Daniel's earlier chapters actually end with papal Rome as the final superpower. Both Daniel 2 and 7 reveal the chronology of Babylon, Media-Persia, Greece, pagan Rome, and papal Rome, while Daniel 8 reveals

---

307 Nicholas Cheetham, *A History of the Popes* (New York: Dorset Press, 1982), 244.

308 Frank J. Coppa, *The Modern Papacy Since 1789* (London: Longman, 1998), 31.

309 Norman Davies, *Europe: A History* (New York: HarperPerennial, 1998), 944. See also J. Derek Holmes, *The Papacy in the Modern World, 1914–1978* (New York: Crossroad, 1981), 52–56, which also describes the Lateran Treaty.

310 Coppa, 175.

311 Cheetham, 279–280.

Media-Persia, Greece, four kingdoms, pagan Rome, and papal Rome. Thus, since papal Rome is the final power in each of these chapters, we must conclude that Daniel 11 would also finish its respective chronology with this very same power.

In several past articles, Seventh-day Adventist pioneer Elder James White also confirmed that the last power in Daniel 11, i.e., the "king of the north," must be referring to the Roman Empire (in its papal phase). Adventist history will also demonstrate that Elder White and another Adventist pioneer, Elder Uriah Smith, presented differing perspectives on the identity of the "king of the north." Having initially believed that the "king of the north" was the papacy,[312] Elder Smith later changed his position by conveying that the "king of the north" would instead consist of the Ottoman-Turkish Empire.[313] In response to this change in position, Elder White noted in the four quotations below that the "king of the north" must still be referring to Rome:

> The field of Daniel's prophecy embraces five universal kingdoms. These are Babylon, Medo-Persia, Grecia, and Rome, and the eternal kingdom of God. The ground of the four perishable kingdoms, reaching to, and introducing the immortal kingdom, is covered by four distinct lines of prophecy. These are given in chapters two, seven, eight, and eleven. The eleventh chapter of Daniel closes with the close of the fourth monarchy with these words: [Daniel 11:45–12:3 quoted]. ... The student of prophecy is thus born down the stream of time from Babylon in the height of the glory of that kingdom, past Media and Persia, the kingdom of Grecia, and *the Roman Empire which comes to its end at the second coming of Christ.*[314]

> Let us take a brief view of the line of prophecy four times spanned in the book of Daniel. ... [The] same ground is passed over in chapters two, seven, eight, and eleven, with this exception, that Babylon is left out of chapters eight and eleven. We first pass down

---

312 See Uriah Smith, *Review and Herald*, 18 May 1862: "[Regarding the] ... plan of removing the seat of the Papacy to Jerusalem. ... Is not the above item significant, taken in connection with Daniel 11:45?"

313 See Uriah Smith, *Daniel and the Revelation* (Nashville, TN: 1949), 289–299.

314 James White, "The Time of the End," *Signs of the Times* (22 July 1880), 1. When Elder White refers to "Rome," he is describing Rome in both its pagan and papal phases.

the great image of chapter 2, where Babylon, Persia, Greece, and Rome are represented by the gold, the silver, the brass, and the iron. All agree that these feet are not Turkish but Roman. And as we pass down to the lion, the bear, the leopard, and the beast with ten horns, representing the same as the great image, again all will agree that it is not Turkey that is cast into the burning flame, but the Roman beast. So of chapter 8, all agree that the little horn that stood up against the Prince of princes is not Turkey but Rome. In all these lines thus far Rome is the last form of government mentioned. ... *Now comes the point in the argument upon which very much depends. Does the eleventh chapter of the prophecy of Daniel cover the ground measured by chapters two, seven, and eight? If so, then the last power mentioned in that chapter is Rome.*[315]

Elder Smith has given a very fine talk on the eleventh chapter of Daniel, and his interpretation seems plausible, but IF the legs of iron, and the feet of iron and clay in the second chapter represent Rome, and IF the non-descript, ten-horned beast, and the little horn of the seventh chapter represent Rome, and IF the little horn which waxed exceeding great of the eighth chapter represents Rome, the King of the North represents Rome also. These are four parallel prophecies, brethren, reaching down to the coming of our Lord.[316]

And there is a line of historical prophecy in chapter eleven, where the symbols are thrown off, beginning with the kings of Persia, and reaching down past Grecia and Rome, to the time when that power 'shall come to his end, and none shall help him.' If the feet and ten toes of the metallic image are Roman, if the beast with ten horns that was given to the burning flame of the great day be the Roman beast, if the little horn which stood up against the Prince of princes be Rome, and if the same field and distance are covered by these four prophetic chains, then the last power of the eleventh chapter which is to 'come to his end and none shall help him,' is Rome. But if this be Turkey, as some teach, then the toes of the image of the second chapter are Turkish, the beast with ten horns of the seventh chapter represents Turkey, and it was Turkey that stood up against

---

315 James White, *Review and Herald*, 29 Nov 1877.
316 James White quoted in M.C. Wilcox, *King of the North* (Mountain View, CA: Pacific Press, 1910), 44.

the Prince of princes of the eighth chapter of Daniel. True, Turkey is bad enough off; but its waning power and its end is the subject of the prophecy of John [5th & 6th trumpets] and not Daniel.[317]

To supplement Elder White's observations (which are absolutely correct), a resurrected papacy is also the final power mentioned in both Revelation 13 and Revelation 17. Again, the "king of the north" is the parallel of both the composite "beast" whose "deadly wound was healed" (Revelation 13:1–3) and the "scarlet-coloured beast" who supports the "great whore" called "Babylon," which "was, and is not," and "shall ascend out of the bottomless pit" (Revelation 17:1–11). Since Daniel and Revelation are sister books, we can conclude that the specific prophecies of Daniel 11:40–45, Revelation 13:1–3, and Revelation 17:1–11 each describe a resurrected, resurgent papacy after the year 1798.

The second reason for identifying the "king of the north" as the papacy is because this symbol is actually one of several symbols used by God in Scripture to identify the antichrist power. In fact, there are at least eight different prophetic symbols used to describe the power of papal Rome: (1) the "feet" of "iron and clay" (Daniel 2:43); (2) the "little horn" (Daniel 7:8, 8:9); (3) the "abomination of desolation" (Daniel 11:31, Matthew 24:15); (4) the "man of sin" (2 Thessalonians 2:3); (5) the "son of perdition" (2 Thessalonians 2:3); (6) the composite "sea beast" (Revelation 13:1–10); (7) the "great whore" called "Babylon" who rides the "scarlet-coloured beast" (Revelation 17:1–11); and, finally (8) the "king of the north" (Daniel 11:40). Therefore, because this specific power is described by so many different symbols in the Bible, it makes sense that the phrase "king of the north" would also be one of these symbols.

A third reason can also be found in understanding the direction of the "north" itself, which is the highest of the four directions. We know from the Bible that this direction symbolizes the location of God's throne (Psalm 48:1–2), and when the prophet Isaiah commented on the fall of Satan, he quoted this fallen angel as saying that he would "exalt" his "throne above the stars of God" and "sit also upon the mount of the congregation, in the sides of the north" (Isaiah 14:13). In essence, by striving to sit in the "sides of the north," Satan desired to be God and claim the prerogatives that are due alone to God. Similarly, the papal power has also blasphemously attempted to assume the prerogatives of God, claiming to be equal with God and have the power to forgive sins. Thus, since this power would

---

317 James White, *Review and Herald*, 3 Oct 1878.

strive to sit in the highest place of the church by making these false claims, we must conclude that it must constitute the "king of the north."

A fourth reason can be found in the example of the relationship between ancient Babylon and ancient Israel in the Old Testament. It is interesting to note that the prophet Jeremiah observed that ancient Babylon came from the direction of the "north" to conquer ancient Israel:

> Behold, I will send and take all the families of the north, saith the LORD, and Nebuchadrezzar the king of Babylon, my servant, and will bring them against this land, and against the inhabitants thereof, and against all these nations round about, and will utterly destroy them, and make them an astonishment, and an hissing, and perpetual desolations. (Jeremiah 25:9)

In another powerful reference, Jeremiah stated that "the LORD said unto me, Out of the north an evil shall break forth upon all the inhabitants of the land" (Jeremiah 1:14); as a result, Israel was called to "flee out of the midst of Jerusalem ... for evil appeareth out of the north, and great destruction" (Jeremiah 6:1). And, because both Daniel 7:4 and Jeremiah 50:43–44 describe ancient Babylon as a "lion," Jeremiah confirmed that this power would come from the "north" to take ancient Israel captive:

> Set up the standard toward Zion: retire, stay not: for I will bring evil from the north, and a great destruction. The lion is come up from his thicket, and the destroyer of the Gentiles is on his way; he is gone forth from his place to make thy land desolate; and thy cities shall be laid waste, without an inhabitant. (Jeremiah 4:6–7)

Thus, all of these passages describe how ancient Babylon had been viewed as a conqueror from the direction of the "north." Geographically, the ancient city of Babylon was actually due east of Jerusalem; yet, in order to conquer the kingdoms of Assyria and Israel, Babylon would need to move "north" around the desert that separated them from Judeo-Palestine. They would crush the Assyrian Empire at Nineveh in 612 B.C., an Egyptian garrison in the Battle of Carchemish in 605 B.C., and later level the city of Jerusalem in the same year; therefore, in marching on Jerusalem, they came from the direction of the "north."

This observation is quite significant, because we have proven that the papacy is the New Testament spiritual counterpart to ancient Babylon (spiritual Babylon of Revelation 17),[318] and the Christian Church is the New Testament spiritual counterpart to ancient Israel (spiritual Israel).[319] Thus, since ancient Babylon came from the direction of the "north" to conquer ancient Israel, we may conclude in a spiritual sense that spiritual Babylon would be the spiritual "king of the north," coming from the spiritual "north" in symbol while attempting to conquer spiritual Israel, i.e., the Christian Church.[320]

The fifth and final reason as to why I believe that the papacy is the "king of the north" stems from a concept we have discussed several times already—the "replacement principle."[321] Once again, as stated earlier, Daniel 11:5–15 labeled Seleucid-Syria as this power; yet, again, when pagan Rome came from the "north" to incorporate Syria into its empire (63 B.C.), it "replaced" this kingdom as the new "king of the north." Furthermore, when papal Rome had "replaced" pagan Rome, it also became the "king of the north" by transition.

Now, some may wonder if pagan Rome would also be the "king of the south," since it also conquered Hellenistic Egypt (31–30 B.C.); yet, even though it would conquer Egypt, it would not become the "king of the south" because of the fact that it had conquered Hellenistic Syria first to become the "king of the north," and therefore could not be both the "king of the north" and the "king of the south" simultaneously. And, again, when papal Rome would "replace" pagan Rome, it would also assume the role of the "king of the north" by transition. Therefore, this "replacement principle" is another logical reason as to why the papacy would be the "king of the north."

Overall, as we conclude this particular chapter, we should offer a brief review of the five reasons presented as to why the "king of the north" of Daniel 11:40 can be none other than a resurrected, resurgent papal Rome in the "time of the end" after 1798:

---

318 We have demonstrated in our review of Revelation 17 that spiritual Babylon is in fact a description of the papal power (Revelation 17:1–11). Please see chapter 6 of this work.

319 See the following verses that prove that the church is spiritual Israel: Matthew 21:42–44, 1 Peter 2:9–10, Romans 2:28–29, 9:6–8, Galatians 3:26–29, Ephesians 2:8–22, and James 1:1. This list is certainly not an exhaustive one.

320 Louis F. Were, *The King of the North at Jerusalem* (St. Maries, ID: LMN Publishing, 2002), 38–42.

321 See footnote 304 in this current chapter.

(1) The final power in each of Daniel's prior prophecies, as well as those of Revelation, end with a description of papal Rome, so naturally chapter 11 must also end with this same power. Therefore, since the final power is the papacy, and the symbol used to describe this final power in Daniel 11:40 is the "king of the north," then we must conclude that the "king of the north" and the papacy are one and the same. This conclusion is confirmed by Seventh-day Adventist pioneer Elder James White.

(2) There are a number of different prophetic symbols used in the Bible to describe the papacy: the feet of iron and clay (Daniel 2), the little horn (Daniel 7 & 8), the abomination of desolation (Daniel 11 & Matthew 24), the man of sin (2 Thessalonians 2), the son of perdition (2 Thessalonians 2), the composite sea beast (Revelation 13), and the harlot riding a scarlet-colored beast (Revelation 17). The phrase "king of the north" is simply another prophetic symbol used in conjunction with these other symbols to describe the papal power.

(3) The direction of the "north" is symbolic of the location of God's throne (Psalm 48:1–2), where Satan had desired to sit in order to claim the prerogatives of God (Isaiah 14:13). Since papal Rome also blasphemously claims to assume the prerogatives that are due alone to God, it would also strive to sit in the direction of the "north" in a spiritual sense, and would thus constitute the spiritual "king of the north."

(4) Ancient Babylon came from the "north" directionally to conquer ancient Israel; as its spiritual counterpart, spiritual Babylon, i.e., the papacy, will also attempt to conquer spiritual Israel (the New Testament Church) from the spiritual "north" (by occupying the position of God), and thus fulfill the description of the "king of the north."

(5) The "replacement principle" dictates that when pagan Rome conquered the first "king of the north," Seleucid-Syria (63 B.C.), it would "replace" that kingdom as the new "king of the north." Now, when papal Rome replaced pagan Rome, the same transition would take place; the papacy would also "replace" pagan Rome as the new "king of the north." And, during the "time of the end," the "king of the north" would also be the papal power, yet in its resurgent, resurrected, "healed wound" phase of existence after the year 1798.

—— FIFTEEN ——

An Examination of Daniel 11:40 "The King of the North vs. the King of the South—Part 3"

W e have demonstrated thus far that the prophecies contained in Daniel 11:1–39 have been fulfilled through past historical trends. Yet, we will discover that a majority of the prophetic events found in the specific passage of Daniel 11:40–45 still have a future application. In essence, this passage contains certain prophetic events that will apply especially to our current day; it is therefore essential that we develop an accurate understanding of its meaning.

Thus, in order to accomplish a proper interpretation of Daniel 11:40–45, we will divide it up into several manageable sections, and this particular chapter will examine the passage of Daniel 11:40. We will discover that it actually outlines that the "king of the north," a resurrected, resurgent papacy, will launch an aggressive warfare against the "king of the south," which we will demonstrate to be its former global political rival of Soviet atheistic communism.

> And at the time of the end shall the king of the south push at him: and the king of the north shall come against him like a whirlwind, with chariots, and with horsemen, and with many ships; and he shall enter into the countries, and shall overflow and pass over. (Daniel 11:40)

And at the time of the end. The phrase "time of the end" will actually set the prophetic context of verses 40–45. We have already demonstrated that the "time of the end" actually began in the year 1798, when the papacy received its "deadly wound" by the hand of revolutionary France. Once again, Daniel was told to seal up the words of his prophecy until the "time of the end" (Daniel 12:4, 9). He was then told that the "end," or "time of the end," would come after the "time," "times," and a "half" (Daniel 12:7), which referred to the 1,260-year reign of papal Rome (A.D. 538–1798). In other words, the end of the 1,260-year reign of the papacy would mark the beginning of the "time of the end," which would extend from 1798 to the second advent of Christ:

> But that part of his prophecy which related to the last days, Daniel was bidden to close up and seal 'to the time of the end.' … But since 1798 the book of Daniel has been unsealed, knowledge of the prophecies has increased, and many have proclaimed the solemn message of the judgment near.[322]

We should also understand that whenever we address post-1798 prophecy, or even New Testament prophecy for that matter, we are usually dealing with concepts that are not local and literal in nature, but rather global and spiritual in nature. For example, when we consider the concept of "Babylon" in the Old Testament, we are usually dealing with the literal kingdom of ancient Babylon that had conquered Israel in 605 B.C. In the New Testament, however, "Babylon" does not symbolize a literal nation, but rather a system of religious confusion controlled by the papal Roman Empire, which would also include its "harlot daughters" of apostate Protestantism and spiritualism.

Another example of this concept can be found when we consider "Israel" from both the Old and New Testaments. The concept of "Israel" in the Old Testament is usually referring to the literal nation located in Palestine, which actually comprised the chosen people of God in that particular time period. Yet, when we examine the New Testament concept of "Israel," we find clear evidence that it does not refer to a literal nation, but a "spiritual nation," a "spiritual Israel," which is a symbol of the Christian Church in the New Testament dispensation. This "spiritual Israel" actually consists of all faithful followers of Christ, irrespective of the biological or ethnic orientation of an individual.[323]

Most churches today espouse some form of theology that emphasizes the false notion that the literal nation of Israel will be reinstated as the chosen people of God. Yet, when we examine the passage of Daniel 9:24–27, we will discover that ancient Israel had lost its national favor with God after the crucifixion of Christ (A.D. 31) and the stoning of Stephen (A.D. 34). A proper understanding of this particular prophecy clearly demonstrates that the "Israel" of God now consists of all faithful believers in Christ. We

---

322 Ellen G. White, *The Great Controversy* (Mountain View, CA: Pacific Press, 1950), 356.

323 See Matthew 21:42–44, 1 Peter 2:9–10, Romans 2:28–29, Ephesians 2:8–22, Romans 9:6–8, Galatians 3:26–29, and James 1:1.

should now take the time to cover this prophecy in an abbreviated sense, because it will not only help us to understand the concept of "spiritual Israel," but also the concept of the "glorious land" (Daniel 11:41), which will be examined in our next chapter.

> Seventy weeks are determined upon thy people and upon thy holy city, to finish the transgression, and to make an end of sins, and to make reconciliation for iniquity, and to bring in everlasting righteousness, and to seal up the vision and prophecy, and to anoint the most Holy. (Daniel 9:24)

Daniel was told in the above passage that "seventy weeks" of probationary time would be given to his people ("thy people"), the literal nation of Israel, to "make an end of sins" and "anoint the most Holy" (Christ). The "seventy weeks" would translate into 490 prophetic "days," and since a prophetic "day" equates to a literal year of time (Numbers 14:34, Ezekiel 4:6), these 490 prophetic "days" would equate to 490 literal years. Therefore, ancient Israel would have a 490-year period of probationary time to prove their fidelity to God and accept Christ as the "Messiah." If they failed to comply with these conditions, they would forfeit their status as the chosen people of God.

> Know therefore and understand, that from the going forth of the commandment to restore and to build Jerusalem unto the Messiah the Prince shall be seven weeks, and threescore and two weeks: the street shall be built again, and the wall, even in troublous times. (Daniel 9:25)

According to the above passage, this 490-year period would begin with the decree to restore and rebuild Jerusalem, which actually took place in 457 B.C. under the reign of the Persian king Artaxerxes (Ezra 6:14, 7:11–25). 69 prophetic weeks would span from the time of this decree to the appearance of the "Messiah," and would equate to 483 prophetic "days," or 483 literal years. Thus, this 483-year period would extend from 457 B.C. to the year A.D. 27 (not counting the year zero when going from B.C. to A.D.). Therefore, the first 69 weeks of the "seventy weeks" would span from 457 B.C. to A.D. 27, the very year that Christ would be baptized as the "Messiah" by John the Baptist (See chart on page 45).

Luke 3:1–3 reveals that John the Baptist began baptizing in the 15th year of the reign of Tiberius Caesar. History will show that Tiberius reigned from A.D. 14 to A.D. 37; yet, he did serve as co-emperor for two years with his predecessor Caesar Augustus before becoming sole emperor in A.D. 14. Therefore, his 15th year would actually be taken from A.D. 12 and not A.D. 14, which would bring us to the year A.D. 27.[324] This is the actual year that Christ was baptized by John in the Jordan River to begin His public ministry as the long-awaited "Messiah." So, the first 69 weeks of the 70 weeks' prophecy would span from 457 B.C. to A.D. 27.

> And he shall confirm the covenant with many for one week: and in the midst of the week he shall cause the sacrifice and the oblation to cease, and for the overspreading of abominations he shall make it desolate, even until the consummation, and that determined shall be poured upon the desolate. (Daniel 9:27)

Many dispensationalist Christians apply the above passage to a future antichrist power that will supposedly appear during the last seven years of earth's history. Yet, in reality, this passage is describing the 70th week that began where the 69 weeks' left off in A.D. 27. The text actually applies to Jesus Christ, not the antichrist, and describes how Christ would come as the "Messiah" to confirm the "covenant" of salvation with the Jewish nation. This final "week" would translate into seven literal years of time, and begin in the year A.D. 27.

According to this passage, in the "midst," or middle, of the week, i.e., 3½ years into this final seven-year period, Christ would cause the "sacrifice and the oblation to cease." This means that, 3½ years into His public ministry, Jesus would be crucified on Calvary, thus ending the sacrificial system of the Jewish economy. When Christ was crucified, the veil in the temple was rent from top to bottom (Matthew 27:51), thus signifying an end to the earthly sacrifices that had pointed to Him. So, 3½ years from A.D. 27 would bring us to the year A.D. 31 when Christ would be crucified; yet, 3½ years would still remain to complete the period of "seventy weeks." This last 3½-year period would continue from A.D. 31 and end in A.D. 34, when the deacon Stephen was stoned by the religious leaders of Israel (Acts 7:51–60).

This notable event would signify the end of Israel's probation as God's chosen people. After this point we see a major evangelistic thrust by the apostles to bring the Gospel to the Gentiles. After Stephen was stoned (Acts 7), Philip baptized an Ethiopian eunuch (Acts 8), Paul was converted as the apostle to the Gentiles (Acts 9), Peter evangelized the house of the

---

324 See pages 125–126 for a review of this time prophecy and the confirmation of the 15th year of the reign of the Roman emperor Tiberius Caesar.

Gentile Cornelius (Acts 10), and eventually the apostles realized that the Gentiles were converting to the Gospel (Acts 11).

These points all signify that the probationary time of literal Israel had expired in A.D. 34, which meant that "Israel" would then become a "spiritual" nation consisting of all true believers in Christ, and not be limited to a geographical area or a specific biological group of people. And, because literal Israel would continue in rebellion against God, their spiritual status with Him would remain "desolate, even until the consummation," i.e., the final destruction of sin and sinners. Therefore, literal Israel as a nation had lost their favor with God in A.D. 34, and will never again be reinstated as His chosen people. "Israel" is now a "spiritual nation," made up of both biological Jewish and Gentile converts who have faith in Christ as their Savior. This evidence confirms that we are now dealing with global, spiritual concepts in Bible prophecy, especially in the passage of Daniel 11:40–45.

The king of the south shall push at him. Our next task will be to identify the power called the "king of the south." Earlier in verses 5–15 and verses 25–28 of Daniel 11, we saw that the "king of the south" consisted of Hellenistic Egypt. Since the literal nation of Egypt has no chance of becoming a major superpower in end-time prophecy, and the prophetic symbols in Daniel 11:40–45 are global and spiritual in nature, we must search for the global, spiritual meaning behind the prophetic symbol of "Egypt" as the "king of the south." It must be a description of an end-time power that would threaten the global agenda of a resurrected papacy. When we examine the case of Pharaoh in the time of Moses, we can unlock the prophetic symbol of "spiritual" Egypt:

> And afterward Moses and Aaron went in, and told Pharaoh, Thus saith the LORD God of Israel, Let my people go, that they may hold a feast unto me in the wilderness. And Pharaoh said, Who is the LORD, that I should obey his voice to let Israel go? I know not the LORD, neither will I let Israel go. (Exodus 5:1–2)

In stating that he didn't "know" the Lord, Pharaoh was essentially denying the existence of the true God, which is a description of "atheism." Pharaoh himself was not an absolute atheist; he did believe in idolatrous "gods," not to mention the fact that the pharaohs themselves were worshipped as "gods." Yet, the principle we need to understand here is that Pharaoh did not claim to believe in the true God, implying that he did not believe that the true God actually existed. This is the essence of "atheism," i.e., a denial of the actual existence of the true God. Based on this line of reasoning, we can conclude that "spiritual Egypt" is a symbol of "atheism." In a statement from her powerful book *The Great Controversy*, Ellen White confirmed this conclusion:

> Of all nations presented in Bible history, Egypt most boldly denied the existence of the living God and resisted His commands. No monarch ever ventured upon more open and highhanded rebellion against the authority of Heaven than did the king of Egypt. ... This is atheism, and the nation represented by Egypt would give voice to a similar denial of the claims of the living God and would manifest a like spirit of unbelief and defiance.[325]

Now that we understand the "king of the south," i.e., "spiritual" Egypt, to be a symbol of atheism, we should remember that it is also a political power. The use of the term "king" signifies that the "king of the south" must be referring to an empire of some sort. Since the "king of the south" is synonymous with "spiritual" Egypt, and "spiritual" Egypt is a symbol of atheism, then the "king of the south" must be referring to an atheistic power that would promote this deceptive philosophy on a worldwide scale. When we examine the scope of history after 1798, there is only one empire, namely the former Soviet Union (1917–1991), which had espoused "atheism" on a global scale. Therefore, the "king of the south" is a symbol of Soviet atheistic communism, because there has been no greater example of an atheistic empire in recent history other than the Soviet Union.

Some have thought that the horrific manifestation of atheism in revolutionary France from 1793–1797 was an actual fulfillment of this prophecy;[326] yet, two reasons clearly show that this could not be the case: (1) this event took place before 1798, and Daniel 11:40–45 describes events after 1798; and (2) after the year 1798 France would not become an atheistic superpower, even during the dictatorial reign of Napoleon Bonaparte. Thus, the former Soviet Union is the only empire that can fulfill the role of the "king of the south" after 1798. Similar to ancient Egypt, this powerful atheistic empire had "pushed" against the authority of the "king of the north," the papacy, by openly denying the existence of God during its specific era as a superpower (1945–1991). Therefore, we could rephrase this sub-passage to say that "the king of the south [Soviet atheistic communism] shall push at [war against] him [the "king of the north," the papacy]."

---

325 White, *Great Controversy*, 269.

326 Louis F. Were, *The King of the North at Jerusalem* (St. Maries, ID: LMN Publishing, 2002), 66–68. For account on atheism and the French Revolution, see White, *Great Controversy*, 265–288.

And the king of the north shall come against him like a whirlwind, with chariots, and with horsemen, and with many ships; and he shall enter into the countries, and shall overflow and pass over. This sub-passage describes how the "king of the north" would eventually overrun the "king of the south." With the help of the United States during the Cold War,[327] papal Rome conspired to cause the collapse of the Soviet Union because of its stronghold on Eastern Europe and its global influence as a model of atheistic communism. The late Catholic scholar Malachi Martin actually confirmed this concept by stating that the papacy did view Soviet communism as a serious threat to its long-term religio-political interests around the globe.[328]

In this particular commentary we will not take the time to discuss specific events in the papal involvement of the demise of the Soviet Union. Yet, it will prove useful to mention several quotations that will demonstrate that the papacy had joined together with the United States in the common cause of destroying this atheistic superpower. Frank Coppa observed that,

> In 1982 the pope [John Paul II] met President Ronald Reagan of the United States, who had likewise survived an assassination attempt in 1981, and the two experienced a meeting of minds. ... The pope and the American president supposedly conspired in a 'holy alliance' not only to support the outlawed Solidarity movement after the martial crackdown of 1981 in Poland, but sought to precipitate the end of Soviet domination of the whole of Eastern Europe. Both were to see their vision fulfilled, as well as the collapse of communism in the Soviet Union.[329]

Interestingly, Mr. Coppa also noted that, after the Soviet Union had collapsed by Christmas of 1991, "in an interview, the ousted Soviet leader" Mikhail "Gorbachev concluded that Pope John Paul II had played a 'major political role' in undermining communism in Eastern Europe."[330] As a result of this collapse, the papacy would then "enter into the countries" and "overflow and pass over," initiating an influx of Catholicism into many of the former Soviet republics. Interestingly, "Near the end of 1991, Pope John Paul II convoked a synod of European bishops, both from the East

---

327 See Carl Bernstein, "The Holy Alliance," *Time*, 24 Feb 1992, 28–35, quoted in Frank J. Coppa, *The Modern Papacy Since 1789* (London: Longman, 1998), 12.

328 Malachi Martin, *The Keys of this Blood* (New York, NY: Simon & Shuster, 1990), 15.

329 Coppa, 12.

330 Ibid, 243.

and West, to assess the opportunities presented by the political changes to promote a new evangelization of Europe."[331] This success of the Holy See against communism is one of many examples where the papal power has exerted a powerful global influence in the worldwide political arena. Mr. Coppa concluded that,

> Despite difficulties, the Holy See remains an active member of the international community, maintaining one of the largest diplomatic establishments. Although its primary realm is that of conscience with spiritual ends and objectives, this does not prevent, and indeed enables, the Holy See to wield considerable influence in diplomatic affairs and global relations.[332]

Therefore, recent events have shown that papal Rome, together with the Cold War efforts of the United States, caused the collapse of Soviet atheistic communism by the end of 1991. Soviet communism had "pushed" at papal Rome for a time; yet, the papacy responded like a "whirlwind" to "overflow" and "pass over," causing the disintegration of this atheistic superpower as a powerful fulfillment of Daniel 11:40. As a result, many of the "countries" that once comprised this former communist empire have now become ripe mission fields for Catholicism. Overall, the collapse of the Soviet Union is a powerful example of the global influence of Rome in the worldwide political arena.

Symbol in Daniel 11:40	Interpretation
"Time of the end"	1798 to the second advent of Christ
"King of the south"	Soviet atheistic communism (1917 to 1991)
"Push against him"	Soviet promotion of atheism
"King of the north"	"Healed" papacy (after 1929)
"Like a whirlwind"	Papacy destroys Soviet Union with the help of USA (1991)
"Enter into countries"	Catholicism brought to several former Soviet bloc nations

---

331 Ibid.
332 Ibid, 249.

—— SIXTEEN ——
An Examination of Daniel 11:41
"The King of the North in
the Glorious Land"

In this particular chapter we will examine the passage of Daniel 11:41 and discover that the papacy (the "king of the north") will seek to "enter" into the "glorious land." In essence, the "glorious land" will prove to be both a general description of "spiritual" Israel (the Christian Church) and a specific description of non-Catholic, Protestant Christianity, which would include Seventh-day Adventism. In essence, Daniel 11:41 will offer a description of how papal Rome will seek to regain control of Christendom through the recapture of non-Catholic, Protestant Christianity back into the fold of Catholicism.

> He shall enter also into the glorious land, and many countries shall be overthrown: but these shall escape out of his hand, even Edom, and Moab, and the chief of the children of Ammon. (Daniel 11:41)

He shall enter also into the glorious land, and many countries shall be overthrown. Earlier in Daniel 11:16 we had associated the "glorious land" with the literal nation of Israel; yet, because we are dealing with global, spiritual concepts in verses 40–45, we must conclude that the "glorious land" in verse 41 is a description of a "spiritual" Israel consisting of all faithful believers from every Christian denomination.[333] Yet, since the papacy will not need to "enter" its own domain of Catholicism, it would need to especially focus on non-Catholic Christianity.

Therefore, the papacy will fully "enter" the "glorious land" by securing the allegiance of all non-Catholic Christian groups, which would especially include Protestantism. Ever since the Protestant Reformation, papal Rome has desired to re-secure the allegiance of Protestantism on Roman Catholic

---

333 Louis F. Were, *The King of the North at Jerusalem* (St. Maries, ID: LMN Publishing, 2002), 60–61.

terms.[334] The *American*, a Catholic periodical, confirmed this point, stating that "Protestantism is rebellion against the authority of Christ vested in His Church."[335] According to this source, Protestants "conveniently forget that they separated from us, not we from them; and that it is for them to return to unity on Catholic terms, not for us to seek union with them, or to accept it, on their terms."[336] *Look Magazine*, another Catholic periodical, also stated that,

> To the church of Rome, there can be no specious equalitarianism with other faiths. As one of the Vatican's chief spokesman on unity says, 'The Catholic Church can never consent to putting herself on the same plane with other confessions.' Christian unity to Catholics means only one thing—the return of non-Catholics to the fold of Rome.[337]

For the papacy, the unification of Christendom can be achieved only on Catholic terms through the return of non-Catholic, Protestant Christianity to the "fold" of Catholicism. Furthermore, Ellen White even confirmed that Rome has the agenda to destroy Protestantism:

> The Roman Church is far-reaching in her plans and modes of operation. She is employing every device to extend her influence and increase her power in preparation for a fierce and determined conflict to regain control of the world, to re-establish persecution, and to undo all that Protestantism has done.[338]

When we consider recent events in the Protestant-Catholic relationship overall, we will discover that Protestantism itself is actually initiating a potential reconciliation with Rome. In her powerful work entitled *The Great Controversy*, Ellen White confirmed that Protestant America would ultimately be first and foremost in attempting to realign itself with the papacy:

---

334 See both Kevin Morgan, *Sabbath Rest* (Brushton, NY: Teach Services, 2002), 66–71 and G. Edward Reid, *Sunday's Coming*, 2nd Edition (Hagerstown, MD: Review and Herald, 2005), 123–142. See also Ellen G. White, *The Great Controversy* (Mountain View, CA: Pacific Press, 1950), 563–581.

335 *American*, 4 Jan 1941, Vol. 64, page 363, in Morgan, 71.

336 Ibid.

337 *Look Magazine*, 21 July 1959.

338 White, *Great Controversy*, 565–566.

The Protestants of the United States will be foremost in stretching their hands across the gulf to grasp the hand of spiritualism; they will reach over the abyss to clasp hands with the Roman power; and under the influence of this threefold union, this country will follow in the steps of Rome in trampling on the rights of conscience.[339]

There are many Protestant leaders and organizations that are quite aggressive in their desire to unify with the Catholic Church. Sincere in the belief that "Catholicism differs less widely from Protestantism than in former times,"[340] these Evangelical Protestant leaders and organizations claim that the Roman Church does not have the same spirit of intolerance and persecution that it possessed during its Dark Age reign. The modern ecumenical movement, which has come into existence largely through the effort of Evangelical Protestant Christianity, desires to bring Catholics and Protestants together under the false pretense of Christian unity. In reality, this agenda can only have one result—the complete entrance of the papacy "into the glorious land" of Christendom through the vehicle of Sunday legislation.

A thorough study of the modern ecumenical movement is certainly beyond the scope of this specific work; yet, it will prove useful to highlight some key examples of ecumenical organizations and notable Protestant leaders that have gone on record by saying that they desire a re-unification with the Roman Catholic Church. In one such example, Michael de Semlyen, in his work entitled *All Roads Lead to Rome*, made the following ecumenical observation by quoting the February 1988 edition of *New Covenant Magazine*:

> Leading evangelical John Stott, an advisor to the World Council of Churches, told the Nottingham Conference [in 1977] that 'the visible unity of all professing Christians should be our goal ... and evangelicals should join others in the Church of England in working towards full communion with the Roman Catholic Church.'[341]

In another example, the periodical *First Things* ran a 1994 article called "Evangelicals & Catholics Together," where ecumenical leaders stated that

---

339 Ibid, 588.

340 Ibid, 571.

341 *New Covenant Magazine*, February 1988, quoted in Michael de Semlyen, *All Roads Lead to Rome* (Bucks, England: Dorchester House Publishers, 1993), 30–31.

"We are Evangelical Protestants and Roman Catholics who have been led through prayer, study, and discussion to common convictions about Christian faith and mission."[342] "As Evangelicals and Catholics, we pray that our unity in the love of Christ will become ever more evident as a sign to the world of God's reconciling power."[343]

In another article entitled "The 'Hypermodern' Foe: How the Evangelicals and Catholics Joined Forces," Laurie Goodstein observed that "evangelical and … Catholic leaders have spent more than a decade laying the groundwork for a religious realignment." She noted that "In a recent poll of evangelicals, the pope had higher favorability ratings (59 percent) than either Jerry Falwell (44 percent) or Pat Robertson (54 percent)," and actually quoted one particular Protestant leader as saying, "There is many an evangelical now who believes that they have more in common with the Catholics down the street than they do with mainline Protestants."[344]

Pat Robertson is one popular evangelical leader who has voiced a strong desire for unity between Evangelical Protestantism and Catholicism. After meeting with the late Pope John Paul II during his 1995 visit to the United States, Mr. Robertson stated that "this meeting was historic. I am hopeful this meeting will result in a new openness and harmony between Evangelicals and Catholics in this country and around the world."[345] Another source quoted him as calling "the Pope 'a humble and caring servant of the Lord.' He said, 'We want to build bridges with the Catholic Church.' The August 12 *Christianity Today* said Robertson has helped to shape the Charismatic movement as a wide, ecumenical and comfortable phenomenon."[346] The *Christian American* also cited him as saying, "Frankly, I feel I have a lot more in common with this pope [John Paul II] than with liberal Protestants."[347]

"Promise Keepers" is another well-known ecumenical organization that "seeks to unite Christian men of all races, denominations, ages,

---

342 "Evangelicals & Catholics together: the Christian mission in the third millennium," *First Things*, 43 (may 1994), 15–22. Please see this particular document in its entirety at the following website: http://www.firstthings.com/ftissues/ft9405/articles/mission.html.

343 Ibid.

344 See the following internet source where this article is located: http://www.yuricareport.com/dominionism/howcatholicsjoinedevangelicals.html.

345 See http://www.wayoflife.org/fbns/patrobertson.Htm.

346 *Calvary Contender*, 1 Sept 1996.

347 *Christian American*, October 1993, in Morgan, 67.

cultures, and socio-economic groups."[348] Its mission statement actually articulates that "We believe that God wants to use Promise Keepers as a spark in His hand to ignite a nationwide movement calling men from all denominational, ethnic, and cultural backgrounds to reconciliation, discipleship, and godliness."[349] Belief number six in its "Statement of Faith" relates the following organizational principle:

> All believers in the Lord Jesus Christ are members of His one international, multi-ethnic and transcultural body called the universal church. Its unity is displayed when we reach beyond racial and denominational lines to demonstrate the Gospel's reconciling power.[350]

Vic Bilson, sponsor of a website called the "Jeremiah Project," observed that Promise Keepers is supported by "Evangelicals, Catholics, Lutherans, Presbyterians, Methodists, Episcopalians, Charismatics, Catholics," and "Mormons."[351] He stated that "These groups have been divided by major doctrinal differences for many years. But now these differences are being dropped for the sake of unity."[352] Mr. Bilson concluded that,

> The Promise Keepers' movement is part of an ecumenical trend of down-playing doctrine for unity that puts aside essential theological issues in order to promote a unity which is not biblical unity. Are false doctrines being addressed? Are the people in these churches challenged to flee their false religious systems? The answer is 'No.' Key foundational issues have been dropped, all for the sake of supposed unity.[353]

We should note that Christ did in fact pray that His people would strive for unity (John 17:20–23); yet, we should understand that no Christian should ever seek to achieve unity at the expense of biblical truth. Ellen White confirmed this principle:

---

348 See http://www.promisekeepers.org/faqscore28.
349 See http://www.promisekeepers.org/faqscore21.
350 See http://www.promisekeepers.org/faqscore22.
351 See www.jeremiahproject.com/prophecy/ecumen01.html.
352 Ibid.
353 Ibid.

Jesus prayed that his followers might be one; but we are not to sacrifice the truth in order to secure this union, for we are to be sanctified through the truth. Human wisdom would change all this, pronouncing this basis too narrow. Men would try to effect unity through concession to popular opinion, through compromise with the world, a sacrifice of vital godliness. But truth is God's basis for the unity of his people.[354]

Another ecumenical organization just recently created is called "Christian Churches Together in the USA" (CCT), and is committed to bringing Protestant and Catholic Christians across denominational barriers to achieve unity of purpose. Jerry Filteau of the *Catholic News Service* noted that "U.S. Catholic bishops ... took a historic ecumenical step by joining" this "new national ecumenical forum" on November 17, 2004.[355] The official website of CCT actually states the organization's core purpose with the following language:

[CCT is] To enable churches and national Christian organizations to grow closer in Christ in order to strengthen our Christian witness in the world. ... Christian Churches Together in the USA is a proposed new forum growing out of a deeply felt need to broaden and expand fellowship, unity and witness among the diverse expressions of Christian faith today.[356]

Furthermore, no ecumenical commentary would be complete without giving mention to the recent collaboration between Lutherans and Catholics in signing a joint doctrinal statement on the issue of "justification by faith." In his book entitled *Sabbath Rest*, pastor and author Kevin Morgan stressed the importance of this pivotal ecumenical event by quoting Erin Pioutek's observations from a 1999 article in a publication called *The Observer*, located in South Bend, Indiana:

---

354 Ellen G. White, "Sanctification Through the Truth," *Review and Herald*, 12 April 1892, paragraph 19. See also White, *Great Controversy*, 45–46.

355 Jerry Filteau, "Bishops Join New U.S. Ecumenical Forum," *Catholic News Service*, 18 Nov 2004. Please see site: http://www.christianchurchestogether. org/press releases.htm. This statement is also quoted in G. Edward Reid, *Sunday's Coming*, 2nd Edition (Hagerstown, MD: Review and Herald, 2005), 136.

356 http://www.christianchurchestogether.org/default.htm.

On Oct. 31, 1999, for the first time in 487 years, the Catholic and Lutheran churches signed a joint doctrinal statement, the 'Joint Declaration on the Doctrine of Justification.' ... The signing took place in Augsburg, Germany, where in 1530, the Augsburg Confession—the founding document of the Lutheran Church—was drafted. The document was signed by delegations from the Vatican and the Lutheran World Federation (LWF), a global communion of Lutheran Churches, including the evangelical Lutheran Church in America.[357]

Bishop H. George Anderson of the Lutheran Evangelical Church, a representative who actually signed this famous joint declaration in Augsburg, told the *St. Anthony Messenger Press* that it was a significant step in bringing the two faiths together:

'Our relationship as two contemporary Churches—Catholic and Lutheran—is clouded always by the fact that these 16th-century theologians condemned the other Church on a variety of matters, and justification was one of the key ones. ... There has always been the question: Are these folks on the other side [Lutheran or Catholic] really orthodox Christians or are they heretical in some way? The statement that the condemnations of the 16th century no longer apply to the Churches clears the air and provides, in the words of the pope, a cornerstone for future ecumenical progress.'[358]

The World Methodist Council also signed into this Lutheran-Catholic agreement on Sunday, July 23, 2006 during its World Methodist Conference in Seoul, Korea. In an official statement, the council stated that "We welcome this agreement with great joy ... It is our deep hope that in the near future we shall also be able to enter into closer relationships with Lutherans and the Roman Catholic Church."[359] The website "ABC Online" added that "Methodist churches have joined a landmark agreement that has brought

---

357 Erin Piroutek, *The Observer*, University Wire, South Bend, Indiana, 1 Nov 1999, quoted in Morgan, 70.

358 Please see the following website for the quotation: http://www.americancatholic.org/Messenger/Jun2000/feature2.asp#F4. This is the official website of *St. Anthony Messenger Press*, a Catholic-American publication.

359 See http://www.cathnews.com/news/607/124.php.

Catholics and Lutherans closer together, taking Pope Benedict's key goal of greater harmony among Christians a step forward."[360]

We can clearly see overwhelming evidence to support the fact that there is a concerted effort on the part of Protestantism to realign itself with Roman Catholicism. Well-known evangelical leader Robert Schuller was even quoted as saying that "It's time for Protestants to go to the shepherd [the pope] and say 'what do we have to do to come home?'"[361] This conciliatory spirit shows that past Protestant contempt toward Romanism, in "protest" against her policies, is virtually non-existent today. In three consecutive quotations below, Ellen White confirmed this modern ecumenical, conciliatory path of Protestantism:

Romanism is now regarded by Protestants with far greater favor than in former years. In those countries where Catholicism is not in the ascendancy, and the papists are taking a conciliatory course in order to gain influence, there is an increasing indifference concerning the doctrines that separate the reformed churches from the papal hierarchy; the opinion is gaining ground that, after all, we do not differ so widely upon vital points as has been supposed, and that a little concession on our part will bring us into a better understanding with Rome. The time was when Protestants placed a high value upon the liberty of conscience which had been so dearly purchased. They taught their children to abhor popery and held that to seek harmony with Rome would be disloyalty to God. But how widely different are the sentiments now expressed![362]

Protestants have tampered with and patronized popery; they have made compromises and concessions which papists themselves are surprised to see and fail to understand. Men are closing their eyes to the real character of Romanism and the dangers to be apprehended from her supremacy. The people need to be aroused to resist the advances of this most dangerous foe to civil and religious liberty.[363]

---

360 See http://www.abc.net.au/news/newsitems/200607/s1694339.htm.
361 *Calvary Contender*, 15 Nov 1987 and the *Los Angeles Herald Examiner*, 19 Sept 1987, quoted in Morgan, 71.
362 White, *Great Controversy*, 563.
363 Ibid, 566.

The Roman Church now presents a fair front to the world, covering with apologies her record of horrible cruelties. She has clothed herself in Christlike garments; but she is unchanged. Every principle of the papacy that existed in past ages exists today. The doctrines devised in the darkest ages are still held. Let none deceive themselves. The papacy that Protestants are now so ready to honor is the same that ruled the world in the days of the Reformation, when men of God stood up, at the peril of their lives, to expose her iniquity. She possesses the same pride and arrogant assumption that lorded it over kings and princes, and claimed the prerogatives of God. Her spirit is no less cruel and despotic now than when she crushed out human liberty and slew the saints of the Most High.[364]

Overall, the modern ecumenical movement has the so-called agenda of emphasizing unity between all Christians, Catholic and Protestant, at the expense of doctrinal differences. This agenda can only have one result, the exaltation of the papal institution of Sunday sacredness, which will allow the papacy to completely "enter into the glorious land" by securing the allegiance of Protestant Christianity. Once this takes place, the Dark Age spirit of religious intolerance and persecution will be revived against those who refuse to submit to Roman Catholic authority.

Therefore, the legislation of Sunday sacredness is the vehicle that Catholicism will use to fully "enter into the glorious land" and secure the allegiance of all of Christendom. Many Roman Catholic sources have clearly stated the desire to legislate Sunday as a public day of rest, and have commented that when Protestants also follow in this same path, they are essentially acknowledging the authority of Rome. John Gilmary Shea confirmed this particular assertion:

For ages all Christian nations looked to the Catholic Church, and, as we have seen, the various states enforced by law her ordinances as to worship and cessation of labor on Sunday. Protestantism, in discarding the authority of the Church, has no good reason for its Sunday theory, and ought logically to keep Saturday as the Sabbath. Strange as it may seem, the state, in passing laws for the due sanctification of Sunday, is unwittingly acknowledging the authority of the Catholic Church, and carry out more or less faithfully its prescriptions. The Sunday, as a day of the week set apart for the

---

364 Ibid, 571.

obligatory public worship of Almighty God … is purely a creation of the Catholic Church.[365]

In an article entitled "Sacking Sunday," the *Catholic Twin Circle* penned that "All Americans would do well to petition the President and the Congress to make a Federal law—an amendment to the Constitution if need be—to re-establish the Sabbath [Sunday] as a national Day of Rest."[366] The late Pope John Paul II, in his famous apostolic letter *Dies Domini*, emphasized that "Christians will naturally strive to ensure that civil legislation respects their duty to keep Sunday holy."[367] In the very same document, he continued to stress the Catholic importance of Sunday sacredness by confirming that,

> When, through the centuries, she has made laws concerning Sunday rest, the Church has had in mind above all the work of servants and workers, certainly not because this work was any less worthy when compared to the spiritual requirements of Sunday observance, but rather because it needed greater regulation to lighten its burden and thus enable everyone to keep the Lord's Day holy. In this matter, my predecessor Pope Leo XIII in his Encyclical *Rerum Novarum* spoke of Sunday rest as a worker's right which the State must guarantee.[368]

Furthermore, in a 1998 article from *The Detroit News*, Mark Puls and Charles Hurt made some interesting observations regarding John Paul's comments on the sanctification of Sunday:

> Sundays have come to be 'felt and lived only as a weekend,' John Paul lamented Sunday. 'It [should be] the weekly day in which the church celebrates the resurrection of Christ. In obedience to the Third Commandment, Sunday must be sanctified, above all, by participation in Holy Mass.' … In his letter, the pope goes on to say a violator should be 'punished as a heretic.'[369]

---

365 John Gilmary Shea, "The Observance of Sunday and Civil Laws for its Enforcement," *The American Catholic Quarterly Review 8*, January, 1883, page 139.

366 "Sacking Sunday," *Catholic Twin Circle*, 25 Aug 1985.

367 Pope John Paul II, *Dies Domini*, Apostolic Letter, 31 May 1998, page 112.

368 Ibid, 109–110.

369 Mark Puls and Charles Hurt, "Pope's Call for Worship Welcomed," *The Detroit*

In a powerful example of Evangelical-Protestant support for Sunday legislation, *Christianity Today* editor Harold Lindsell, in his 1976 article called "The Lord's Day and Natural Resources," made the following declaration:

> The proper use of the Lord's Day [Sunday], wholly apart from any religious implications, can come about by free choice or it can be legislated. It is highly unlikely that it will be accomplished by voluntary action by the citizenry generally. Therefore the only way to accomplish the objective is by force of legislative fiat through the duly elected officials of the people.[370]

Pat Robertson even made the false proclamation that the absence of Sunday legislation in America is an insult to God:

> Higher civilizations rise when people can rest, think, and draw inspiration from God. Laws in America that mandated a day of rest [Sunday laws] from incessant commerce have been nullified as a violation of the separation of church and state. ... As an outright insult to God and His plan, only those policies that can be shown to have a clearly secular purpose are recognized.[371]

Interestingly, the "Lord's Day Alliance" (LDA) is one particular organization that exists with the sole purpose of promoting the sanctification of Sunday. The homepage of their official website clearly advocates that "The Lord's Day Alliance of the United States exists to encourage Christians to reclaim the Sabbath—the Lord's Day—as a day of spiritual and personal renewal, enabling them to impact their communities with the Gospel."[372] In other words, "The LDA has been the one national organization whose sole purpose is to maintain and cultivate the first day of the week as a time for rest, worship, Christian education and spiritual renewal."[373]

We should also take the time to briefly mention another powerful entity, the "Christian Coalition of America" (CCA), the "largest and

---

News, 7 July 1998.

370 Harold Lindsell, Editor, "The Lord's Day and Natural Resources," *Christianity Today*, 7 May 1976, page 12.

371 *The Collected Works of Pat Robertson* (New York: Inspirational Press, 1994), 481–482.

372 See http://www.ldausa.org/.

373 Ibid.

most active conservative grassroots political organization in America," which vows to offer "people of faith the vehicle to be actively involved in shaping their government—from the County Courthouse to the halls of Congress."[374] Aspiring "to give Christians a voice in their government again," CCA proudly claims to "actively lobby Congress and the White House on numerous issues" in order to "continuously work to identify, educate and mobilize Christians for effective political action! Such action will preserve, protect and defend the Judeo-Christian values that made this the greatest country in history."[375] Please notice this summary statement from their official website:

> Christian Coalition of America is a political organization, made up of pro-family Americans who care deeply about becoming active citizens for the purpose of guaranteeing that government acts in ways that strengthen, rather than threaten, families. As such, we work together with Christians of all denominations, as well as with other Americans who agree with our mission and with our ideals.[376]

There is another movement worthy of mention that could potentially play a significant role in future Sunday legislation—the "Ten Commandments Day" movement. The official website of this specific organization states that it exists for the sole purpose of focusing on the importance of the Ten Commandments, and has the agenda of pushing for an official American holiday that will recognize the Decalogue:

> The focal point … is the first annual Ten Commandments Day that will be held on Sunday May 7, 2006. On this date we are calling on all religious leaders who are concerned about traditional Judeo-Christian values to host special celebrations and/or deliver stirring messages centering on the Ten Commandments.[377]

The website continued by stating that "With the Ten Commandments day, we will offer a powerful display of unity, as we, with one voice, declare our unwavering support for the bedrock principles that made our country

---

374 See http://www.cc.org/about.cfm.

375 Ibid.

376 Ibid.

377 See www.tencommandmentsday.com/.

great—the Ten Commandments."[378] The leaders of this movement also made the following observation:

> Recent rulings have threatened the very fabric and foundation of our…faith. The Ten Commandments, which have served as the moral foundation and anchor of our great country, are systematically being removed from public places. Public displays of the Ten Commandments have been a powerful visual testimony to the fact that the United States of America is 'one nation under God.' Their removal from public places shows that those with a secular humanist agenda are intent on destroying the moral heritage of our nation.[379]

There have been a number of significant evangelical leaders who have also openly pledged their support of this movement, which would include: Paul Crouch (founder, president of Trinity Broadcasting Network), Benny Hinn (a popular charismatic faith healer), Roberta Combs (Christian Coalition), James Dobson (Focus on the Family), Jerry Falwell (Liberty Alliance), Pat Robertson (Christian Broadcasting Network), George Morrison (chairman, Promise Keepers), and Frances Roth (Committee for Biblical Principles in Government).[380]

This organization is also soliciting national support from all God-fearing people: "We are inviting all Christians, churches, synagogues, ministry leaders, religious book stores and everyone who is interested in preserving traditional values to join us in [this] national and global movement." "Please take a stand and join the coalition of thousands of cross cultural interdenominational community leaders … and heads of denominations who are committed to bringing the Word of God back to our nation. Join us for Ten Commandments Day!"[381]

Although a general promotion of the Ten Commandments is a positive enterprise, we can see that the overall tendency of this movement could further empower the modern ecumenical movement to promote a possible Sunday "Sabbath." Evangelical Christianity would address the Sabbath question by emphasizing that the "Christian Sabbath" is "Sunday," which could eventually help to facilitate a national Sunday law in America. The first official "Ten Commandments Day" actually took place on a Sunday—

378 Ibid.
379 Ibid.
380 Ibid.
381 Ibid.

May 7, 2006, and will continue every first Sunday in May on an annual basis. Therefore, the "Ten Commandments Day" movement could ultimately prove to be a powerful impetus in contributing to the eventual legislation of Sunday.

Once again, we can clearly see that the modern ecumenical movement is initiating a Protestant reconciliation with Catholicism. Both of these groups have the common ground of Sunday sacredness and desire to legislate Sunday as a national day of rest. It is quite possible that the Christian Coalition, Lord's Day Alliance, and the Ten Commandments Day movement could all be used as potential political forces to make Sunday legislation a reality. The passing of time will reveal the specifics as to how a national Sunday law will come into being; yet, we can rest assured that it will take place in the very near future. Ellen White confirmed this in the two quotations below:

> In the movements now in progress in the United States to secure for the institutions and usages of the church the support of the state, Protestants are following in the steps of papists. Nay, more, they are opening the door for the papacy to regain in Protestant America the supremacy which she has lost in the Old World. And that which gives greater significance to this movement is the fact that the principal object contemplated is the enforcement of Sunday observance—a custom which originated with Rome, and which she claims as the sign of her authority. It is the spirit of the papacy—the spirit of conformity to worldly customs, the veneration for human traditions above the commandments of God—that is permeating the Protestant churches and leading them on to do the same work of Sunday exaltation which the papacy has done before them.[382]

> And let it be remembered, it is the boast of Rome that she never changes. ... And had she but the power, she would put them [instruments of persecution] in practice with as much vigor now as in past centuries. Protestants little know what they are doing when they propose to accept the aid of Rome in the work of Sunday exaltation. While they are bent upon the accomplishment of their purpose, Rome is aiming to re-establish her power, to recover her lost supremacy. Let the principle once be established in the United States that the church may employ or control the power

---

382 White, *Great Controversy*, 573.

of the state; that religious observances may be enforced by secular laws; in short, that the authority of church and state is to dominate the conscience, and the triumph of Rome in this country is assured.[383]

In times past, the Roman Church has used both force and compromise to gain entrance into non-Catholic Christian groups; but this enactment of Sunday legislation in the near future will signal the complete entrance of the papacy into the "glorious land" of the Christian Church. As all non-Catholic Christian groups comply with Sunday sacredness, this will confirm Rome's status as head of all Christendom once again. At this point in time, the "man of sin" and "son of perdition" will be fully "revealed," "Who opposeth and exalteth himself above all that is called God, or that is worshipped; so that he as God sitteth in the temple of God, shewing himself that he is God" (2 Thessalonians 2:3–4).[384]

Thus, we can conclude that, when the sub-passage of Daniel 11:41 describes the entrance of the "king of the north" into the "glorious land," it describes the legal enforcement of Sunday sacredness, which will unify all of Christendom, i.e., both Catholic and non-Catholic/Protestant Christianity, and eventually the entire world, under the authority of the papacy.

As an important side note, we should also observe that the Seventh-day Adventist Church denomination is also a well-known Protestant movement, and is therefore also part of the "glorious land." Ellen White even referred to this particular movement as the "Israel of God."[385] Interestingly,

---

383 Ibid, 581.

384 Ibid, 383, 389–390, 563–581. We are dealing with global, spiritual concepts when interpreting prophetic symbols in the New Testament. Thus, the earthly "temple" would consist of the church. See 1 Corinthians 3:16–17, 2 Corinthians 6:14–18, and Revelation 3:12.

385 See the following two quotations: "Those who have seen the truth and felt its importance, and have had an experience in the things of God ... should make them [their children] acquainted with the great pillars of our faith, the reasons why we are Seventh-day Adventists,—why we are called, as were the children of Israel, to be a peculiar people, a holy nation, separate and distinct from all other people on the face of the earth" (Ellen G. White, *Testimonies for the Church*, 9 vols. [Boise, ID: Pacific Press, 1948], 5:330); "In order to be purified and to remain pure, Seventh-day Adventists must have the Holy Spirit in their hearts and in their homes. The Lord has given me light that when the Israel of today humble themselves before Him ... He will hear their prayers" (Ibid, 9:164). See also Ellen G. White, *Ministry of Healing* (Boise, ID: Pacific Press, 1942), 405, and Ellen G. White, *Prophets and Kings* (Boise, ID: Pacific Press,

the Roman Catholic Church actually claims that the Seventh-day Adventist Church is the only consistent Protestant movement, which stems from the fact that this specific denomination observes the true seventh-day Sabbath of the Bible (Saturday), and not the first day of the week (Sunday). The next four quotations below demonstrate that Catholic leaders actually commend the consistency of Seventh-day Adventists:

> We also say that of all Protestants, the Seventh-day Adventists are the only group that reason correctly and are consistent with their teachings. It is always laughable to see the Protestant churches, in pulpit and legislature, demand the observance of Sunday, of which there is nothing in the Bible.[386]

> Perhaps the boldest thing, the most revolutionary change the church ever did, happened in the first century. The holy day, the Sabbath, was changed from Saturday to Sunday ... not from any directions noted in the Scriptures, but from the Church's sense of its own power. ... People who think the Scriptures should be the sole authority, should logically become 7th Day Adventists, and keep Saturday holy.[387]

> The [Catholic] church changed the observance of the Sabbath to Sunday. ... The Protestant claiming the Bible to be the only guide of faith, has no warrant for observing Sunday. In this matter the Seventh-day Adventist is the only consistent Protestant.[388]

> If the Bible is the only guide for the Christian, then the Seventh-day Adventist is right, in observing the Saturday with the Jew. Is it not strange that those who make the Bible their only teacher, should inconsistently follow in this matter the tradition of the Catholic Church? [389]

1943), 74, 370–372.

386 Peter Tramer, Editor, *The Catholic Extension Magazine*, 22 May 1934.

387 *St. Catherine Catholic Church Sentinel*, Algonac, Michigan, Volume 50, Number 22, 21 May 1995.

388 *The Catholic Universe Bulletin*, 14 Aug 1942, 4.

389 Betrand L. Conway, *The Question Box* (New York: The Paulist Press, 1903), 254–255.

Therefore, the Seventh-day Adventist Church is the only global religious movement that proclaims the true Bible Sabbath on a worldwide scale; furthermore, the "tidings" out of the "east" and "north" from Daniel 11:44 is a global Gospel message promoted by this very same movement (Revelation 14:6–12), which will prove to hinder the work of the papacy in its agenda to exalt Sunday sacredness. We will discover later that Daniel 11:44–45 describes the papal effort to also bring Seventh-day Adventism into compliance.

And many countries shall be overthrown: but these shall escape out of his hand, even Edom, and Moab, and the chief of the children of Ammon. As the papacy strives to enter into the "glorious land" of the Christian Church through Sunday legislation, this sub-passage states that "many countries shall be overthrown." Interestingly, the word "countries" here is italicized in the *King James Version* of the Bible, which means that the actual word isn't in the original text. We could therefore render the verse to say that "many shall be overthrown," meaning that "many" people will yield to Sunday legislation and be "spiritually" overthrown by receiving the "mark" of the beast.

Notice that some will "escape" from the grasp of the papacy—"Edom, and Moab, and the chief of the children of Ammon." In ancient times, these three groups were neighboring enemies of Israel who consisted of both worldly, half-hearted believers in God and idolatrous heathen nations. And, because Israel had eventually intermarried with these three groups, it had experienced a rapid spiritual declension.[390] As we seek to find the modern-day, "spiritual" equivalent of this three-fold group, we can see that "Edom," "Moab," and the "chief of the children of Ammon" will actually symbolize both half-hearted, worldly, professed Christians and non-Christian, heathen peoples.

Yet, by the very fact that they "escape" from the influence of the papacy means that they would experience a true heart-felt conversion, renounce their worldliness, leave their apostate, false religious systems, and make their stand for God. Isaiah observed that "it shall come to pass in that day, that the LORD shall set his hand again the second time to recover the remnant of his people. ... they shall lay their hand upon Edom and Moab; and the children of Ammon shall obey them" (Isaiah 11:11, 14). Thus, from Isaiah's passage it appears that these three groups will obey the gospel call of God's remnant (Revelation 14:6–12), and come out of spiritual Babylon (Revelation 14:8, 18:1–4). They will make their stand for Jesus Christ by

---

390 Ellen G. White, "Mingling Error with Truth," *Review and Herald*, March 10, 1910.

obeying the true Bible Sabbath, and refuse to submit to the papal agenda of Sunday legislation.[391]

We should remember that a majority of God's sincere followers are still in the "fallen" churches and apostate religions that make up spiritual Babylon; yet, when the whole earth is lightened with the glory of God through the loud cry of the latter rain (Revelation 18:1), these faithful, sincere believers who are truly searching after the true God will respond to this heavenly call, "escape" this system of religious confusion, and avoid the mark of the beast.[392] Ellen White confirmed this assertion in the two quotations below:

> The Sabbath will be the great test of loyalty, for it is the point of truth especially controverted. When the final test shall be brought to bear upon men, then the line of distinction will be drawn between those who serve God and those who serve Him not. While the observance of the false sabbath [Sunday] in compliance with the law of the state, contrary to the fourth commandment, will be an avowal of allegiance to a power that is in opposition to God, the keeping of the true Sabbath, in obedience to God's law, is an evidence of loyalty to the Creator. While one class, by accepting the sign of submission to earthly powers, receive the mark of the beast, the other choosing the token of allegiance to divine authority, receive the seal of God.[393]

> Servants of God ... will hasten from place to place to proclaim the message from heaven. By thousands of voices, all over the earth, the warning will be given. ... The message will be carried not so much by argument as by the deep conviction of the Spirit of God. ... Now the rays of light penetrate everywhere, the truth is seen in its clearness, and the honest children of God sever the bands which have held them. Family connections, church relations, are powerless to stay them now. Truth is more precious than all besides.

---

391 See Louis F. Were, *The King of the North at Jerusalem* (St. Maries, ID: LMN Publishing, 2002), 69–70. See Acts 15:14–18 with Amos 9:11–15 and Isaiah 11:11–16. In Acts 15:14–18, James equates the fulfillment of Amos 9:11–15 with the influx of Gentile converts.

392 White, *Great Controversy*, 383, 390.

393 Ibid, 605.

Notwithstanding the agencies combined against the truth, a large number take their stand upon the Lord's side.[394]

Overall, Daniel 11:41 illustrates that papal Rome will attempt to enter into the "glorious land" of the Christian Church (Christendom) through the vehicle of Sunday legislation. Yet, "Edom," "Moab," and the "chief of the children of Ammon" will "escape" the influence of the papacy by leaving both spiritual Babylon and the other heathen, non-Christian religions of the world. They will stand true to Jesus Christ, be faithful to the seventh-day Sabbath, and refuse to submit to the papal agenda of Sunday legislation.

Daniel 11:41 Symbol	Interpretation
"Glorious Land"	Christian Church made up of all faithful Christians from Catholic, Protestant, and non-Catholic Christianity
"Enter the glorious land"	Papal Rome controls Christendom with Sunday legislation (future)
"Edom, Moab, Ammon"	Worldly people, members of heathen, non-Christian religions, and spiritual Babylonians who heed the call to come out of religious apostasy

---

394 Ibid, 612.

— SEVENTEEN —

An Examination of Daniel 11:42–43 "The King of the North vs. the Libyans and the Ethiopians"

S o far in our examination of Daniel 11:40–45, we have established the following prophetic trends: (1) the "king of the north" describes a resurrected papacy (verse 40); (2) the "king of the south" equates to Soviet atheistic communism, which collapsed in 1991 through the influence of the Roman Catholic Church (verse 40); (3) the future entrance of papal Rome into the "glorious land" of the Christian Church through the legislation of Sunday sacredness (verse 41); and (4) the "escape" of "Edom," "Moab," and the "chief of the children of Ammon," which is a description of how God's faithful followers will exit all apostate religions, refuse submission to Sunday legislation, and render obedience to the true Bible Sabbath (verse 41).

This particular chapter will discuss the specific passage of Daniel 11:42–43. Our examination of these two passages will reveal two main prophetic trends: (1) the papal seizure of "all the precious things of Egypt," which symbolizes the submission of both the former Soviet nations and remaining communist countries to papal authority (verse 42–43); and (2) the submission of the "Libyans" and "Ethiopians," which symbolizes Islamic compliance to papal authority (verse 43).

> He shall stretch forth his hand also upon the countries: and the land of Egypt shall not escape. But he shall have power over the treasures of gold and of silver, and over all the precious things of Egypt: and the Libyans and Ethiopians shall be at his steps. (Daniel 11:42–43)

He shall stretch forth his hand also upon the countries: and the land of Egypt shall not escape. But he shall have power over the treasures of gold and of silver, and over all the precious things of Egypt. This sub-passage offers a description of how the "countries," including "spiritual

Egypt," will "not escape" the power of the papacy. Overall, these phrases have two main applications. In a primary application, they describe the fact that the former communist countries of Eastern Europe will eventually be brought under the control of Roman Catholicism. These nations have actually proven to be a ripe mission field for the Catholic Church.[395] There is also a striking similarity between the liturgical ceremonies of Roman Catholicism and the various forms of Eastern Orthodoxy, which will aid Rome in this process.

When we examine the predominant religions of Eastern Europe, we will discover that a majority espouse either Roman Catholicism or a native version of Eastern Orthodoxy. The Eastern European adherents to Roman Catholicism include Croatia, Hungary, Latvia, Poland, Slovakia, and Slovenia. The Eastern European adherents to the local form of Orthodoxy include Belarus, Bulgaria, Greece, Macedonia, Moldova, Romania, Russia, Serbia, and the Ukraine. There are also three Islamic adherents (Albania, Bosnia-Herzegovina, and Turkey), two Protestant adherents (Estonia and Lithuania), and one atheistic adherent (the Czech Republic).[396] Overall, 15 of the 21 nations just mentioned espouse either Catholicism or Orthodoxy.[397]

There has also been considerable effort on the part of the Catholic Church to seek an ecumenical alliance with Eastern Orthodox Christianity. A website called "Catholic Answers" cited that "While Catholics and Eastern Orthodox are separate for the moment, what unites us is still far greater than what divides us, and there are abundant reasons for optimism regarding reconciliation in the future."[398] This Roman Catholic website went on to say that "John Paul II, the first Slavic pope, has made the reconciliation of Eastern and Western Christendom a special theme of his pontificate," having actually sought "to promote unity between Catholics and Orthodox."[399]

Furthermore, the September 12, 1978, edition of *The Montgomery Advertiser* made a powerful observation concerning the ecumenical efforts

395 Frank J. Coppa, *The Modern Papacy Since 1789* (London: Longman, 1998), 243.

396 Roman Catholicism is a close second to atheism. See the website: www.cia.gov/cia/publications/factbook/geos/ez.html.

397 For religion statistics on these countries, please see www.phrasebase.com/countries/index.php?variable=people_religion.html.

398 www.catholic.com/library/eastern_orthodoxy.asp.

399 Ibid.

of Roman Catholics, Protestants, and Eastern Orthodoxy in the following quotation:

> Heads of the American Protestant and Eastern Orthodox churches who were meeting with pope John Paul II on Friday haled [sic, hailed] their first, broadly representative discussion as a landmark on the road to greater unity. ... The Rev. Donald Jones, a United Methodist and chairman of the University of South Carolina religious studies department, termed it 'the most important ecumenical meeting of the century' ... The Rev. Paul A. Crow, Jr., of Indianapolis, ecumenical officer of the Christian Church (Disciples of Christ), called it a 'new day in ecumenism' opening a future in which God 'is drawing us together.'[400]

Therefore, given the predominance of Roman Catholicism in the former communist regions of Eastern Europe, its actual similarities with Eastern Orthodoxy, and the fact that there have been ecumenical efforts to unite Catholicism with Orthodoxy, we can see that Rome will eventually "stretch forth his hand also upon the countries," and "have power over the treasures of gold and of silver, and over all the precious things of Egypt" by bringing these nations into compliance.

We should also take the time to briefly mention growing influence of Roman Catholicism in the European Economic Union overall, which contains a total of 25 member nations and will increase to 27 by January 1, 2007. Interestingly, 17 of the EEU member nations are for the most part Roman Catholic in religious orientation; these nations include Austria, Belgium, France, Germany, Ireland, Italy, Luxembourg, Netherlands, Portugal, Spain, United Kingdom, Hungary, Lithuania, Malta, Poland, Slovakia, and Slovenia. There are five professed Lutheran countries: Denmark, Finland, Sweden, Estonia, and Latvia. Four countries are Orthodox: Greece, Cyprus, Bulgaria, and Romania. The Czech Republic is the lone atheistic country (39.8%), but Roman Catholicism is a close second (39.2%).[401] This growing economic alliance could possibly be a

---

400 *The Montgomery Advertiser*, 12 Sept 1987, quoted in Morgan, 66.

401 See the following websites for statistical information on the Economic Union: http://en.wikipedia.org/wiki/European_Union and www.phrasebase.com/countries/. As a side note, Germany is equally Catholic and Protestant (each at 34%), and the United Kingdom is 66% of a combination of Anglican and Roman Catholic.

potential vehicle for the Roman Catholic Church to promote Sunday legislation on the European continent.

There is also a second meaning to the phrase "the land of Egypt shall not escape." We should remember that there are currently five remaining communist countries in the world that are still a part of "spiritual" Egypt—China, Cuba, Laos, North Korea, and Vietnam. Being in Latin America, Cuba could easily accept Roman Catholicism; yet, the other four countries on the Asian continent might be somewhat more difficult to bring into compliance, especially China and North Korea. At some point the papacy will have to bring these remaining members of "spiritual" Egypt under its religio-political authority.

Here is another important observation that mandates consideration. The arena of scientific evolution is a major component of the atheistic worldview. It should be noted that the papacy has gone on record by espousing evolutionary thinking as a viable option to explain the existence of our universe. Of course, this perspective strikes at the heart of the seventh-day Sabbath, which clearly defines God as the Creator of the universe. In his encyclical letter entitled *Humani Generis*, Pope Pius XII conveyed that the Catholic Church does not forbid consideration of the doctrine of evolution:

> The Teaching Authority of the Church does not forbid that, in conformity with the present state of human sciences and sacred theology, research and discussions, on the part of men experienced in both fields, take place with regard to the doctrine of evolution, insofar as it inquiries into the origin of the human body as coming from pre-existent and living matter.[402]

In a recent address to the Pontifical Academy of Sciences, the late Pope John Paul II confirmed the observation made above by Pope Pius XII in espousing scientific evolution:

> In his encyclical *Humani Generis* (1950), my predecessor Pius XII had already stated that there was no opposition between evolution and the doctrine of the faith about man and his vocation. ... Taking into account the state of scientific research at the time as well as of the requirements of theology, the encyclical *Humani Generis* considered the doctrine of 'evolutionism' a serious hypothesis, worthy

---

402 Pope Pius XII, *Humani Generis*, Encyclical Letter, 12 Aug 1950.

of investigation and in-depth study equal to that of the opposing hypothesis.[403]

In the same address, John Paul II goes on say that,

Today, almost half a century after the publication of the encyclical, new knowledge has led to the recognition of the theory of evolution as more than a hypothesis. … It is indeed remarkable that this theory has been progressively accepted by researchers, following a series of discoveries in various fields of knowledge. The convergence, neither sought nor fabricated, of the results of work that was conducted independently is in itself a significant argument in favor of this theory.[404]

More recently, a movement called "The Clergy Letter Project" has emerged that has the agenda of promoting the combination of the Bible and scientific evolution. Having received over ten thousand signatures from supportive clergy around America as of November, 2006, the website of this project makes the following observation concerning the alleged harmony between the Bible and evolution:

We the undersigned, Christian clergy from many different traditions, believe that the timeless truths of the Bible and the discoveries of modern science may comfortably coexist. We believe that the theory of evolution is a foundational scientific truth, one that has stood up to rigorous scrutiny and upon which much of human knowledge and achievement rests. To reject this truth or to treat it as 'one theory among others' is to deliberately embrace scientific ignorance and transmit such ignorance to our children. We believe that among God's good gifts are human minds capable of critical thought and that the failure to fully employ this gift is a rejection of the will of our Creator. … We urge school board members to preserve the integrity of the science curriculum by affirming the teaching of the theory of evolution as a core component of human knowledge. We ask that science remain science and that religion

---

403 Pope John Paul II, Address to the Pontifical Academy of Sciences, 22 Oct 1996. Please see the following website where this address is posted: www. newadvent.org/library/docs_jp02tc.htm.

404 Ibid.

remain religion, two very different, but complementary, forms of truth.[405]

These quotations clearly demonstrate the valid possibility that Rome's support of evolutionary theory, when combined with the support of other clergy across multi-denominational lines, might very well be an avenue to where atheistic evolutionists could be brought into line with Sunday legislation.

Therefore, when this passage states that the "land of Egypt shall not escape," it is also a description of the papal subjugation of all the remaining professed atheistic communist countries, which could also include an attempt to win sympathy from the followers of atheistic evolution. Because spiritual Babylon also consists of both apostate Protestantism and spiritualism, in addition to Catholicism,[406] the component of spiritualism may be the vehicle to bring the popular religions of both communist and non-communist Asia (such as Buddhism and Hinduism, for example) into compliance with Sunday legislation, because of their spiritualistic tendencies.

And the Libyans and the Ethiopians shall be at his steps. This phrase conveys that the "Libyans" and "Ethiopians" will also be at Rome's "steps." Because these two nations have really no chance of becoming superpowers that will play a significant role in end-time prophecy, we should once again attempt to ascertain the "spiritual" meaning behind these symbols. When we consider modern Libya, we will find that it is almost exclusively an Islamic nation (97%).[407] Furthermore, modern Ethiopia is also predominately Islamic (45–50%), just edging out Ethiopian Orthodoxy (35–40%).[408] Therefore, the "spiritual" nations of "Libya" and "Ethiopia" are in fact powerful symbols of modern Islam.

We should also understand that the Islamic religion is right at Rome's "steps" as a worthy spiritual competitor. As the fastest growing religion in the world today, it has recently exceeded Roman Catholicism in global membership; as of January of 2005, this religion has claimed 21% of the global population (approximately 1.3 billion people), while Catholicism

---

405 Please see the following website for the Clergy Letter Project: www.butler. edu/clergyproject/religion_science_collaboration.htm.

406 See pages 78–84 on a description of the three-fold nature of spiritual Babylon, which is led by Roman Catholicism and includes Apostate Protestantism and Spiritualism.

407 See www.phrasebase.com/countries/index.html.

408 For statistics on Ethiopia: www.careinternational.org.uk/cares work/where/ ethiopia/ethiopia_stats.html.

has claimed 18% (approximately 1.1 billion people). Out of the 258 countries in our modern world, Islam has claimed dominance in 55 countries (21%), while Catholicism has claimed 69 countries (27%).[409] Overall, these statistics clearly prove that Catholicism and Islam are right next to each other in spiritual competition.

It is also quite interesting that both Libya and Ethiopia are located on the continent of Africa. Recent statistics demonstrate that approximately 40–45% of the African population claims adherence to the Islamic faith, while 17–20% claim the Catholic faith. Overall, nearly 30% of all Muslims in the world today live on the continent of Africa.[410] Once again, these alarming statistics confirm that Islam and Catholicism are right at each other's "steps" as close spiritual competitors.

In essence, the papacy will eventually have to contend with the powerful spiritual rival of Islam that claims one out of every five people in the world. And, Daniel 11:42–43 clearly tells us that the papacy will ultimately be successful in this quest; since the entire world will eventually "wonder after the beast" (Revelation 13:3), the powerful global force of Islam will follow in papal Rome's "steps" through an eventual compliance with Sunday legislation.

We should also take the time to mention that there has been a considerable amount of ecumenical dialogue as of late between both Catholic and Muslim leaders here in the United States. On January 5, 2006, the official website of the "United States Conference of Catholic Bishops" discussed a recent meeting between Catholic and Muslim leaders called the "Midwest Regional Dialogue." In the following quotation below, the USCCB website commented that,

> At a time of continuing public debate on the role of religion in American life, the Midwest Regional Dialogue of Catholics and Muslims met at the headquarters of the Islamic Society of North America (ISNA) in Plainfield, Indiana, on December 13 and 14, 2005, to identify core values and to seek creative ways to address the challenges of faithful living in the USA today. ... Basing their convictions on divine revelation, Catholics and Muslims come

---

409 See www.census.gov/main/www/poplock.html, www.gem-werc.org/resources.html, and the well-known website www.phrasebase.com/countries/index.php?variable=people_religion.html for statistics on Catholicism and Islam.

410 See the following websites for African statistics on the popularity of Islam: www.zpub.com/un/pope/relig.html and www.islam.about.com/library/weekly/aa120298.htm.

together as bearers of living faith traditions that offer guidance in the way of peace, reconciliation, and the virtuous life.[411]

Overall, this "dialogue brought to the fore the need to understand one another's positions and proposals with greater clarity and theological depth," and concluded by "urging Muslims and Catholics to make common cause" in "identifying common values through dialogue with Christians and Jews." There are also "Future plans ... for a national level dialogue of Catholics and Muslims for 2007 ... at the Catholic Theological Union in Chicago." In addition to this specific meeting, a "number of interfaith panels are planned" in the near future that can only result in bringing these two rival faiths closer together.[412]

This ecumenical dialogue clearly demonstrates that papal Rome is expending a considerable amount of energy to unify with Islam, which could ultimately pave the way for an eventual Islamic compliance with Sunday legislation here in the United States. These two religions also share common ground on the subject of the virgin Mary, which will certainly help to bring these two faiths even closer. In his book entitled *A Woman Rides the Beast*, author Dave Hunt observed that,

> It is easy to imagine Buddhists, Hindus, New Agers, and liberals—as well as both Catholics and Protestants—uniting in a world religion, but the billion Muslims pose a special problem. Mary, however, seems to be the unique one through whom even they could be united into a universal faith.[413]

Mr. Hunt also observed that *The Tablet*, a British-Catholic periodical, stated that a "Marian revival is spreading throughout Africa, with alleged apparitions of the virgin Mary finding a following among Muslims."[414] He quoted *The Christian World Report* as saying that "African Muslims ... are seeing apparitions of the virgin Mary and 'are not required to become Christians' to follow her."[415] He also noticed that *Our Sunday Visitor*

---

411 See www.usccb.org/comm/archives/2006/06-003.shtml.

412 Ibid.

413 Dave Hunt, *A Woman Rides the Beast: The Roman Catholic Church and the Last Days* (Eugene, OR: Harvest House, 1994), 457–458. This is not a Seventh-day Adventist source, but offers some tremendous information.

414 *The Tablet*, 29 Feb 1992, quoted in Hunt, 458.

415 *The Christian World Report*, May 1992, in Hunt, 458.

emphasized the "honor given to Mary in Islam's Koran," citing the connection between her and "Mohammad's favorite daughter, Fatima."[416]

Referring to a source entitled "Mary and the Moslems," Mr. Hunt also quoted Bishop Fulton J. Sheen as predicting that "Islam would be converted to Christianity 'through a summoning of the Moslems to a veneration of the Mother of God.'"[417] He cited Bishop Sheen as stating further that,

> The Koran … has many passages concerning the Blessed Virgin. First of all, the Koran believes in her Immaculate Conception and also her Virgin Birth. … Mary, then, is for the Moslems the true *Sayyida*, or Lady. The only possible serious rival to her in their creed would be Fatima, the daughter of Mohammed himself. But after the death of Fatima, Mohammed wrote: 'Thou shalt be the most blessed of all the women in Paradise, after Mary.'[418]

Medieval history speaks of several militant crusades conducted by the Roman Church against the rising forces of Islam. Rome will rekindle an end-time crusade against Islam by securing its allegiance either through force or compromise. Since we know that Rome and the United States will eventually unify to enforce papal worship on a global scale through Sunday legislation, we should observe that the U.S. war in Iraq may in fact prove to be an entering wedge for Rome to secure the homage of the Middle Eastern Islamic nations. The progression of time will reveal what American involvement in Iraq will bring; yet, overall, the papacy will certainly put forth considerable effort to bring Islam into compliance with Sunday legislation, thus fulfilling the prophecy that the "Libyans" and the "Ethiopians" will follow in her "steps."

Overall, we can see that the passage of Daniel 11:42–43 reveals the following prophetic events: (1) the papal subjugation of the former Soviet nations and remaining communist countries; and (2) the papal subjugation of Islam through the doctrine of the virgin Mary, current ecumenical dialogue, and the potential entering wedge of the current U.S. occupation of Iraq. Eventually, these groups will comply with the papal Roman agenda to enforce Sunday legislation on a global scale.

---

416 *Our Sunday Visitor*, 29 May 1994, 5, in Hunt, 458.

417 Fulton J. Sheen, "Mary and the Moslems," *The World's First Love* (Garden City Books, 1952), in Hunt, 458.

418 Ibid.

Daniel 11	Interpretation
Verse 42	"Land of Egypt, not escape" Remaining Communist countries submit to Sunday legislation
Verse 43	"Libyans" and "Ethiopians" Symbols of Islamic religion
	"At his steps" Islam, Catholicism in spiritual competition, Islamic nations submit to Sunday legislation and follow in Rome's steps

—— EIGHTEEN ——
An Examination of Daniel 11:44–45
"The King of the North and the Glorious Holy Mountain"

U p to this point, we have established that the passage of Daniel 11:40–43 demonstrates that the papacy will ultimately seek to bring atheistic communism (verses 40 and 42), Christendom ("spiritual" Israel, verse 41), and Islam (verse 43) into compliance with global Sunday legislation. Yet, there is one remaining spiritual rival left in the world today that is preventing complete Roman Catholic domination—the movement of Seventh-day Adventism. The Seventh-day Adventist Church is the only major spiritual force in the modern world that promotes the true Bible Sabbath in opposition to Rome's "mark" of Sunday sacredness. Therefore, at some point the papacy will attempt to bring this particular movement into compliance with Sunday legislation. We will soon discover that an attempted papal subjugation of Seventh-day Adventism is the actual theme of Daniel 11:44–45.

> But tidings out of the east and out of the north shall trouble him: therefore he shall go forth with great fury to destroy, and utterly to make away many. (Daniel 11:44)

But tidings out of the east and out of the north shall trouble him. Earlier in verse 43 we saw the "escape" of "Edom," "Moab," and "Ammon" from papal authority; we will discover that this sub-passage describes how this "escape" will actually take place—through "tidings" given from the "east" and "north." When we consider the word "tidings," the apostle Paul used it synonymously with the word "gospel," stating, "How beautiful are the feet of them that preach the gospel of peace, and bring glad tidings of good things!" (Romans 10:15). Therefore, the word "tidings" describes a specific "gospel" message that will "trouble" the papacy, i.e., seek to hinder her desire for global domination.

An understanding of the "north" and "east" will confirm this conclusion. We have already established that the "north" is a symbol of God's dwelling place (Psalm 48:1–2, Isaiah 14:12–14). Concerning the "east," the Bible reveals that the sealing angel comes from the east (Revelation 7:1–3), God's glory comes from the east (Ezekiel 43:1–5), Israel entered the earthly sanctuary from the east (Ezekiel 43:1–5), Jesus returns the second time from the east (Matthew 24:27), and, in the Battle of Armageddon, the spiritual river "Euphrates" will be dried up to prepare the way for the "kings of the east" (Christ and the heavenly angels) at the second advent of Christ (Revelation 16:12).[419] Thus, being similar to the "north," the direction of the "east" is also symbolic of God's dwelling place.

As we piece these concepts together, we can conclude that the phrase "tidings out of the east and out of the north" describes a specific Gospel message of heavenly origin that will oppose the work of papal Rome as this power attempts to bring the world into compliance with Sunday legislation. Christ prophesied that "this gospel of the kingdom shall be preached in all the world for a witness unto all nations; and then shall the end come" (Matthew 24:14). And, as a result, the three-fold group called "Edom," "Moab," and "Ammon" will heed the call of this global Gospel message, and "escape" from the grasp of the papacy by refusing to submit to Sunday legislation.

Furthermore, as we traverse through the Word of God, only one worldwide Gospel message can be found—the three angel's messages of Revelation 14:6–12. Therefore, we can conclude that the "tidings out of the east and out of the north" and this three-fold, global Gospel message are one and the same entity. Going a step further, there is only one religious movement in the world today that proclaims this specific message—the Seventh-day Adventist Church. And, because this specific message will "trouble" the papacy by pointing out her apostasies and exposing her false doctrines, the Seventh-day Adventist Church will eventually become the special recipients of her wrath.

John the Revelator offered a firsthand account of this end-time, three-fold message by stating that he "saw another angel fly in the midst of heaven, having the everlasting gospel to preach unto them that dwell on the earth, and to every nation, and kindred, and tongue, and people" (Revelation 14:6). This "first angel" cried, "Fear God, and give glory to him; for the hour of his judgment is come: and worship him that made heaven, and earth, and the sea, and the fountains of waters" (Revelation 14:7).

419 See Matthew 25:31 and Revelation 16:12. See also Louis F. Were, *The Kings that Come from the Sunrising* (Sarasota, FL: H.K. LaRondelle, 1988), 31–36.

The message of the "first angel" can be divided into four basic parts. The first part, "fear God," conveys a total consecration of the heart and soul to Christ. Moses asked Israel, "what doth the LORD thy God require of thee, but to fear the LORD thy God, to walk in all his ways, and to love him, and to serve the LORD thy God with all thy heart and with all thy soul" (Deuteronomy 10:12). To "fear God" also implies that, like Job, the faithful will not be living in known sin: "There was a man in the land of Uz, whose name was Job; and that man was perfect and upright, and one that feared God, and eschewed evil" (Job 1:1).

The second part of the "first angel" conveys that we should "give glory" to God. In seeking to understand this phrase, we should recognize that we are "fearfully and wonderfully made" (Psalm 139:14); thus, to "give glory" to God means that we will strive to live in harmony with God's health message as outlined in the Bible, just as Daniel and his three friends did in Babylonian captivity (Daniel 1:1–20). Since our bodies are the temple of the Holy Spirit, we should seek to maintain a healthy lifestyle and not defile our body temples with unhealthy food or drink (Genesis 1:29, Leviticus 11:1–23). The apostle Paul confirmed in the following two passages that, "Whether therefore ye eat, or drink, or whatsoever ye do, do all to the glory of God" (1 Corinthians 10:31). "What? know ye not that your body is the temple of the Holy Ghost which is in you, which ye have of God, and ye are not your own? For ye are bought with a price: therefore glorify God in your body, and in your spirit, which are God's" (1 Corinthians 6:19–20).

The third part of the "first angel" proclaims that the "hour" of God's judgment "is come." In our review of Daniel 8 (chapter 4), we discovered that the specific passage of Daniel 8:14 outlines an "hour" of judgment that actually began in the year 1844. Ever since this time, Christ has been conducting an investigative judgment that will result in the "cleansing" of the heavenly sanctuary. Therefore, in emphasizing that the "hour" of God's "judgment" has arrived, the third part of the "first angel" will proclaim a "sanctuary message," outlining the solemn reality that we are living in a sobering time of judgment.

The fourth and final part of the "first angel" conveys that we should "worship him that made heaven, and earth, and the sea, and the fountains of waters." When we consider this phrase, we should note that it is strikingly similar to the language of the Sabbath commandment, which states that "in six days the LORD made heaven and earth, the sea, and all that in them is, and rested the seventh day: wherefore the LORD blessed the sabbath day, and hallowed it" (Exodus 20:11). These two synonymous passages actually contain God's "seal," i.e., His name, office, and territory;[420] therefore, this last component of the "first angel" will call the world to receive God's "seal" by returning to the worship of Christ, our Creator,[421] through faithful Sabbath observance.

With the "first angel" having finished the proclamation of the seventh-day Sabbath as the "seal" of God, the "second angel" would then proclaim that "Babylon is fallen, is fallen, that great city, because she made all nations drink of the wine of the wrath of her fornication" (Revelation 14:8). This particular message would announce the "fall" of spiritual Babylon by exposing her false doctrines and apostasies, especially the heresy of Sunday sacredness. This proclamation will also be repeated by another "mighty angel" who will light the whole "earth" with "his glory." Coming "down from heaven" with "great power," he will issue one final worldwide call for God's faithful followers to leave the "fallen" churches of spiritual Babylon (Revelation 18:1–4).[422]

As the first two angels finish their work, the "third angel" will finally announce that "If any man worship the beast and his image, and receive his mark in his forehead, or in his hand, The same shall drink of the wine of the wrath of God" (Revelation 14:9). After announcing the fearful consequences of receiving the "mark" of the beast (Revelation 14:9–11), this angel mentions the qualities of God's faithful followers: "Here is the patience of the saints: here are they that keep the commandments of God, and the faith of Jesus" (Revelation 14:12).

When considering the three angels' messages, we must understand that God will not allow anyone to suffer His wrath (Revelation 15:1, 16:1) until they have made a conscious decision to reject His law. Once again,

---

420 Please see chapter five for an in-depth review on the "seal" of God and the "mark" of the beast.

421 The following passages outline Jesus Christ as our Creator: Genesis 1:26, John 1:1–3, 10, Ephesians 3:9, Colossians 1:16–17, and Hebrews 1:1–2, 8–10.

422 See Ellen G. White, *The Great Controversy* (Mountain View, CA: Pacific Press, 1950), 603: "This scripture [Revelation 18:1–4] points forward to a time when the announcement of the fall of Babylon, as made by the second angel of Revelation 14 (verse 8), is to be repeated, with the additional mention of the corruptions which have been entering the various organizations that constitute Babylon. ... A terrible condition of the religious world is here described. With every rejection of truth the minds of the people will become darker, their hearts more stubborn, until they are entrenched in an infidel hardihood. In defiance of the warnings which God has given, they will continue to trample upon one of the precepts of the Decalogue, until they are led to persecute those who hold it sacred."

as this three-fold message of truth goes forth in the power of the "mighty angel" of Revelation 18, the whole "earth" will be lit with "his glory." This means that every sincere individual will be shown the real issue of the final conflict between good and evil, and be faced with a conscious decision to either accept or reject God's Sabbath. Ellen White confirmed this principle with a powerful observation:

> With the issue thus clearly brought before him, whoever shall trample upon God's law to obey a human enactment receives the mark of the beast. ... But not one is made to suffer the wrath of God until the truth has been brought home to his mind and conscience, and has been rejected. There are many who have never had an opportunity to hear the special truths for this time. The obligation of the fourth commandment has never been set before them in its true light. He who reads every heart and tries every motive will leave none who desire a knowledge of the truth, to be deceived as to the issues of the controversy. The decree is not to be urged upon the people blindly. Everyone is to have sufficient light to make his decision intelligently.[423]

Therefore he shall go forth with great fury to destroy, and utterly to make away many. Because the "tidings" from the "east" and "north," the "everlasting gospel" of the three angels' messages (Revelation 14:6–12), will call people out of her apostate system, the papacy will be "troubled" in her quest to globalize Sunday sacredness. As a result, she will "go forth with great fury to destroy" anyone who will proclaim this Gospel message and maintain fidelity to the Bible Sabbath.[424] Ellen White confirmed that "Especially will the wrath of man be aroused against those who hallow the Sabbath of the fourth commandment; and at last a universal decree will denounce these as deserving of death."[425] In a similar statement, she also noted that,

> As the Sabbath has become the special point of controversy throughout Christendom, and religious and secular authorities

---

423 Ellen G. White, *The Great Controversy*, (Mountain, View, CA: Pacific Press, 1950), 604–605.

424 See Ibid, 588, 625–626 for further details on the end-time persecution against the faithful.

425 Ellen G. White, *Prophets and Kings* (Mountain View, CA: Pacific Press, 1943), 512.

have combined to enforce the observance of the Sunday, the persistent refusal of a small minority to yield to the popular demand will make them objects of universal execration. It will be urged that the few who stand in opposition to an institution of the church and a law of the state ought not to be tolerated; that it is better for them to suffer than for whole nations to be thrown into confusion and lawlessness. ... [A] decree will finally be issued against those who hallow the Sabbath of the fourth commandment, denouncing them as deserving of the severest punishment and giving the people liberty, after a certain time, to put them to death. ... The people of God will then be plunged into those scenes of affliction and distress described by the prophet as the time of Jacob's trouble.[426]

As stated earlier, the Seventh-day Adventist movement is the most prominent global spiritual force in the world today that proclaims both the binding claims of the seventh-day Sabbath and the Gospel "tidings" of the three angels' messages from the "east" and "north." Therefore, because this movement will especially oppose the global agenda of papal Rome, all faithful Sabbath-keepers who follow the message of this movement in the final crisis will be the special recipients of her wrath; eventually they will be deemed worthy of death because of their refusal to comply with Sunday legislation. Yet, because of their fidelity to God, this faithful last-day group will ultimately experience a great deliverance at the second advent of Christ.

---

426 White, *Great Controversy*, 615–616. See also Ellen G. White, "The Final Test of God's People," *Signs of the Times*, February 22, 1910, paragraph 5. Notice the following statement from White, *Prophets and Kings*, 605: "The decree that will finally go forth against the remnant people of God will be very similar to that issued by Ahasuerus against the Jews. Today the enemies of the true church see in the little company keeping the Sabbath commandment, a Mordecai at the gate. The reverence of God's people for His law is a constant rebuke to those who have cast off the fear of the Lord and are trampling on His Sabbath." See also White, *Great Controversy*, 604: "Fearful is the issue to which the world is to be brought. The powers of earth, uniting to war against the commandments of God, will decree that 'all, both small and great, rich and poor, free and bond' (Revelation 13:16), shall conform to the customs of the church by the observance of the false sabbath. All who refuse compliance will be visited with civil penalties, and it will finally be declared that they are deserving of death."

And he shall plant the tabernacles of his palace between the seas in the glorious holy mountain; yet he shall come to his end, and none shall help him. (Daniel 11:45)

And he shall plant the tabernacles of his palace between the seas in the glorious holy mountain; yet he shall come to his end, and none shall help him. In an attempt to eradicate God's faithful last-day Sabbath-keepers, Rome will strive to "plant" the "tabernacles" of her "palace between the seas in the glorious holy mountain." First, a "tabernacle," or temple, is a place where God dwells and can symbolize a "church." Second, a "palace" depicts a place where a king or ruler dwells, and can symbolize the "state." Third, we have established that "seas" symbolize the nations of the world (Revelation 17:15), so the phrase "between the seas" can be rephrased "among the nations of the world." Therefore, these three concepts together symbolize the papal agenda for a global union of church and state through Sunday legislation, which will attempt to force all faithful Sabbath-keepers into compliance.

This scenario can be further demonstrated through an understanding of the "glorious holy mountain." As we consider the meaning of this particular phrase, we must again remember that we are dealing with global, spiritual concepts in Daniel 11:40–45; therefore, the "glorious holy mountain" could not be referring to a literal mountain, but rather a "spiritual" mountain. In fact, it is actually synonymous with Mt. Zion, as God had stated through the prophet Joel that "I am the LORD your God dwelling in Zion, my holy mountain" (Joel 3:17). Thus, the "glorious holy mountain" and "Mt. Zion" are one and the same—they both symbolize God's dwelling place. Interestingly, "Mt. Zion" is actually described as being located "on the sides of the north" in a symbolic sense (Psalm 48:1–2). Before his fall, Satan had been in the "holy mountain of God" (Ezekiel 28:14), desiring to "sit upon the mount of the congregation, in the sides of the north" (Isaiah 14:13). In essence, these passages clearly describe that the "glorious holy mountain" of "Mt. Zion" is a "spiritual" mountain, located "in the sides of the north," symbolizing God's dwelling place in heaven.

Therefore, the phrase "he shall plant the tabernacles of his palace between the seas in the glorious holy mountain" describes the end-time effort of the papacy to sit in the dwelling place of God by demanding global worship. As we have emphasized all along, this worship will be compelled through a global union of church and state, which will require all people to receive Rome's legislated "mark" of Sunday sacredness.

Yet, there will be a faithful, obedient last-day group who will refuse to submit to papal authority; this group will not presume to stand on the "glorious holy mountain" in the place of God, but rather would seek refuge and deliverance on this spiritual "mountain." The prophet Joel confirmed this concept by stating that "in mount Zion and in Jerusalem shall be deliverance, as the LORD hath said, and in the remnant whom the LORD shall call" (Joel 2:32).

Furthermore, because this "glorious holy mountain" is also a symbol of deliverance, "Mt. Zion" can also symbolize the faithful people of God. God told the prophet Isaiah to "say unto Zion, thou art my people" (Isaiah 51:16). In describing the faithful, the apostle Paul told the Hebrew church that "ye are come into mount Sion, and unto the city of the living God, the heavenly Jerusalem, and to an innumerable company of angels, To the general assembly and church of the firstborn, which are written in heaven" (Hebrews 12:22–23).

Therefore, the faithful people of God who refuse to submit to papal authority will also make up the "glorious holy mountain" of "Mt. Zion." Being faithful to the seventh-day Sabbath, this special group will seek deliverance from the papacy on this "spiritual mountain" when persecution explodes on all faithful Sabbath-keepers. And, when Christ returns the second time, He will rescue this group in the Battle of Armageddon, which, incidentally, means "mountain of rendezvous."[427]

The apostle John caught a glimpse of this very special last-day group, stating that "I looked, and, lo, a Lamb stood on the mount Sion, and with him an hundred forty and four thousand, having his Father's name written in their foreheads" (Revelation 14:1). Thus, the 144,000, who are basically last-day, Sabbath-keeping "spiritual" Israelites, will experience a great deliverance on the "glorious holy mountain" of "Mt. Zion" (spelled "Sion" by John), after remaining faithful to God during the final crisis. This group will have the "Father's name" in their "foreheads," a concept that is synonymous with the "seal" of God's Sabbath:

> And I saw another angel ascending from the east, having the seal of the living God: and he cried with a loud voice to the four angels, to whom it was given to hurt the earth and the sea, Saying, Hurt not the earth, neither the sea, nor the trees, till we have sealed the

427 The term "armageddon" actually comes from two Hebrew words, "har" (mountain) and "megiddo" (rendezvous, gathering), which implies that Christ will "rendezvous" with His faithful followers on His spiritual "mountain" when He returns the second time.

servants of our God in their foreheads. And I heard the number of them which were sealed: and there were sealed an hundred and forty and four thousand of all the tribes of the children of Israel. (Revelation 7:2–4)

When we compare these two passages that describe the 144,000, we can see that the "Father's name" and the "seal of the living God" are one and the same. We have already demonstrated that God's "seal" is the actual Sabbath commandment, which incidentally contains God's "name" within its borders. Since these last-day Sabbath-keepers stand on "Mt. Zion," they are the "glorious holy mountain" on earth in a spiritual sense. The papacy will try to "plant" itself "in" this "mountain" by forcing this group to comply with Sunday legislation;[428] yet, they will remain faithful to God during the "great tribulation" (Revelation 7:14), experience a final deliverance, and stand triumphantly on "Mt. Zion," i.e., the "sea of glass," in the eternal kingdom of God. Once again, John caught a glimpse of this victorious group:

And I saw as it were a sea of glass mingled with fire: and them that had gotten the victory over the beast, and over his image, and over his mark, and over the number of his name, stand on the sea of glass, having the harps of God. And they sing the song of Moses the servant of God, and the song of the Lamb, saying, Great and marvellous are thy works, Lord God Almighty; just and true are thy ways, thou King of saints. (Revelation 15:2–3)

In a powerful quotation from her book *The Great Controversy*, Ellen White associated "Mt. Zion" with the "sea of glass," which is actually located in front of God's throne; she commented on how the 144,000 would stand before this throne with Christ and sing the song of deliverance after their victory over the "mark" of the beast:

Upon the crystal sea before the throne, that sea of glass as it were mingled with fire ... are gathered the company that have 'gotten the victory over the beast, and over his image, and over his mark, and over the number of his name.' With the Lamb upon Mount Zion, 'having the harps of God,' they stand, the hundred and forty and four thousand that were redeemed from among men. ... And they sing 'a new song' before the throne, a song which no man

---

428 Louis F. Were, *The King of the North at Jerusalem* (St. Maries, ID: LMN Publishing, 2002), 77–81.

can learn save the hundred and forty and four thousand. It is the song of Moses and the Lamb—a song of deliverance. None but the hundred and forty-four thousand can learn that song; for it is the song of their experience—an experience such as no other company have ever had.[429]

We should note that the Seventh-day Adventist message will actually develop the "glorious holy mountain" of the 144,000. This group will essentially consist of both faithful Seventh-day Adventists and "Edom," "Moab," and the "chief of the children of Ammon" who come out of all false religious systems, who at that point will not be "defiled with women" (Revelation 14:4). In addition to faithful Seventh-day Adventists, "Edom," "Moab," and "Ammon" will include former communists, former Catholics, former Protestants from the "fallen" churches, former Muslims, former Jews, and former followers of any other false religion who respond to the Gospel "tidings" of the three angels' messages from the "east" and "north" and "escape" the influence of the papacy. As a result, this special group will render obedience to the seventh-day Sabbath in the face of Sunday legislation and experience a great deliverance at the second advent of Christ.

Overall, the 144,000 will be faithful Sabbath-keepers who stand through the final crisis, and live to be translated alive without ever seeing death when Christ returns again. Before their final deliverance, however, papal Rome will attempt to "plant" itself "in" this "glorious holy mountain" by forcing these faithful Sabbatarians to capitulate to worldwide Sunday legislation. After discovering that she cannot force this special group to honor her false Sabbath, even in the midst of coercive global legislation, she "shall go forth with great fury" to eliminate them through a global death decree. This will be the final "great tribulation," the "time of trouble, such as never since there was a nation" (Matthew 24:21, Daniel 12:1), where the 144,000 will be forced to flee to the solitary places in the mountains, as they seek refuge from the wrath of antichrist. Ellen White noted that this final time of persecution would be the complete fulfillment of Daniel chapter 11:

We have no time to lose. Troublous times are before us. The world is stirred with the spirit of war. Soon the scenes of trouble spoken of in the prophecies will take place. The prophecy in the eleventh of Daniel has nearly reached its complete fulfillment. Much of the history that has taken place in fulfillment of this prophecy

429 White, *Great Controversy*, 648–649.

will be repeated. In the thirtieth verse a power is spoken of that 'shall be grieved, and return, and have indignation against the holy covenant.'[430]

Yet, although papal Rome would make one last thrust to eliminate those who refuse to comply with Sunday legislation, "he shall come to his end," and "none shall help him." In this final great tribulation, at the grand climax of the Battle of Armageddon, Christ will return to destroy spiritual Babylon and deliver all those whose names are written in the Lamb's book of life.[431]

Once again, having subjugated atheistic communism, Protestant, non-Catholic Christianity, and Islam, papal Rome's biggest foe at the end of time will be that of Seventh-day Adventism. The Seventh-day Adventist movement does not possess any of papal Rome's false doctrines, and promotes both the seventh-day Sabbath and the Gospel "tidings" of the three angels' messages from the "east" and "north," and will thus become the primary target of papal Rome's agenda to achieve and secure global worship through the legal enforcement of Sunday sacredness.

Yet, faithful Seventh-day Adventists and Sabbath-keepers will fearlessly proclaim the Gospel "tidings" of the three angels' messages from the "east" and "north" to call God's faithful believers out of spiritual Babylon, which will prove to "trouble" the papacy. Through the power of this message, "Edom," "Moab," and the "chief of the children of Ammon" will "escape" and make their stand with the faithful people of God. Eventually, the 144,000, the "glorious holy mountain" of "Mt. Zion," made up of both faithful Seventh-day Adventists and Sabbath-keepers who have left spiritual Babylon and exited all the apostate religious systems of the world, will experience a final deliverance and be translated alive at the second advent of Christ. Ellen White confirmed this wonderful promise of deliverance:

> I saw the leading men of the earth consulting together … giving orders that unless the saints should yield their peculiar faith, give up the Sabbath, and observe the first day of the week, the people were at liberty after a certain time to put them to death. … Satan wished to have the privilege of destroying the saints of the Most High; but … God would be honored by making a covenant with those who had kept His law … and Jesus would be honored by

---

430 Ellen G. White, *Manuscript Releases*, 21 vols. (Legacy of Light, 2000), 13:394.
431 Were, 106–109. See also Daniel 12:1–2, Revelation 16:12, 17:16, and 18:1–24.

translating, without their seeing death, the faithful, waiting ones who had so long expected Him.[432]

Daniel 11 Interpretation

Verse 44   "Tidings" from the "east" and "north"
(Loud cry of three angels' messages)

"Great fury to destroy"
(Papal persecution against message)

Verse 45   "Plant tabernacles of palace"
(Church-State union, global death decree)

"Between seas"
(Sunday laws in all nations of world)

"Glorious holy mountain"
(Desire of papacy to sit in place of God,
144,000 faithful to Bible Sabbath)

"Come to his end"
(Papacy destroyed by Christ's Coming)

432 Ellen G. White, *Early Writings* (Hagerstown, MD: Review and Herald, 1945), 282–283.

— NINETEEN —
An Summary of Daniel 11:40–45
A Chronological Review and
the Danger of Literalism

I n this specific chapter we will take the time to offer a general review of what we have discovered from the passage of Daniel 11:40–45. We must understand that, even though all of the passages of Daniel 11 are very important and should be understood, this specific section is most important because it addresses events that are both concurrent to our modern day and will transpire in the very near future.

> And at the time of the end shall the king of the south push at him: and the king of the north shall come against him like a whirlwind, with chariots, and with horsemen, and with many ships; and he shall enter into the countries, and shall overflow and pass over. (Daniel 11:40)

Daniel 11:40 offers a description of how the "king of the north" will overrun and destroy the "king of the south." Since the "king of the north" symbolizes a resurrected, resurgent papacy after 1798, and the "king of the south" symbolizes Soviet atheistic communism, it is quite conclusive that this passage refers to the papal agenda to cause the collapse of the Soviet Union. History will clearly demonstrate that, with the help of the United States, papal Rome was quite instrumental in hastening the demise of communism in Eastern Europe, which ultimately took place by the end of 1991. With this collapse, Rome was able to "enter into the countries," i.e., the former Soviet nations, which have proven to be ripe evangelistic fields for Roman Catholicism. Therefore, the specific passage of Daniel 11:40 is a description of the collapse of the Soviet Union by the hand of a resurrected papacy.

> He shall enter also into the glorious land, and many countries shall be overthrown: but these shall escape out of his hand, even

Edom, and Moab, and the chief of the children of Ammon.
(Daniel 11:41)

Daniel 11:41 offers a description of how the "king of the north"
would next enter into the "glorious land." We have discovered that the
"glorious land" is a symbol of "spiritual" Israel, which can also be called
"Christendom" and would consist of all true believers in Christ from every denomination. Thus, the papacy would strive to enter into "spiritual"
Israel by regaining control of all Christian groups outside of her domain of
Catholicism, especially the movement of Protestantism.

This entrance into the "glorious land" will ultimately be accomplished
through two major vehicles—the modern ecumenical movement and
Sunday legislation. Overall, when the papacy is successful in moving the
majority of Christendom to appeal to civil power for the actual legislation of Sunday, an event which is still future to our day, then her entrance
into the "glorious land" will be complete. Yet, this passage also states that
some shall "escape" papal influence, i.e., "Edom," "Moab," and the "chief
of the children of Ammon," a phrase which symbolizes a group of people
who will heed the call of the three angels' messages (Revelation 14:6–12,
Daniel 11:44), leave the apostate religions of the world, fully convert to
Christ, render obedience to the seventh-day Sabbath, and refuse to submit
to Sunday legislation.

> He shall stretch forth his hand also upon the countries: and the
> land of Egypt shall not escape. But he shall have power over the
> treasures of gold and of silver, and over all the precious things of
> Egypt: and the Libyans and the Ethiopians shall be at his steps.
> (Daniel 11:42–43)

Daniel 11:42–43 offers a description of how the "king of the north"
would "stretch forth his hand" on the "countries," having "power over" the
"precious things of Egypt." These phrases review that the former Soviet bloc
nations, the "countries" and the "precious things of Egypt," are brought into
line with the Roman Catholic agenda of Sunday legislation. Also, the "land
of Egypt" would "not escape," meaning that all the remaining communist
nations of the world will also come into compliance with Sunday legislation. Overall, this passage implies that, after having entered Christendom
in verse 41 through Sunday legislation, the rest of the nations of the world
will come into compliance with this very same legislation; in other words,
Sunday legislation will be moved to the global level. This would also include

the "Libyans" and "Ethiopians," who would be "at" Rome's "steps." These two symbols are indicative of the powerful global force of Islam, which is a close spiritual competitor of the papacy; yet, they shall "be at his steps," meaning that eventually Islam will come into line with the papal agenda of promoting Sunday legislation in the Islamic nations of the world.

> But tidings out of the east and out of the north shall trouble him: therefore he shall go forth with great fury to destroy, and utterly to make away many. (Daniel 11:44)

Daniel 11:44 offers a description of what will take place once Sunday legislation is enacted around the world. As the papacy regains control of the nations of the world through Sunday sacredness, there will be "tidings" from the "east" and "north" that will "trouble" her. These "tidings" are essentially a description of a specific global Gospel message, the three angels' messages of Revelation 14:6–12. This message from heaven will swell into a "loud cry," where the people of the earth will hear the call to exit the false religions of the world, which will be given by God's faithful followers. Those who respond to this message will sever their ties with all apostate religion, make a final stand for Jesus Christ, honor the seventh-day Sabbath, and refuse to submit to Sunday legislation. As a result, this message will awaken the wrath of the papacy to persecute those who resist her authority. This papal wrath will be especially focused on the Seventh-day Adventist movement, which incidentally is the only global spiritual force that promotes both the seventh-day Sabbath and the three angels' messages.

> And he shall plant the tabernacles of his palace between the seas in the glorious holy mountain; yet he shall come to his end, and none shall help him. (Daniel 11:45)

Daniel 11:45 offers a description of how papal Rome will "plant" the "tabernacles" of her "palace" between the "seas" in the "glorious holy mountain." These phrases describe a global union (seas) of church (tabernacles) and state (palace), where papal Rome and the "kings of the earth" (Revelation 17:1–2) unite to enforce Sunday legislation on a global scale. Yet, one specific group, the "glorious holy mountain," i.e., the "144,000," will ultimately refuse to comply with this global agenda. Made up of faithful Seventh-day Adventists and Sabbath-keepers who exit the false religions of the world, this special group has been raised up by the three angels' messages, and are "sealed" with the Sabbath.

Because of their fidelity to God, the "144,000" will ultimately become the special target of papal wrath; they will pass through an experience that no other group has been called to endure—the final crisis of the "time of trouble" (Daniel 12:1), also referred to as the "great tribulation" (Matthew 24:21). Yet, they will remain faithful in this final crisis by refusing to comply with Sunday legislation; they will ultimately triumph with Christ on "Mt. Zion" and live to be translated alive without ever dying at the second advent of Christ. And, while the "144,000" experience a great deliverance, the papacy will "come to his end," and "none shall help him," meaning that this power will ultimately be destroyed by the power and glory of Christ's return (2 Thessalonians 2:7–8).

In some theological circles, it has been suggested that Daniel 11:40–45 might have a literal application. This would mean that, instead of espousing the global, spiritual application to the prophetic symbols found in this particular passage, they would have local, literal meanings. Therefore, Egypt, Libya, and Ethiopia would symbolize Rome's desire for control of the Islamic Middle East. The phrases "glorious land" and "glorious holy mountain" would refer to literal Israel and Mt. Zion, while "between the seas" would refer to the Mediterranean Sea and the Sea of Galilee. The papacy would be seen as planting the "tabernacles" of her "palace" in this region, moving her capital seat from Rome to Jerusalem.

This move would supposedly facilitate a reconstruction of the temple, and the papacy would again claim to be the vicegerent of Christ, sitting in the "temple of God." From this central location, she would dictate world affairs and mandate global Sunday legislation. These literalists advocate that, because the world would look to the papacy for spiritual leadership, the deception would be monumental. Therefore, similar to the modern view of dispensationalism, adherents of literalism combine the papal antichrist and Sunday legislation with temple reconstruction and the re-exaltation of Israel to global prominence, which, they claim, could prove to be a major avenue of deception.

From a certain perspective, this view might be a valid possibility as a means of deceiving the world; yet, we should observe that Ellen White did not mention a papal move to the city of Jerusalem, nor did she mention that Satan, during his counterfeit of the second advent of Christ, would appear at Jerusalem specifically, but rather around the world:

As the crowning act in the great drama of deception, Satan himself will personate Christ. The ... great deceiver will make it appear that Christ has come. In different parts of the earth, Satan will manifest himself among men as a majestic being of dazzling brightness, resembling the description of the Son of God given by John in the Revelation ... and then, in his assumed character of Christ, he claims to have changed the Sabbath to Sunday, and commands all to hallow the day which he has blessed. He declares that those who persist in keeping holy the seventh day are blaspheming his name by refusing to listen to his angels sent to them with light and truth. This is the strong, almost overmastering delusion.[433]

Again, there is no mention of Jerusalem specifically in this observation; neither did Jesus mention this specific location when warning us of the appearance of false Christs just before His return (Matthew 24:23–27). Therefore, great care must be exercised in considering a literal interpretation of Daniel 11:40–45. Because of the deceptive dispensationalist beliefs of a secret rapture, the restoration of literal Israel and temple reconstruction, and a temporal, earthly millennium, we must use extra caution in espousing literal, local interpretations of prophecy.

The possibility of the papacy moving its seat to literal Jerusalem in literal Israel in order to rebuild the literal temple seems highly unlikely because of the fact that, in doing so, it would essentially label itself as the antichrist power to the dispensationalist Christian. Again, Ellen White did not mention any significance with Jerusalem or Israel at the end of time, other than the fact that many individual Jews would be converted to the truth before the close of probation.[434] Therefore, it seems more likely that we should focus on the global, spiritual application of Daniel 11:40–45, and reject any literal interpretation.[435]

It has also been suggested in some theological circles that the "glorious land" of Daniel 11:41 is actually a symbol of the United States, while the "glorious holy mountain" is descriptive of the corporate Seventh-day Adventist

---

433 Ellen G. White, *The Great Controversy*, (Mountain View, CA: Pacific Press, 1950), 624.

434 Ellen G. White, *Evangelism* (Hagerstown, MD: Review and Herald, 1973), 577–579.

435 See Steve Wohlberg, *End Time Delusions: The Rapture, the Antichrist, Israel, and the End of the World* (Shippensburg, PA: Destiny Image Publishers, Inc., 2004), Louis F. Were, *The King of the North at Jerusalem*, (St. Maries, ID: LMN Publishing, 2002), and Louis F. Were, *The Battle for the Kingship of the World: Will the King of the North Invade the Holy City?* (Berrien Springs, MI: First Impressions, n.d.).

Church, which was founded and has its headquarters in America, located "between the seas," i.e., between both the Atlantic and Pacific Oceans.

Now, Revelation 13:11–17 clearly reveals that America and its apostate Protestant majority will have a crucial role in end-time prophecy; yet, to draw these specific conclusions would be doing so without any sound biblical evidence or logical reasoning, and thus should lead us to reject this particular viewpoint. This false interpretation goes against the "global," "spiritual" perspective that we have established for New Testament prophetic interpretation. God does not limit prophecy to local, geographical areas (in this case, the United States), but rather deals with global, spiritual principles. Thus, the "glorious land" would symbolize "spiritual Israel" and not the United States, and the "glorious holy mountain" would symbolize the desire of antichrist to sit in the place of God by receiving global worship through the mark of the beast, and the final deliverance of those who resist this situation, namely the 144,000, not the corporate Seventh-day Adventist church.

Overall, the passage of Daniel 11:40–45 reveals the global agenda of papal Rome to either eliminate or subjugate every rival spiritual force in the world that could potentially challenge her agenda to exalt Sunday sacredness on a global scale. Warring against communism, Protestantism, Islam, and Seventh-day Adventism, eventually every country in the world will comply with Sunday legislation. Yet, the message of Seventh-day Adventism, which promotes the seventh-day Sabbath and the three angels' messages, will raise up a final generation called the "144,000." This special last-day group will be made up of faithful Seventh-day Adventists and Sabbath-keepers who come out of the apostate religions of the world and make their stand for Jesus Christ. Furthermore, they will ultimately triumph by refusing to submit to Sunday legislation, and, because of their fidelity to God during the greatest test ever given to mankind, also receive a glorious deliverance at the second advent of Jesus Christ.

— TWENTY —
A Review of Daniel 12
"When Michael Stands Up"

Having finished our textual analysis of Daniel 11, we will now offer a brief survey of Daniel 12. We will discover that this particular chapter will complete the specific passage of Daniel 11:40–45, and serve as the actual conclusion for the entire vision of chapter 11. Overall, Daniel 12 will establish the following prophetic trends: (1) the close of human probation, "time of trouble," and final deliverance of God's people (verse 1); (2) the "special resurrection" and the eternal reign of the righteous (verses 2–3); (3) the unsealing of Daniel's prophecies in the "time of the end" (verses 4–10, 13); and (5) the 1,290-year and 1,335-year time prophecies (verses 11–12).

> And at that time shall Michael stand up, the great prince which standeth for the children of thy people: and there shall be a time of trouble, such as never was since there was a nation even to that same time: and at that time thy people shall be delivered, every one that shall be found written in the book. (Daniel 12:1)

And at that time shall Michael stand up, the great prince which standeth for the children of thy people. Here we see that an individual named "Michael" will "stand" for the people of God at the end of time. In seeking to understand the identity of "Michael," we should first realize that his actual name means "one like God."[436] Furthermore, in Jude 9, "Michael" is also called the "archangel," a term which can mean either "head messenger" or "leader of the angels."[437] Other passages also reveal that "Michael" had resurrected Moses into heaven,[438] and cast Satan out of heaven

436 James Strong, *Strong's Exhaustive Concordance* (Grand Rapids, MI: Baker, 1997), S.V. "Michael."

437 Ibid, "Archangel."

438 See Deuteronomy 34:5–6, Jude 9, and Matthew 17:1–3 for evidence on the

(Revelation 12:7–9). He is also called the "first prince" (Daniel 10:13—margin), "your prince" (Daniel 10:21), and the "great prince" (Daniel 12:1). In this particular passage, He will stand up for the faithful during the "time of trouble" and deliver those whose names are written in the Lamb's book of life (Daniel 12:1). Piecing these clues together, there is only one individual that could meet these identifiers: Jesus Christ. And, interestingly enough, when Christ returns again, He will come with the "voice of the archangel, and the trump of God" (1 Thessalonians 4:16).[439]

We will now examine what it means for "Michael" (Christ) to "stand up." Before unlocking the meaning of this phrase, we must first observe that there are four different sets of passages that describe Christ as being at the "right hand" of God: (1) nine passages state that He is "seated" at the "right hand" of God;[440] (2) one passage reveals that He is simply "at" God's "right hand" (Romans 8:34); (3) one passage states that He is "on" God's "right hand" (1 Peter 3:22); and (4) one passage describes Christ as "standing" at God's "right hand" (Acts 7:55–56).

In order to understand what it means for "Michael" to "stand up," we must examine the fourth category mentioned above, which describes Christ as "standing" at God's "right hand." In that particular passage, the deacon Stephen, as he was being stoned to death, saw "Jesus standing on the right hand of God, And said, Behold, I see the heavens opened, and the Son of man standing on the right hand of God" (Acts 7:55–56). This is the only passage in the Bible that describes Christ as "standing" on God's "right hand," and it is mentioned in the context of Stephen's execution, which took place in A.D. 34 and actually signified the close of probation for ancient Israel.[441] Because Christ was "standing" and not "sitting" when this

---

· resurrection of Moses.

439 Jesus' title as "Michael the Archangel" does not mean that He is a literal "angel" or a created being. (1) Christ is fully God (Philippians 2:5–6, Isaiah 9:6, John 1:1–3, Hebrews 1:8–10, 1 Timothy 3:16, Genesis 1:26); (2) Christ has power over death and the grave (John 11:20–25, Revelation 1:18); (3) Christ is leader of the heavenly angels (Joshua 5:13–15, Revelation 19:11–16, Matthew 25:31); (4) Christ is our Prince (Isaiah 9:6, Acts 5:31); and (5) Christ will also deliver the righteous at His second advent (Matthew 24:27–31).

440 See Colossians 3:1, Ephesians 1:20, Mark 16:19, Acts 2:33–34, Hebrews 1:3, 8:1, 10:12, and 12:2.

441 On pages 180–183 of this book we had discussed the 70-weeks' prophecy of Daniel 9:24–27, which had actually outlined a 490-year period of probation for ancient Israel, from 457 B.C. to A.D. 34, ending with the stoning of Stephen. Thus, when Stephen was stoned, Christ "stood up," signifying the final close of probation for ancient Israel as a nation.

event took place, "standing" up can be associated with a close of probation. Therefore, as we apply this principle to Daniel 12:1, when "Michael" shall "stand up," it will signify the close of probation for earth, and the commencement of the "time of trouble."[442]

And there shall be a time of trouble, such as never was since there was a nation even to that same time. This phrase signifies that when Christ concludes His intercessory ministry in the heavenly sanctuary (Revelation 22:11–12), the infamous "time of trouble" will commence. And, "When this time of trouble comes, every case is decided; there is no longer probation, no longer mercy for the impenitent."[443] This specific time period is to be the greatest crisis that God's people will ever be called to endure:

> The 'time of trouble, such as never was,' is soon to open upon us; and we shall need an experience which we do not now possess and which many are too indolent to obtain. It is often the case that trouble is greater in anticipation than in reality; but this is not true of the crisis before us. The most vivid presentation cannot reach the magnitude of the ordeal. In that time of trial, every soul must stand for himself before God.[444]

And at that time thy people shall be delivered, every one that shall be found written in the book. Although God's faithful, last-day believers will be called to endure the "time of trouble," they will experience a final deliverance when Christ returns again. The names of this faithful group, i.e., the "144,000," are to be immortalized in the book of life, and, when Christ comes again, they will stand on "Mt. Zion," the "sea of glass," with the "Lamb," having conquered the "beast," his "image," "his mark," and the "number of his name" (Revelation 14:1, 15:2–3).

And many of them that sleep in the dust of the earth shall awake, some to everlasting life, and some to shame and everlasting

---

442 See Ellen G. White, *Early Writings* (Hagerstown, MD: Review and Herald, 1945), 36–37. In this quotation, Ellen White associated the close of probation with Christ "standing up" at the end of His intercession in the heavenly sanctuary. See also Ellen White, *The Great Controversy* (Mountain View, CA: Pacific Press, 1950), 613.

443 See Ellen G. White, *Testimonies for the Church*, 9 vols. (Boise, ID: Pacific Press, 1986), 5:213.

444 White, *Great Controversy*, 622.

contempt. And they that be wise shall shine as the brightness of the firmament; and they that turn many to righteousness as the stars for ever and ever. (Daniel 12:2–3)

And many of them that sleep in the dust of the earth shall awake, some to everlasting life, and some to shame and everlasting contempt. In this passage, we see that "many" people will "awake" from the "sleep" of death to reap either "everlasting life" or "everlasting contempt."[445] When we compare this passage to John 5:38–39, which states that "all" people will be resurrected, we must conclude that the "many" people mentioned here would not be referring to the "all" who are resurrected at Christ's second advent; rather, this passage would refer to a "special resurrection" which will take place just prior to the general resurrection that will occur when Christ returns.

This text also implies that this "special resurrection" will involve two distinct groups who are on opposite sides. The first group will consist of God's faithful followers who have died in the faith of the "third angel's message" (Revelation 14:9–12); after describing this specific message, John the Revelator was given the admonition, "Blessed are the dead which die in the Lord from henceforth" (Revelation 14:13), which demonstrates a special blessing for those who keep the "third angel's message." Since this particular message began in the year 1844, this "special resurrection" would consist of the faithful who have died since that year while believing in this specific message.

As she was shown this "special resurrection" in vision, Ellen White confirmed that "The graves were opened, and those who had died in faith under the third angel's message, keeping the Sabbath, came forth from their dusty beds, glorified, to hear the covenant of peace that God was to make with those who had kept His law."[446] In a similar statement below, she also stated that,

> Graves are opened, and 'many of them that sleep in the dust of the earth ... awake, some to everlasting life, and some to shame and everlasting contempt.' Daniel 12:2. All who have died in the faith

---

445 There are 66 passages in the Bible that equate death with an unconscious "sleep" until the resurrection. A few examples would be John 11:11–14, Acts 7:59–60, 1 Corinthians 15:3–6, 16–24, 51–55, 1 Thessalonians 4:15–18, 2 Peter 3:4, and Psalm 13:3.

446 White, *Early Writings*, 285.

of the third angel's message come forth from the tomb glorified, to hear God's covenant of peace with those who have kept His law.[447]

The second group to experience this "special resurrection" will consist of people who were involved in the crucifixion of Christ, and also others who were especially vehement in their persecution of faithful Christians over the centuries. John the revelator confirmed this, saying, "Behold, he cometh with clouds; and every eye shall see him, and they also which pierced him" (Revelation 1:7). Christ also told Caiaphas that "Hereafter shall ye see the Son of man sitting on the right hand of power, and coming in the clouds of heaven" (Matthew 26:64). Thus, Caiaphas, along with many others, will be raised in this "special resurrection" to see Christ come again in glory:

> All who have died in the faith of the third angel's message come forth from the tomb glorified, to hear God's covenant of peace with those who have kept His law. 'They also which pierced Him' (Revelation 1:7), those that mocked and derided Christ's dying agonies, and the most violent opposers of His truth and His people, are raised to behold Him in His glory and to see the honor placed upon the loyal and obedient.[448]

And they that be wise shall shine as the brightness of the firmament; and they that turn many to righteousness as the stars for ever and ever. This passage describes the faithful people of God over the centuries of redemptive history who will reign for ever and ever with Christ in the eternal kingdom. Though maligned and mistreated by the people of this world (Hebrews 11:31–40), they have remained faithful to Christ and have sought to understand God's truth, winning many souls to the Lord in the process. As a result, they will be given immortality and receive a crown of glory that will never fade away.

> But thou, O Daniel, shut up the words, and seal the book, even to the time of the end: many shall run to and fro, and knowledge shall be increased. (Daniel 12:4)

But thou, O Daniel, shut up the words, and seal the book, even to the time of the end: many shall run to and fro, and knowledge shall be

---

447 White, *Great Controversy*, 637.
448 Ibid.

increased. Again, Daniel was told to seal up his book until the "time of the end,"[449] which would begin after the 1,260-year papal Dark Age persecution. Thus, the book of Daniel would be "unsealed" after the year 1798, and would result in both a greater understanding of Bible prophecy and a tremendous increase and advancement in modern technology.[450]

> Then I Daniel looked, and, behold, there stood other two, the one on this side of the bank of the river, and the other on that side of the bank of the river. And one said to the man clothed in linen, which was upon the waters of the river, How long shall it be to the end of these wonders? (Daniel 12:5–6)

Then I Daniel looked, and, behold, there stood other two, the one on this side of the bank of the river, and the other on that side of the bank of the river. And one said to the man clothed in linen, which was upon the waters of the river, How long shall it be to the end of these wonders? Daniel describes two "men" who are conversing about the vision of chapter 11; one asks the other how much time will transpire before the "wonders" of this vision actually come to an "end."[451]

> And I heard the man clothed in linen, which was upon the waters of the river, when he held up his right hand and his left hand unto heaven, and sware by him that liveth for ever that it shall be for a time, times, and an half; and when he shall have accomplished to scatter the power of the holy people, all these things shall be finished. (Daniel 12:7)

And I heard the man clothed in linen, which was upon the waters of the river, when he held up his right hand and his left hand unto heaven, and sware by him that liveth for ever that it shall be for a time, times, and an half; and when he shall have accomplished to scatter the power of the holy people, all these things shall be finished. In this passage, Daniel is told that a "time," "times," and a "half" would transpire, and then the "end" of these prophetic "wonders" would come. We have already identified that the "time," "times," and a "half" refer to the 1,260-year Dark Age reign

---

449 See pages 93, 179–180.

450 Ibid, 356. Again, see pages 93, 179–180 for an explanation of Daniel 12:4–9. See also Ellen G. White, *The Desire of Ages* (Mountain View, CA: Pacific Press, 1945), 234–235.

451 These men were either two "angels" or Christ and an "angel."

of the papacy, which, once again, spanned from A.D. 538 to 1798. After this prophetic period is accomplished, then the "end," or "time of the end," would actually begin, and span from the year 1798 to the end of time.

> And I heard, but I understood not: then said I, O my Lord, what shall be the end of these things? And he said, Go thy way, Daniel: for the words are closed up and sealed till the time of the end. (Daniel 12:8–9)

And I heard, but I understood not: then said I, O my Lord, what shall be the end of these things? And he said, Go thy way, Daniel: for the words are closed up and sealed till the time of the end. After hearing that the "end" of "wonders" would take place after the 1,260-year papal reign, Daniel was told that his book would be "sealed" up and not fully understood until the "time of the end." His prophecies would be "unsealed" only after the year 1798; after this pivotal year, these visions would then be examined and understood by faithful Bible students who diligently seek after their meaning.[452]

> Many shall be purified, and made white, and tried; but the wicked shall do wickedly: and none of the wicked shall understand; but the wise shall understand. (Daniel 12:10)

Many shall be purified, and made white, and tried; but the wicked shall do wickedly: and none of the wicked shall understand; but the wise shall understand. Similar to Daniel 11:33–35, this passage states that "many" would be "tried" during the 1,260-year Dark Age period; yet, when Daniel's prophecies are unsealed after 1798, the "wise" would understand them.

> And from the time that the daily sacrifice shall be taken away, and the abomination that maketh desolate set up, there shall be a thousand two hundred and ninety days. (Daniel 12:11)

And from the time that the daily sacrifice shall be taken away, and the abomination that maketh desolate set up, there shall be a thousand two hundred and ninety days. Before attempting to understand this 1,290-day prophecy, we should reiterate that (1) the "daily" refers to the replacement of pagan Rome with papal Rome; (2) the "abomination of

---

452 White, *Great Controversy*, 356.

desolation" refers to the elevation of the papal power and its subsequent removal of both paganism and Christ's intercessory ministry; and (3) the specific time prophecy of 1,290 prophetic "days" actually translates into 1,290 literal years of actual time.

In essence, this passage states that the 1,290-year prophecy would begin with the elevation of the papacy to power, the complete destruction of paganism, and the papal usurpation of Christ's intercessory ministry. Furthermore, because this text is quite similar in wording to Daniel 8:11–12 and Daniel 11:31, and these two passages refer to the Dark Age papal reign, we must conclude that the 1,290-year prophecy must also refer to this same period. Since this particular reign ended in 1798, we must also conclude that the 1,290-year prophecy would end in this same year. Spanning 1290 years into the past from 1798 will take us to A.D. 508. This particular year was very significant in the elevation of the papacy and the final destruction of paganism, as the Frankish king Clovis become a powerful tool in behalf of the Catholic Church:

> What happened in 508? In 496, Clovis, king of the Franks, became a Roman Catholic. All the other Germanic tribes who had dismantled the Roman Empire were Arians and therefore in opposition to the pope in Rome. Clovis defeated the Visigoths and became the first civil power to join up with the rising Church of Rome. France, therefore, is called the oldest daughter of the Roman Catholic Church.[453]

> After his great victory over the Goths in 507 ... together with his Burgundian allies, Clovis came to Tours, probably in the middle of 508, to hold a victory celebration. There he met Byzantine envoys who presented to him the decree naming him an honorary consul [of Rome].[454]

Gerhard Pfandl commented by saying that "The joining of the civil and religious powers (Franks and papacy) at that time was an important step in 'setting up the abomination of desolation,' which refers to the unscriptural teachings of the papacy and their enforcement through the union of

---

453 Gerhard Pfandl, *Time Prophecies in Daniel 12* (Biblical Research Institute, May 2005), 8. Please see pages 23–24, and 158–160 of this book for discussions on the rise of Clovis.

454 Herwig Wolfram, *The Roman Empire and Its Germanic Peoples* (Berkeley, CA: University of California Press, 1997), 222, quoted in Pfandl, *Time Prophecies in Daniel 12*, 8.

church and state."[455] He also observed that "It is one of the ironies of history that France, the power that helped the papacy at the beginning of the 1,290 years, was the power that brought about its demise at the end of this time period, when Napoleon in 1798 had Pope Pius VI taken prisoner."[456] Therefore, the 1,290-year prophecy would begin in 508 when Clovis, a pagan, barbarian king, having converted from paganism to Catholicism, fully committed his political and military support to the cause of the Roman Catholic Church; it would terminate in 1798, in the very same year that the 1,260-year prophecy had ended.[457]

> Blessed is he that waiteth, and cometh to the thousand three hundred and five and thirty days. (Daniel 12:12)

Blessed is he that waiteth, and cometh to the thousand three hundred and five and thirty days. This passage introduces a third time prophecy which spans 1,335 prophetic "days," i.e., 1,335 literal years. Up to this point we have seen a 1,260-year period (which went from 538 to 1798) and a 1,290-year period (which went from 1798 back to 508). In essence, we have gone from 538 to 1798 (1260 years) and back from 1798 to 508 (1,290 years). Thus, because we last left off at the year 508 with the 1,290-year prophecy, we must use this pivotal year as the starting point of the 1,335-year prophecy. Moving forward 1335 years from 508, we will arrive at the year 1843, which turned out to be a significant year in Adventist history because of the initial proclamation of the "three angels' messages" (Revelation 14:6–12).

The late Adventist theologian Louise Were confirmed this conclusion by stating, "Beginning at the same date as the 1,290 days ... A.D. 508, 1,335 days (literal years) extend to 1843–4, the time when the world-wide proclamation was given, 'The hour of His Judgment is come'

---

455 Pfandl, *Time Prophecies in Daniel 12*, 8–9.

456 Ibid, 9.

457 See Stephen N. Haskell, *The Story of Daniel the Prophet* (Brushton, NY: Teach Services, Inc., 1999), 263–265, Pfandl, *Time Prophecies in Daniel 12*, 6–9, *Seventh-day Adventist Bible Commentary*, 12 vols. (Hagerstown, MD: Review and Herald, 1955, 2002), 4:880–881, William H. Shea, *Daniel: A Reader's Guide* (Nampa, ID: Pacific Press, 2005), 273–275, Uriah Smith, *Daniel and the Revelation* (Nashville, TN: Southern Publishing, 1945), 323–330, Dr. Alberto R. Treiyer, *Apocalypse: Seals & Trumpets* (Dr. Alberto R. Treiyer, 2005), 113–114, and Louis F. Were, *The King of the North at Jerusalem* (St. Maries, ID: LMN Publishing, 2002), 120–123. See also pages 23–24, 158–160 of this book discussing Clovis' career.

(Revelation 14:6, 7)."[458] Because the final year of the 2,300-year prophecy of Daniel 8:14 spanned from the fall of 1843 to the fall of 1844, we can safely conclude that the end of the 1,335-year prophecy parallels this same termination point, also ending in the period of 1843–1844. James White confirmed that "Evidences are conclusive that the 1,335 days ended with the 2,300, with the Midnight Cry in 1844."[459] Ellen White also noted that the "great test on time was in 1843 and 1844."[460] In the following quotation below, Adventist pioneer Uriah Smith also advocated that the 1,335-year prophecy actually began in A.D. 508:

> Now it is manifestly wrong to date the 1,290 days from the setting up of the papacy, when the prophecy says they are to date from the taking away of paganism, which was thirty years previous. We therefore date the 1,290 days from the year 508; and as the 1,335 days are spoken of in connection with these, no possible reason can be given why they do not commence at the same point. The 1,290 and 1,260 end together in 1798.[461]

Unfortunately, some have misused a particular statement from the pen of Ellen White in order to justify a potential future application of this specific time prophecy. In reality, Mrs. White had actually commented on a particular individual who had been teaching certain doctrinal errors, stating, "We told him of some of his errors in the past, that the 1,335 days were ended and numerous errors of his."[462] Upon first glance, it would appear that Mrs. White had espoused a future application to this 1,335-year prophecy; yet, Gerhard Pfandl offered a perfectly harmonious explanation of this specific quotation:

> Some believe that in this statement she [Mrs. White] places the 1,335 days in the future. However, the sentence is generally understood to mean, 'We told him of some of his errors in the past, [we told him] that the 1,335 days were ended and [we told him] numerous errors of his.' Otherwise we must ask, why Ellen White

458 Were, *King of the North at Jerusalem*, 120.
459 James White, "The Judgment," *Review and Herald*, 29 Jan 1857, quoted in Pfandl, *Time Prophecies in Daniel 12*, 5. See also Shea, *Daniel*, 276–277.
460 White, *Testimonies for the Church*, 1:73.
461 Uriah Smith, "Short Interviews with Correspondents," *Review and Herald*, 24 Feb 1863, quoted in Pfandl, *Time Prophecies in Daniel 12*, 5–6.
462 Ellen G. White, *Manuscript Releases*, 21 vols. (Legacy of Light, 2000), 6:251.

reprimanded brother Hewit and not her husband and all the other pioneers who taught that the 1,335 years were ended?[463]

Given these explanations, there have been some recent trends in Seventh-day Adventism that continue to promote a future application to the 1,260-, 1,290-, and 1,335-day prophecies of Daniel 12. In this future application, these three periods are no longer calculated to be literal years of time, meaning that the 1,260-, 1,290-, and 1,335-day periods are actually literal days. Furthermore, these three periods are seen to have the same starting point, which would be the passing of a national Sunday law here in America. In other words, each of these three periods would begin with the pivotal point of Sunday legislation in the United States, and then end with three different significant events that would transpire at the end of time, before the faithful enter into the eternal world.[464]

Therefore, the 1,260 literal days, or 3½ literal years, would transpire from the passing of a national Sunday law and span until the time that probation would close for the entire human race. We must notice that, if this theory were to be true, we could ascertain the time for the close of probation, once a Sunday law is passed. Yet, Ellen White clearly noted in the three quotations below that God has never revealed, nor will He ever reveal to finite human beings, when the close of human probation will take place:

> God has not revealed to us the time when this message will close, or when probation will have an end. Those things that are revealed we shall accept for ourselves and for our children; but let us not seek to know that which has been kept secret in the councils of the Almighty.[465]

> [There] is no command for anyone to search the Scripture in order to ascertain, if possible, when probation will close. God has no such message for any mortal lips. He would have no mortal tongue declare that which He has hidden in His secret councils.[466]

> Men need to be aroused to realize the solemnity of the time, the nearness of the day when human probation shall be ended. God

463 Pfandl, *Time Prophecies in Daniel 12*, 5.
464 Kenneth Cox, *Daniel* (Coldwater, MI: Remnant Publications, 2005), 155.
465 Ellen G. White, *Selected Messages from the Writings of Ellen G. White*, 3 vols. (Hagerstown, MD: Review and Herald, 1980, 1986), 1:191.
466 Ibid, 1:192.

gives no man a message that it will be five years or ten years or twenty years before this earth's history shall close. He would not give any living being an excuse for delaying the preparation for His appearing.[467]

Also, according to proponents of this "futurist" theory, the 1,290-day period is considered to extend from the Sunday law to the universal death decree.[468] Yet, again, Ellen White spoke of this specific event, but never mentioned exactly when it would happen:

> Then I saw the leading men of the earth consulting together, and Satan and his angels busy around them. I saw a writing, copies of which were scattered in different parts of the land, giving orders that unless the saints should yield their peculiar faith, give up the Sabbath, and observe the first day of the week, the people were at liberty after *a certain time* to put them to death.[469]

This "futurist" theory also extends the 1,335-day prophecy from the national Sunday law to the second advent of Christ.[470] Yet, once again, Jesus stated that God has not revealed when He will return again: "But of that day and that hour knoweth no man, no, not the angels which are in heaven, neither the Son, but the Father" (Mark 13:32).[471] We should again confirm that time has no longer been a test for God's people since 1844; Ellen White noted that,

> I have borne the testimony since the passing of the time in 1844, that there should be no definite time set by which to test God's people. The great test on time was in 1843 and 1844; and all who have set time since these great periods marked in prophecy were deceiving and being deceived.[472]

---

467 Ellen G. White, *Maranatha* (Hagerstown, MD: Review and Herald, 1976), 108.

468 Cox, 155.

469 White, *Early Writings*, 282–283, italics mine.

470 Cox, 155.

471 Ellen White does mention that after the close of probation, the 144,000 do in fact hear the day and hour of Christ's coming; yet, this takes place after probation has closed, and has not been identified from any Bible text. See White, *Early Writings*, 15.

472 Ellen G. White, *Life Sketches of James and Ellen White* (Legacy of Light, 2000), 221–222.

In light of this clear evidence, we can therefore conclude that the 1,260-year prophecy clearly found its fulfillment in the Dark Age career of the papacy, which spanned from A.D. 538 to 1798. Furthermore, both the 1,290-year and 1,335-year prophecies began in the year 508 and ended in 1798 and 1843–1844 respectively, and clearly have their prophetic fulfillment in the past. Thus, we need not search for some future fulfillment of these time prophecies, as, according to Ellen White, after the year 1844, neither prophetic time nor literal time will ever again be a test for God's people. Therefore, any "futurist" view of these three time prophecies of Daniel 12 should be rejected, as these three prophetic periods have clearly met their fulfillment in the past.

> But go thou thy way till the end be: for thou shalt rest, and stand in
> thy lot at the end of the days. (Daniel 12:13)

But go thou thy way till the end be: for thou shalt rest, and stand in thy lot at the end of the days. Daniel was told in this passage that he would "rest" and "stand" in his "lot at the end of the days." This statement actually has two meanings: (1) Daniel would "sleep" in death to "rest" from his labors, and then "stand" in his "lot" during the investigative judgment that would begin at the "end of the days" in 1844; and (2) the prophecies of his book would "rest," meaning that they would not be understood until the "time of the end" (after 1798), but would "speak" at the "appointed time" (Habakkuk 2:2–3), and fulfill their role in the closing work of redemption at the end of this earth's history.

Ellen White especially confirmed this second application by emphasizing that "Daniel is today standing in his lot, and we are to give him place to speak to the people. Our message is to go forth as a lamp that burneth."[473] "His wonderful prophecies, as recorded by him in chapters 7 to 12 of the book bearing his name, were not fully understood even by the prophet himself," but "before his life labors closed, he was given the blessed assurance that 'at the end of the days'—in the closing period of this world's history—he would again be permitted to stand in his lot and place."[474]

Furthermore, "In his vision of the last days ... Daniel has been standing in his lot since the seal was removed and the light of truth has been shining upon his visions. He stands in his lot, bearing the testimony which

---

473 Ellen G. White, "To Our Church Members in Australasia," *Australasian Union Conference Record*, 11 March 1907.

474 Ellen G. White, *Prophets and Kings* (Mountain View, CA: Pacific Press, 1943), 547.

was to be understood at the end of the days."[475] Therefore, "As we near the close of this world's history, the prophecies recorded by Daniel demand our special attention, as they relate to the very time in which we are living. ... 'The wise shall understand' (verse 10), was spoken of the visions of Daniel that were to be unsealed in the latter days."[476]

475 Ellen G. White, *Sermons and Talks*, 2 vols. (Legacy of Light, 2000), 1:225–226.

476 White, *Prophets and Kings*, 547–548. See Daniel 12:10.

—— TWENTY-ONE ——
Putting the Pieces Together
Paraphrasing Daniel 11

H aving accomplished our overall goal of developing a basic chronology of Daniel 11, it will now prove useful to present a general paraphrase of the entire chapter. An interpretation of each phrase will be contained in brackets in order to provide an easy readability, and trace the major historical trends outlined in each specific passage.

"Also I [**the angel Gabriel**] in the first year of Darius the Mede, even I, stood to confirm and to strengthen him [**Daniel**]. And now will I shew thee the truth. Behold, there shall stand up yet three kings in Persia [**Cambyses, False Smerdis, and Darius I OR Cambyses, Darius I, and Xerxes**]; and the fourth [**Xerxes OR Artaxerxes**] shall be far richer than they all: and by his strength through his riches he shall stir up all against the realm of Grecia [**Greek Empire**]" (Daniel 11:1–2).

"And a mighty king [**Alexander the Great**] shall stand up, that shall rule with great dominion, and do according to his will [**conquer a vast territory**]. And when he shall stand up [**at height of his power**], his kingdom shall be broken [**his death, 323 B.C.**], and shall be divided toward the four winds of heaven [**four Hellenistic empires**]; and not to his posterity [**Alexander had no legitimate heirs**], nor according to his dominion which he ruled [**his former kingdom would not be under one ruler**]: for his kingdom shall be plucked up, even for others beside those [**the four former generals of Alexander—Ptolemy, Cassander, Lysimachus, and Seleucus**]" (Daniel 11:3–4).

"And the king of the south [**Ptolemy I Soter**] shall be strong, and one of his princes [**Seleucus I Nicator**]; and he [**Seleucus I**] shall be strong above him [**Ptolemy I**], and have dominion [**gain the territory of Syria**]; his dominion shall be a great dominion [**largest territory of the Hellenistic empires**]. And in the end of years [**after the first and second Syrian Wars**] they [**Ptolemy II Philadelphus and Antiochus I Soter**] shall join

—— 249 ——

themselves together [**conclude peace in 252 B.C.**]; for the king's daughter [**Berenice, daughter of Ptolemy II**] of the south [**Egypt**] shall come to the king of the north [**Antiochus II Theos, Syria**] to make an agreement [**peace through a marriage alliance**]: but she [**Berenice**] shall not retain the power of the arm [**lose her position from the former queen Laodice**]; neither shall he [**Antiochus II**] stand [**assassinated by Laodice**], nor his arm [**Berenice's son**]: but she [**Berenice**] shall be given up [**executed by Laodice**], and they that brought her [**execution of her attendants also**], and he that begat her [**"she begat," her son**], and he that strengthened her in these times [**Antiochus II**]" (Daniel 11:5–6).

"But out of a branch of her [**Berenice's**] roots [**family**] shall one [**Ptolemy III Euergetes**] stand up in his estate [**assume the throne of Egypt**], which shall come with an army [**launch an invasion**], and shall enter into the fortress of the king of the north [**Seleucid Syria**], and shall deal against them [**attempt to exact revenge for his sister's death**], and shall prevail [**win the Third Syrian War**]: And shall also carry captives into Egypt their gods [**recover pagan idols captured from Egypt by the Persians in former conquests**], with their princes [**take captives to Egypt**], and with their precious vessels of silver and of gold [**spoils of war**]; and he [**Ptolemy III**] shall continue more years [**died in 221 B.C.**] than the king of the north [**Seleucus II, died in 226 B.C.**]. So the king of the south [**Ptolemy III**] shall come into his [**Seleucus'**] kingdom [**Syria**], and shall return into his own land [**Egypt**]" (Daniel 11:7–9).

"But his [**Seleucus'**] sons [**Seleucus III Ceraunus Soter and Antiochus III Magnus**] shall be stirred up [**desire to war against Egypt**], and shall assemble a multitude of great forces [**raise a large army**]: and one [**one son, Antiochus III**] shall certainly come, and overflow, and pass through [**start the Fourth Syrian War**]: then shall he [**Antiochus III**] return [**fight against Egypt**], and be stirred up, even to his [**Ptolemy IV Philopater's**] fortress" (Daniel 11:10).

"And the king of the south [**Ptolemy IV**] shall be moved with choler [**raise a large army**], and shall come forth and fight with him [**continue the Fourth Syrian War**], even with the king of the north [**Antiochus III**]: and he [**Antiochus III**] shall set forth a great multitude [**a large army**]; but the multitude [**Antiochus' army**] shall be given into his [**Ptolemy's**] hand [**Ptolemy IV would defeat Antiochus III at the Battle of Raphia, 217 B.C.**]. And when he [**Ptolemy IV**] hath taken away the multitude [**Syrian army**], his heart shall be lifted up; and he shall cast down many ten thousands: but he [**Ptolemy IV**] shall not be strengthened by it [**not complete the conquest of Syria**]. For the king of the north [**Antiochus III**] shall return, and shall set forth a multitude greater than the former [**start the Fifth Syrian War**], and shall certainly come after certain years [**he regrouped from 212–204 B.C.**] with a great army and with much riches [**Antiochus III would defeat Ptolemy V Epiphanes at the Battle of the Panium, 201–200 B.C., driving Egypt out of Judeo-Palestine once and for all**]" (Daniel 11:11–13).

"And in those times [**after the Fifth Syrian War**] there shall many stand up [**make war**] against the king of the south [**Egypt**]: also the robbers of thy people [**Seleucid-Syrian invaders under Antiochus IV Epiphanes**] shall exalt themselves [**attempt to eliminate Judaism**] to establish the vision [**complete the elimination of God's people**]; but they shall fall [**the Seleucid-Syrian Empire would collapse by 64–63 B.C.**]" (Daniel 11:14).

"So the king of the north [**Seleucid Syria, Antiochus IV**] shall come [**invade Egypt, 169–168 B.C.**], and cast up a mount, and take the most fenced cities [**Memphis, Alexandria, and others**]: and the arms of the south [**the Egyptian army**] shall not withstand [**fall prey to a Syrian invasion**], neither his chosen people [**the Jewish people couldn't resist the Syrian occupation of Judea**], neither shall there be any strength to withstand [**Seleucid Syria would dominate Judea and Egypt under Antiochus IV Epiphanes**]" (Daniel 11:15).

"But he [**pagan Rome**] that cometh against him [**Seleucid Syria, Antiochus IV**] shall do according to his own will [**cast Antiochus IV out of Egypt, aid Jewish people against Syria through "Jewish league"**], and none shall stand before him [**will subjugate Syria and become the next "king of the north"**]: and he [**pagan Rome under Pompey the Great**] shall stand in the glorious land [**Judeo-Palestine**], which by his hand shall be consumed [**64–63 B.C.**]. He [**pagan Rome under Julius Caesar**] shall also set his face to enter [**Egypt**] with the strength of his whole kingdom [**all Caesar's military resources**], and upright ones with him [**Jewish forces loyal to Caesar led by Antipater**]; thus shall he do [**begin the Roman subjugation of Egypt**]: and he shall give him the daughter of women [**Cleopatra**], corrupting her [**making her his mistress**]: but she shall not stand on his side, neither be for him [**could not prevent his assassination**]" (Daniel 11:16–17).

"After this [**the occupation of Egypt**] shall he [**Caesar**] turn his face unto the isles [**Mediterranean basin**], and shall take many [**eliminate all political enemies**]: but a prince for his own behalf [**Mark Antony**] shall cause the reproach offered by him to cease [**protect Caesar's political interests in Rome**]; without his own reproach he shall cause it to turn upon him [**defend Caesar against the Roman senate**]. Then he [**Caesar**] shall turn his face toward the fort of his own land [**Rome**]: but he shall stumble and fall, and not be found [**Caesar's assassination, 44 B.C.**]" (Daniel 11:18–19).

"Then shall stand up in his [**Caesar's**] estate a raiser of taxes [**Caesar Augustus, reign 27 B.C. to A.D. 14**] in the glory of the kingdom: but within few days he shall be destroyed, neither in anger, nor in battle [**die a peaceful death, A.D. 14**]. And in his [**Augustus'**] estate shall stand up a vile person [**Tiberius Caesar, reign A.D. 14 to 37**], to whom they shall not give the honour of the kingdom: but he shall come in peaceably [**peaceful transference of power after Augustus' death**], and obtain the kingdom by flatteries [**false flattery of Roman senate**]. And with the arms of a flood shall they [**alleged seditionists**] be overflown from before him, and shall be broken [**executed**]; yea, also the prince of the covenant [**crucifixion of Christ, A.D. 31**]" (Daniel 11:20–22).

"And after the league [**Jewish league, 161 B.C.**] made with him [**pagan Rome**] he shall work deceitfully [**use the league for furthering Roman interests in the eastern regions**]: for he shall come up [**enter Judeo-Syria, 64–63 B.C.**], and shall become strong with a small people [**Judeo-Palestine**]. He shall enter peaceably even upon the fattest places of the province [**Syria, Judea, Egypt**]; and he shall do that which his fathers have not done, nor his fathers' fathers [**Titus' destruction of Jerusalem, A.D. 70**]; he shall scatter among them the prey, and spoil, and riches [**dispersion of Jewish people after the destruction of Jerusalem**]: yea, and he shall forecast his devices against the strong holds [**persecution of Christians**], even for a time [**360 years, 48 B.C. to A.D. 313 OR 31 B.C. to A.D. 330**]" (Daniel 11:23–24).

"And he [**pagan Rome, Octavian, the "king of the north"**] shall stir up his power and his courage against the king of the south [**Egypt and Cleopatra under Mark Antony**] with a great army; and the king of the south [**Antony**] shall be stirred up to battle with a very great and mighty army; but he [**Antony**] shall not stand [**Octavian defeated him in the Battle of Actium, 31 B.C.**]: for they shall forecast devices against him. Yea, they that feed of the portion of his meat shall destroy him [**Cleopatra abandoned Antony during Actium**], and his army shall overflow: and many shall fall down slain [**Antony's army and navy would be defeated**]" (Daniel 11:25–26).

"And both these kings' [**Octavian, Antony**] hearts shall be to do mischief [**they would both desire control of Roman world**], and they shall speak lies at one table [**form false alliances**]; but it shall not prosper [**these agreements wouldn't last**]: for yet the end shall be at the time appointed [**Antony would be defeated in 31 B.C. and commit suicide in**

30 B.C.]. Then shall he [**Octavian, later Caesar Augustus**] return into his land [**Rome**] with great riches [**wealth of Egypt**]; and his [**pagan Rome's, Octavian's**] heart shall be against the holy covenant [**Christianity, Judeo-Palestine**]; and he shall do exploits [**persecute Christians, settle the eastern territories**], and return to his own land [**Rome**]" (Daniel 11:27–28).

"At the time appointed [**between A.D. 313 and 330**] he [**pagan Rome, Constantine the Great**] shall return [**to the eastern territories**], and come toward the south [**move capital of Roman Empire to Constantinople, toward Egypt, but not into Egypt itself**]; but it shall not be as the former [**not for purposes of war, as in time of Caesar and Octavian**], or as the latter [**the last-day war between the "king of the north" and "south" in the time of the end**]. For the ships of Chittim [**Germanic tribal invasions**] shall come against him [**pagan Rome**]: therefore he [**paganism and papalism**] shall be grieved, and return, and have indignation against the holy covenant [**paganism and papalism try to destroy Christianity**]: so shall he do; he shall even return [**make final attempt to survive**], and have intelligence with them that forsake the holy covenant [**paganism enters Christianity, papacy corrupts and persecutes Christians**]" (Daniel 11:29–30).

"And arms [**military might, i.e., Clovis**] shall stand on his part [**in behalf of papal Rome**], and they shall pollute the sanctuary of strength [**remove paganism, corrupt earthly church with false doctrine, usurp Christ's intercession in heavenly sanctuary**], and shall take away the daily sacrifice [**remove paganism, turn people's hearts away from Christ's intercessory ministry**], and they shall place the abomination that maketh desolate [**set up the papacy in power over the church, state, and the conscience of Christians**]. And such as do wickedly against the covenant [**those who turn against the gospel through recantation**] shall he [**papacy, the next "king of the north"**] corrupt by flatteries [**flatter with prospects of position and material gain**]: but the people that do know their God shall be strong, and do exploits [**faithful followers of God will remain faithful, preach the truth and win many true converts**]" (Daniel 11:31–32).

"And they that understand among the people [**faithful Christians**] shall instruct many [**spread the light of truth**]: yet they [**the faithful**] shall fall by the sword [**war**], and by flame [**burned at stake**], by captivity [**prison**], and by spoil [**economic hardships**], many days [**1,260 years, A.D. 538–1798**]. Now when they shall fall, they shall be holpen with a little help [**there will be some helpers of the truth**]: but many shall cleave to them [**the faithful**] with flatteries [**prospects of material, financial gain**]. And some of them of understanding [**the faithful**] shall fall [**be martyred**], to try them, and to purge, and to make them white [purification through trial], even to the time of the end [to the year 1798]: because it is yet for a time appointed [Dark Age papal persecutions, 538–1798]" (Daniel 11:33–35).

"And the king [papal Rome, the "king of the north"] shall do according to his will [exercise power over all of Christendom]; and he shall exalt himself [claim to be head of the Church], and magnify himself above every god [commit blasphemy], and shall speak marvellous things against the God of gods [claim to be equal with God and have the power to forgive sins], and shall prosper till the indignation be accomplished [reign from 538 to 1798]: for that that is determined shall be done [God foresaw that the papacy would rule for 1,260 years]" (Daniel 11:36).

"Neither shall he [papal Rome] regard the God of his fathers [the true God], nor the desire of women [celibacy of Catholic clergy], nor regard any god: for he shall magnify himself above all [papal claim to equality with God]. But in his estate [position] shall he honour the God of forces [use military force to secure homage of Europe]: and a god whom his fathers knew not [virgin Mary] shall he honour with gold, and silver, and with precious stones, and pleasant things [Mary crowned with honor and authority]. Thus shall he do in the most strong holds [Christendom] with a strange god [virgin Mary], whom he shall acknowledge and increase with glory: and he shall cause them [Mary and the saints] to rule over many [Christendom], and shall divide the land for gain [territories divided into dioceses for economic gain]" (Daniel 11:37–39).

"And at the time of the end [sometime after A.D. 1798] shall the king of the south [Soviet atheistic communism] push at him [war against papal interests]: and the king of the north [papal Rome in its "healed wound" state after 1929] shall come against him [Soviet atheistic communism] like a whirlwind, with chariots, and with horsemen, and with many ships [war against Soviet atheistic communism]; and he shall enter into the countries [former Soviet bloc nations], and shall overflow and pass over [destroy the Soviet Union by the end of 1991]" (Daniel 11:40).

"He [papal Rome] shall enter also into the glorious land [Christian Church through Sunday legislation], and many countries shall be overthrown [many individuals and countries will submit to Sunday legislation]: but these shall escape out of his hand [refuse to submit to Sunday legislation], even Edom, and Moab, and the chief of the children of Ammon [spiritual Babylonians, members of non-Christian, heathen religions, and worldly people who exit all apostate religions]" (Daniel 11:41).

"He [papal Rome] shall stretch forth his hand also upon the countries [former Soviet countries]: and the land of Egypt [remaining communist countries around the world] shall not escape [submit to Sunday legislation]. But he [papal Rome] shall have power over the treasures of gold and of silver, and over all the precious things [spiritual and material wealth] of Egypt [former Soviet countries and remaining communist countries who submit to Sunday legislation]: and the Libyans and the Ethiopians [Islamic nations of the world] shall be at his steps [a close spiritual competitor who will eventually submit to Sunday legislation]" (Daniel 11:42–43).

"But tidings out of the east and out of the north [message of Seventh-day Adventism, loud cry of three angels' messages] shall trouble him [hinder work of papacy]: therefore he [papal Rome] shall go forth with great fury to destroy, and utterly to make away many [cast faithful Sabbath-keepers into great tribulation]. And he shall plant the tabernacles of his palace between the seas [secure a global union of church and state among the nations of the world to force worldwide compliance with Sunday legislation] in the glorious holy mountain [144,000, faithful Sabbath-keepers forced to comply with Sunday legislation also]; yet he shall come to his end [144,000 will remain faithful to the Sabbath, and the papacy will be destroyed at second coming of Christ], and none shall help him [her own followers will turn on her, cause her eventual collapse]" (Daniel 11:44–45).

Overall, as we survey Daniel 11:1–45, we can see the larger scope of major trends in human history within the context of biblical prophecy. Clearly the historical trends outlined in this chapter highlight the influence of the different empires of history that had a direct effect on the chosen people of God. We can be greatly encouraged by the fact that this chapter concludes with the eventual triumph of God's faithful followers at the end of time.

—— TWENTY-TWO ——
Summary & Conclusions
Some Final Thoughts on Daniel 11

As we reflect on what we have discovered in our journey to establish a basic historical chronology of Daniel 11; we can draw several conclusions with a high degree of certainty. Overall, this chapter can be divided into five general sections that can be clearly assigned to specific historical trends in human history.

We have discovered that the passage of Daniel 11:1–4 describes Media-Persia (539–331 B.C.), Greece (331–168 B.C.), Alexander the Great (356–323 B.C.), and the four Hellenistic kingdoms that were led by four of Alexander's former generals, which formed shortly after the famous Battle of Ipsus in 301 B.C. These four kingdoms would consist of the following: (1) Greco-Macedonia, led by Cassander; (2) Thrace and Asia Minor, led by Lysimachus; (3) Syria and the East, led by Seleucus; and (4) Egypt and Judeo-Palestine, led by Ptolemy. After the Battle of Corupedium (281 B.C.), where Lysimachus was defeated and killed by Seleucus, these four kingdoms would be reduced to three Hellenistic monarchies that would endure until the rise of pagan Rome: (1) Antigonid Macedonia; (2) Seleucid Syria; and (3) Ptolemaic Egypt.

The passage of Daniel 11:5–15 offers a description of the "Five Syrian Wars" that were fought between Ptolemaic Egypt (the "king of the south") and Seleucid Syria (the "king of the north"); these conflicts actually took place over the region of Judeo-Palestine and spanned the reigns of several Ptolemaic and Seleucid kings over many years. The "First Syrian War" (276–271 B.C.) was fought between Ptolemy II Philadelphus and Antiochus I Soter. The "Second Syrian War" (261–252 B.C.) was fought between Antiochus II Theos and Ptolemy II Philadelphus. The "Third Syrian War" (246–240 B.C.) was fought between Ptolemy III Euergetes and Seleucus II Callinicus. The "Fourth Syrian War" (219–217 B.C.) was fought between Antiochus III Magnus and Ptolemy IV Philopater. The "Fifth Syrian War" (202–199 B.C.) was fought between Antiochus III Magnus and Ptolemy V

Epiphanes. In short, these wars were a result of an initial conflict between Ptolemy I Soter and Seleucus I Nicator over the occupation of the holy land that took place after the Battle of Ipsus (301 B.C.).

As we move into the passage of Daniel 11:16–30, we find a clear transition into the career of pagan Rome (168 B.C. to A.D. 476). This power would "replace" Syria as the next "king of the north" and eventually subjugate the three remaining Hellenistic kingdoms: (1) Greco-Macedonia was subjugated after the Battle of Pydna in 168 B.C.; (2) Judeo-Syria was subjugated by the Roman general Pompey in 64–63 B.C.; and (3) Egypt was subjugated through the influence of both Julius Caesar and Octavian (Caesar Augustus) from 48–30 B.C.

In short, verses 16–30 cover ten general historical trends in pagan Roman history: (1) the subjugation of Palestine by Pompey (verse 16); (2) the involvement of Julius Caesar in Egyptian affairs and his eventual assassination (verses 17–19); (3) the rise of Caesar Augustus, the "raiser of taxes," who died a peaceful death (verse 20); (4) the rise of Tiberius Caesar, the "vile person," under whose reign Christ was crucified (verses 21–22); (5) a Judeo-Roman "league" (verse 23); (6) the Roman subjugation of Syria, Judea, and Egypt, which would include the destruction of Jerusalem in A.D. 70 (verse 24); (7) two separate conflicts over Hellenistic Egypt, i.e., Caesar versus Pompey and Octavian versus Antony (verses 25–28); (8) the rise of Constantine the Great, the end of Christian persecution, and the dedication of Constantinople (verse 29); (9) the Germanic invasions that caused the collapse of western Rome (verse 30); and (10) the eventual triumph of Christianity, the collapse of paganism, and the emergence of papal Rome (verse 30).

The next section, Daniel 11:31–39, offers a clear description of the Dark Age career of the papal Roman Empire (A.D. 538–1798), who "replaced" pagan Rome as the next "king of the north." Five general trends in papal Roman history can be ascertained from this passage: (1) the complete destruction of both paganism and Arian Christianity through the influence of the papacy (verse 31); (2) the 1,260-year Dark Age period of papal Roman persecution against God's faithful followers (verses 32–35); (3) the exaltation of the papal power to the level of God (verses 36–37); (4) the papal Roman exaltation of a "strange god," i.e., the virgin Mary (verse 38), and (5) the division of Europe into dioceses for the purpose of material and financial gain (verse 39).

As we move into Daniel 11:40–45, we see a description of the activities of a resurrected, resurgent papal Rome in its "healed wound" phase of existence after the year 1798. This power is called the "king of the north" because: (1) it is the final power in all prior prophecies of Daniel, and

Daniel 11 is no exception; (2) the phrase "king of the north" is one of many phrases used in the Bible to describe the papacy; (3) the "north" describes the location of God's throne, and since the papacy assumes the place of God, it must be the "king of the north;" (4) ancient Babylon came from the "north" to conquer ancient Israel, and since spiritual Babylon is another description of the papacy, it must also be the spiritual power of the "king of the north;" and (5) the "replacement principle" dictates that when pagan Rome subjugated Syria, it replaced this power as the "king of the north." Therefore, when the papacy replaced paganism, it would then also "replace" both Syria and pagan Rome as the "king of the north."

In Daniel 11:40, we find a continuation of the war between the "king of the north" and the "king of the south." Having already identified the "king of the north" as the papacy, we have defined the "king of the south" as a symbol of Soviet atheistic communism. With the help of the United States, the papacy exercised its global, religio-political influence to hasten the demise of communism in Eastern Europe. By the end of 1991, the Soviet Union had finally collapsed, and the former Soviet bloc nations once again became open to Christian influences; they now serve as ripe evangelistic fields for Roman Catholicism.

The specific passage of Daniel 11:41 actually describes the entrance of the papacy into the "glorious land" of the Christian Church, which would include Catholicism, Eastern Orthodoxy, Protestantism, Seventh-day Adventism, and all versions of non-Catholic Christianity. This will be accomplished through the vehicle of Sunday legislation, because Sunday sacredness is Rome's "mark," or "sign," of authority. As the Christian world unites with Rome on this specific issue, she will once again have full control of the "glorious land" of Christendom. Yet, this passage also states that "Edom," "Moab," and the "chief of the children of Ammon" will "escape" the influence of the papacy; this means that there will be a group of people who will not submit to Sunday sacredness. They will make their stand for Christ and resist Rome's authority by obeying the seventh-day Sabbath. This particular group will consist of both faithful Seventh-day Adventists and faithful Sabbath-keepers around the world who exit the world's apostate religions.

Daniel 11:42–43 describes the papal agenda to bring the former Soviet bloc nations and remaining communist countries of the world into compliance with Sunday legislation. This passage also hints that this papal agenda will eventually spread to all the countries of the world. Even the "Libyans" and "Ethiopians," symbolic of the Islamic nations of the world (concentrated mostly in the Middle East and Africa), will come into compliance with Sunday legislation. Islam is actually right at Rome's "steps" as a close spiritual competitor, but will eventually follow in her "steps" by complying with Sunday legislation. We should remember that Islam and Catholicism hold the common ground of the veneration of the virgin Mary.

The final two verses of Daniel 11, Daniel 11:44–45, describe the papal Roman effort to destroy Seventh-day Adventism and bring God's last-day faithful group, the "144,000," into compliance with global Sunday legislation. In this passage, the "tidings" form the "east" and "north," a Gospel message known as the three angels' messages (Revelation 14:6–12), will "trouble" the papacy, hindering her desire for global domination. The Seventh-day Adventist movement has this specific message within its spiritual borders, and exalts the true seventh-day Sabbath in the face of Sunday exaltation.

As these "tidings" go forth to warn the world of Rome's agenda, she will respond with great wrath to persecute and eliminate all faithful Seventh-day Adventists and other faithful Sabbath-keepers who remain loyal to Jesus Christ. Eventually, the "144,000," the "glorious holy mountain," will triumph in a spiritual sense, remaining faithful through a global union of church and state that will attempt to force them to comply with Sunday sacredness. Because of this great victory, they will be delivered at the second coming of Christ, translated alive without ever dying, after having endured the greatest crisis that any group of God's faithful people have ever been called to endure. And, while Christ delivers the "144,000" at His second advent, He will also destroy the papacy and bring her power to an end once and for all.

Having provided this detailed summary of what we have discovered in our study of Daniel 11, I would like to conclude this work by making a few observations. First, I would like you as the reader to realize that, while I believe that the views presented in this book are solid, I don't believe that they are absolutely infallible. God will give greater light on these prophecies as we continue to progress toward the close of time. Furthermore, when considering the specific passage of Daniel 11:23–28, it is my understanding that these verses address very specific events in the career of pagan Rome; yet, you may choose to assign other historical trends to this particular passage.

Overall, this work is more historical than theological in nature, and is definitely a work in progress. It is essentially the result of my own personal quest to understand Daniel 11. Also, the specific passage of Daniel 11:40–45 is one that we need to pay very close attention to, as we are living in the days of this particular portion of the vision. More specifically, we are between verses 40 and 41; the Soviet Union fell in 1991 (verse 40), and we have not yet seen Rome fully enter the "glorious land" through Sunday legislation—this event is still future (verse 41).

Yet, in light of this fact, we need to make sure that we are preparing for the final crisis that Daniel described in verses 41–45. In addition to helping to provide a workable chronology of Daniel 11, I hope by the grace of God that this work has encouraged you to continue to prepare for the final events of this earth's history, because we have not a moment to lose. Very soon, we, like Daniel, will all have to stand in our lot at the "end of days" (Daniel 12:13), and the central theme that will polarize those who follow Christ and those who follow the antichrist will consist of the Sabbath-Sunday issue. Please notice this final comparison chart that blends the specific chapters of Daniel 2, 7, 8, and 11, along with Revelation 13 and Revelation 17:

Kingdom	Dan. 2	Dan. 7	Dan. 8	Dan. 11	Rev. 13	Rev. 17
Babylon (605 B.C.)	v. 38	v. 4	n/a	n/a	n/a	n/a
Persia (539 B.C.)	v. 39	v. 5	vs. 3–4, 20	v. 2	n/a	n/a
Greece (331 B.C.)	v. 39	v. 6	vs. 5–8, 21	vs. 2–3	n/a	n/a
4 Kingdoms (301 B.C.)	n/a	v. 6	vs. 8, 22	vs. 4–15	n/a	n/a
Pagan Rome (168 B.C.)	v. 40	vs. 7, 19, 23	vs. 9–12, 23–25	vs. 16–30	n/a	n/a
Europe (A.D. 476)	v. 42	vs. 7, 20, 24	n/a	n/a	n/a	n/a
Papacy (538–1798)	vs. 41–43	vs. 8, 20–21, 24–25	vs. 9–12, 23–25	vs. 31–39	vs. 4–10	vs. 1–6
Judgment (1844)	v. 44	vs. 9–14, 22, 26–27	vs. 14, 26	n/a	n/a	n/a
Papacy Healed (1929)	n/a	n/a	n/a	vs. 40–45	vs. 1–3	vs. 7–13
Second Advent (Future)	vs. 34, 45	v. 27	v. 25	n/a	n/a	v. 14

As we bring our study to a close, we must consider some crucial questions—Are we ready to remain faithful to Jesus Christ and the true seventh-day Sabbath, even when under the pressure of a death decree? Will we stand up to both "live" and "proclaim" God's Gospel "tidings" from the "east" and the "north," i.e., the three angels' messages, so that the people of the world will hear the call to come out of spiritual Babylon and into the true message for this time? As we consider the "lot" that God has called us to "stand in" during these last days, we should sense the divine urgency to proclaim these "tidings out of the northeast," the final warning message to a dying world. It is my prayer that this work, through the divine aid of the Holy Spirit, has helped to rekindle this sense of urgency in your heart to both "live" and "give" these gospel "tidings out of the northeast" in these final hours of earth's history. May we allow God to use us in a powerful way during this final era of redemptive history so that we might fulfill our appointed place in His sovereign plan. Amen.

— BIBLIOGRAPHY —
A List of Sources Cited

- *American*, January 4, 1941, Volume 64, 363.

- Bacchiocchi, Samuele. *From Sabbath to Sunday: A Historical Investigation of the Rise of Sunday Observance in Early Christianity*. Rome: Pontifical Gregorian University Press, 1977.

- Bacchiocchi, Samuele. *The Sabbath in the New Testament*. Berrien Springs, MI: University Printers, 1985.

- Baker, G.P. *Justinian: The Last Roman Emperor*. New York: Cooper Square Press, 2002.

- Bainton, Roland H. *Here I Stand: A Life of Martin Luther*. Nashville, TN: Abingdon Press, 1978.

- Barry, William. *The Papacy and Modern Times: A Political Sketch, 1303–1870*. New York: Henry Holt and Company, 1911.

- Bemont, Charles and G. Monod. *Medieval Europe from 395 to 1270*. New York: Henry Holt and Company, 1906.

- Berg, Joseph F. *The Great Apostacy*. Philadelphia, PA: J.B. Lippincott & Company, 1842.

- Bernstein, Carl. "The Holy Alliance." *Time*, 24 Feb 1992, 28–35.

- Bevan, Edwyn R. *The House of Ptolemy: A History of Egypt under the Ptolemaic Dynasty*. Chicago: Ares Publishers, 1985.

- Bevan, Edwyn R. *The House of Seleucus: A History of the Hellenistic Near East Under the Seleucid Dynasty*. 2 Vols. Chicago: Ares Publishers, 1985.

- *Bible Readings for the Home*. Nashville, TN: Southern, 1944.

- Botsford, George Willis and Charles Alexander Robinson, Jr. *Hellenic History*. New York: MacMillan Company, 1950.

- Browning, Robert. *Justinian and Theodora*. New York: Thames and Hudson, 1971.

- Burns, Thomas. *A History of the Ostrogoths*. Bloomington, IN: Indiana University Press, 1984.

- Bury, J.B. *History of the Later Roman Empire: From the Death of Theodosius I to the Death of Justinian*. 2 vols. New York: Dover Publications, 1958.

- Bury, J.B. *The Invasion of Europe by the Barbarians*. New York: W.W. Norton & Company, 1967.

- *Calvary Contender*, 15 Nov 1987.

- *Calvary Contender*, 1 Sept 1996.

- *Catechism of the Catholic Church*. 2nd Ed. Washington, DC: United States Catholic Conference, 1997.

- Cheetham, Nicolas. *A History of the Popes*. New York: Dorset Press, 1982.

- *Christian American*, October 1993.

- Conway, Betrand L. *The Question Box*. New York: The Paulist Press, 1903 Edition.

- Conway, Betrand L. *The Question Box*. New York: The Paulist Press, 1929 Edition.

- Coppa, Frank J. *The Modern Papacy Since 1789*. London: Longman, 1998.

- Cox, Kenneth. *Daniel*. Coldwater, MI: Remnant Publications, 2005.

- Damsteegt, P. Gerard. *Foundations of the Seventh-day Adventist Message and Mission*. Berrien Springs, MI: Andrews University Press, 1995.

- d'Aubigné, J.H. Merle. *History of the Reformation*. 5 vols. Rapidan, VA: Hartland Publications, n.d.

- Davies, Norman. *Europe: A History*. New York: HarperPerennial, 1998.

- de Semlyen, Michael. *All Roads Lead to Rome*. Bucks, England: Dorchester House Publishers: 1993.

- Doukhan, Jacques. *Secrets of Daniel: Wisdom and Dreams of a Jewish Prince in Exile*. Hagerstown, MD: Review and Herald, 2000.

- Doukhan, Jacques. *Secrets of Revelation: The Apocalypse through Hebrew Eyes.* Hagerstown, MD: Review and Herald, 2002.

- Dowling, John. *The History of Romanism.* Pensacola, FL: Vance, 2002.

- Durant, Will. *The Age of Faith.* New York: Simon and Schuster, 1950.

- Durant, Will. *The Age of Napoleon: A History of European Civilization from 1789 to 1815.* New York: Simon and Schuster, 1975.

- Durant, Will. *The Life of Greece.* New York: Simon and Schuster, 1966.

- Edwardson, Christian. *Facts of Faith.* Nashville, TN: Southern, 1943.

- Enright, Thomas. *The American Sentinel*, June 1893.

- *Eusebius' Ecclesiastical History*, Book 10, Chapter 5.

- "Evangelicals & Catholics Together: The Christian Mission in the Third Millennium," *First Things*, 43 (May 1994), 15–22.

- Ferraris, Lucius. "Papa," in *Prompta Bibliotheca*, Volume 6 (1772), Article 2, page 29.

- Filteau, Jerry. "Bishops Join New U.S. Ecumenical Forum," *Catholic News Service*, 18 Nov 2004.

- Fletcher, Richard. *The Barbarian Conversion from Paganism to Christianity.* Berkeley, CA: University of California Press, 1997.

- *Fox's Book of Martyrs.* William Byron Forbush, Editor. Grand Rapids, MI: Zondervan, 1967.

- Freeman, Charles. *Egypt, Greece, and Rome: Civilizations of the Ancient Mediterranean.* Oxford: Oxford University Press, 1996.

- Froom, LeRoy E. *The Prophetic Faith of Our Fathers.* 4 Vols. Washington, DC: Review and Herald, 1946–1954.

- Geiermann, Peter. *The Convert's Catechism of Catholic Doctrine.* St. Louis, MI: B. Herder Book Company, 1949.

- Gibbon, Edward. *The Decline and Fall of the Roman Empire.* 6 vols. New York: Everyman's Library, 1993.

- Gibbons, James Cardinal. Letter to J.F. Snyder of Bloomington, Illinois, signed by H.F. Thomas, the Chancellor for Cardinal Gibbons, dated 11 Nov 1895.

- Gibbons, James Cardinal. *The Catholic Mirror*, 23 Dec 1893.

- Gibbons, James Cardinal. *The Faith of Our Fathers.* New York: P.J. Kennedy & Sons, 1917.

- Goldstein, Clifford. *1844 Made Simple.* Nampa, ID: Pacific Press, 1988.

- Gordon, Paul A. *The Sanctuary, 1844, and the Pioneers.* Nampa, ID: Pacific Press, 2000.

- Grant, Michael. *History of Rome.* New York: Book-of-the Month Club, 1997.

- Grant, Michael. *The Twelve Caesars.* New York: Barnes & Noble, 1975.

- *Hartford Weekly Call*, Hartford, Kansas, 22 Feb 1884.

- Haskell, Steven N. *The Cross and Its Shadow.* Brushton, NY: Teach Services, 2002.

- Haskell, Steven N. *The Story of Daniel the Prophet.* Brushton, NY: Teach Services, 1999.

- Haskell, Steven N. *The Story of the Seer of Patmos.* Brushton, NY: Teach Services, 2004.

- Heather, Peter. *The Fall of the Roman Empire: A New History of Rome and the Barbarians.* New York: Oxford, 2006.

- Heather, Peter. *The Goths.* Oxford: Blackwell Publishing, 1997.

- Holmes, J. Derek. *The Papacy in the Modern World: 1914–1978.* New York: Crossroad Publishing, 1981.

- Holmes, William Gordon. *The Age of Justinian and Theodora.* 2 vols. New York: John Wiley & Sons, 1907, 1919.

- Hunt, Dave. *A Woman Rides the Beast.* Eugene, OR: Harvest House, 1994.

- "Inquisition." *Microsoft® Encarta® Encyclopedia 2000.* © 1993–1999 Microsoft Corporation. All rights reserved.

- James, Edward. *The Franks.* Oxford: Butler & Tanner Limited, 1988.

- James, Edward. *The Origins of France: From Clovis to the Capetians, 500–1000.* London: MacMillan, 1982.

- Jones, Alonzo T. *The Two Republics.* Ithaca, MI: A. B. Publishing, Inc, n.d.

- Joy, James Richard. *Rome and the Making of Modern Europe.* New York: Flood and Vincent, 1893.

- Knight, George R. *Millennial Fever and the End of the World.* Boise, ID: Pacific Press, 1993.

- Lecky, William E. H. *The History of the Rise and Influence of the Spirit of Rationalism in Europe.* Vol. 2. University Press of the Pacific, 2001.

- Lindsell, Harold, Editor, "The Lord's Day and Natural Resources," *Christianity Today,* 7 May 1976, page 12.

- *Look Magazine,* 21 July 1959.

- *Los Angeles Herald Examiner,* 9 Sept 1987.

- Loughborough, J.N. *The Great Second Advent Movement.* Pacific Press, Adventist Pioneer Library, 1992.

- Martin, Malachi. *The Keys of This Blood: Pope John Paul II Versus Russia and the West for Control of the New World Order.* New York: Simon & Schuster, 1990.

- Maxwell, C. Mervyn. *God Cares.* 2 vols. Boise, ID: Pacific Press, 1981.

- Moorhead, John. *The Roman Empire Divided, 400-700.* Harlow, England: Pearson Education Limited, 2001.

- Morgan, Kevin. *Sabbath Rest.* Brushton, NY: Teach Services, 2002.

- Mueller, Ekkehardt. *The Beast of Revelation 17—A Suggestion.* Biblical Research Institute, May 2005.

- *New Covenant Magazine,* February 1988.

- Nichol, Francis D. *The Midnight Cry.* Brushton, NY: Teach Services, 2000.

- O'Brien, John A. *The Faith of Millions.* Huntington, IN: Our Sunday Visitor, 1938.

- *Our Sunday Visitor,* 29 May 1994.

- *Our Sunday Visitor,* 15 Nov 1914.

- *Our Sunday Visitor's Catholic Encyclopedia.* Our Sunday Visitor Publishing Division, 1991.

- Paulien, Jon. "The Hermeneutics of Biblical Apocalyptic," unpublished paper, 2004.

- Pfandl, Gerhard. *Daniel: The Seer of Babylon.* Hagerstown, MD: Review and Herald, 2002.

- Pfandl, Gerhard. *Time Prophecies in Daniel 12.* Biblical Research Institute, May 2005.

- Piroutek, Erin. *The Observer*, University Wire, South Bend, Indiana, 1 Nov 1999.

- "Pius VI." *Microsoft® Encarta® Encyclopedia 2000*. © 1993–1999 Microsoft Corporation. All rights reserved.

- Pope John Paul II, Address to the Pontifical Academy of Sciences, 22 Oct 1996.

- Pope John Paul II, *Dies Domini*, Apostolic Letter, 31 May 1998.

- Pope Leo XIII, "The Reunion of Christendom," Encyclical Letter, 20 June 1894.

- Pope Pius XII, *Humani Generis*, Encyclical Letter, 12 Aug 1950.

- Procopius. *History of the Wars*. Vols. 3–5. Translated by H.B. Dewing. Cambridge, MA: Harvard University Press, 1919–1928.

- Puls, Mark and Charles Hurt, "Pope's Call for Worship Welcomed," *The Detroit News*, 7 July 1998.

- Reid, G. Edward. *Sunday's Coming*. 2nd Edition. Hagerstown, MD: Review and Herald, 2005.

- Rickaby, Joseph. "The Modern Papacy," in *Lectures on the History of Religions*, Vol. 3, lecture 24. London: Catholic Truth Society, 1910.

- "Rome (Italy)." *Microsoft® Encarta® Encyclopedia 2000*. © 1993–1999 Microsoft Corporation.

- *Rome's Challenge: Why Protestants Keep Sunday*, ISBN 0-8280-0378-5.

- "Sacking Sunday," *Catholic Twin Circle*, 25 Aug 1985.

- *Saint Catherine Catholic Church Sentinel*, Algonac, Michigan, Volume 50, Number 22, 21 May 1995.

- "Scarlet Woman." *Webster's New World Dictionary*, College Edition. Cleveland, OH: World Publishing Company, 1957.

- Schaff, Philip. *History of the Christian Church*. 8 vols. Peabody, MA: Hendrickson, 2006.

- Scherman, Katharine. *The Birth of France: Warriors, Bishops, and Long-Haired Kings*. New York: Paragon House, 1987.

- Schwarz, R.W. *Light Bearers to the Remnant*. Boise, ID: Pacific Press, 1979.

- Scott, Samuel Parsons. *The Civil Law*, Volume 12. Cincinnati: Central Trust Company, 1932, pages 11–12.

- *Seventh-day Adventists Believe: A Biblical Exposition of 27 Fundamental Doctrines.* Hagerstown, MD: Review and Herald, 1988.

- *Seventh-day Adventist Bible Commentary.* 12 vols. Hagerstown, MD: Review and Herald, 1957–2000.

- Shea, John Gilmary. "The Observance of Sunday and Civil Laws for its Enforcement," *The American Catholic Quarterly Review 8*, January, 1883.

- Shea, William H. *Daniel: A Reader's Guide.* Nampa, ID: Pacific Press, 2005.

- Sheen, Fulton J. "Mary and the Moslems," *The World's First Love.* Garden City Books, 1952.

- Smith, Uriah. *Daniel and the Revelation.* Nashville, TN: Southern, 1944.

- Smith, Uriah. *Review and Herald,* 18 May 1862.

- Smith, Uriah. "Short Interviews with Correspondents," *Review and Herald,* 24 Feb 1863.

- Strong, James. *Strong's Exhaustive Concordance.* Grand Rapids, MI: Baker, 1997.

- *The Catholic Encyclopedia,* Volume 7 (1910).

- *The Catholic Encyclopedia,* Volume 12 (1907).

- *The Catholic National,* 1 July 1895.

- *The Catholic Record,* London, Ontario, Canada, 1 Sept 1923, Volume XLV.

- *The Catholic Universe Bulletin,* 14 Aug 1942, 4.

- *The Catholic World,* June 1871.

- *The Christian World Report,* May 1992.

- *The Collected Works of Pat Robertson.* New York: Inspirational Press, 1994.

- *The Complete Works of Josephus.* Translated by William Whiston. Lynn, MA: Hendrickson Publishers, 1981.

- *The Interlinear Hebrew-Aramaic Old Testament.* 3 vols. Jay P. Green, Sr., editor. Peabody, MA: Hendrickson, 1985.

- *The Tablet,* 29 Feb 1992.

- Thiele, Edwin R. *The Mysterious Numbers of the Hebrew Kings.* Grand Rapids, MI: Kregel Publications, 1983.

- "Tiberius." *Microsoft® Encarta® Encyclopedia 2000.* © 1993–1999 Microsoft Corporation.

- Tramer, Peter. Editor, *The Catholic Extension Magazine*, 22 May 1934.

- Treadgold, Warren. *A History of the Byzantine State and Society.* Stanford, CA: Stanford University Press, 1997.

- Treiyer, Alberto R. *Apocalypse: Seals & Trumpets.* Dr. Alberto R. Treiyer, 2005.

- Van Biema, David. "Hail, Mary," *Time*, 21 March 2005, 62–69.

- Walbank, F.W. *The Hellenistic World.* Cambridge, MA: Harvard, 1992.

- Walker, Williston. *A History of the Christian Church.* New York: Charles Scribner's Sons, 1918.

- Webster, Hutton. *Early European History.* Boston: D.C. Heath & Company, 1920.

- Were, Louis F. *The Battle for the Kingship of the World: Will the King of the North Invade the Holy City?* Berrien Springs, MI: First Impressions, n.d.

- Were, Louis F. *The King of the North at Jerusalem.* St. Maries, ID: LMN Publishing, 2002.

- Were, Louis F. *The Kings that Come from the Sunrising.* Sarasota, FL: H.K. LaRondelle, 1988.

- Were, Louis F. *The Woman and the Beast in the Book of Revelation.* Sarasota, FL: H.K. LaRondelle, 1993.

- White, Ellen G. *Early Writings.* Hagerstown, MD: Review and Herald, 1943.

- White, Ellen G. *Evangelism.* Hagerstown, MD: Review and Herald, 1973.

- White, Ellen G. *Life Sketches of James and Ellen White.* Legacy of Light, 2000.

- White, Ellen G. *Manuscript Releases.* 21 vols. Legacy of Light, 2000.

- White, Ellen G. *Maranatha.* Hagerstown, MD: Review and Herald, 1976.

- White, Ellen G. "Mingling Error with Truth," *Review and Herald*, 10 March 1910.

- White, Ellen G. *Ministry of Healing.* Boise, ID: Pacific Press, 1942.

- White, Ellen G. *Prophets and Kings.* Nampa, ID: Pacific Press, 1943.

- White, Ellen G. "Sanctification Through the Truth," *Review and Herald*, 12 April 1892, paragraph 19.

- White, Ellen G. *Selected Messages from the Writings of Ellen G. White.* 3 vols. Hagerstown, MD: Review and Herald, 1980, 1986.

- White, Ellen G. *Sermons and Talks.* 2 vols. Legacy of Light, 2000.

- White, Ellen G. *Testimonies for the Church.* 9 vols. Mountain View, CA: Pacific Press, 1948.

- White, Ellen G. *Testimonies to Ministers and Gospel Workers.* Mountain View, CA: Pacific Press, 1962.

- White, Ellen G. *The Acts of the Apostles.* Mountain View, CA: Pacific Press, 1911.

- White, Ellen G. "The Day of the Lord is Near, and Hasteneth Greatly," *Review and Herald*, 24 Nov 1904, paragraph 8.

- White, Ellen G. *The Desire of Ages.* Nampa, ID: Pacific Press, 1940.

- White, Ellen G. "The Final Test of God's People," *Signs of the Times*, 22 Feb 1910, paragraph 5.

- White, Ellen G. *The Great Controversy.* Nampa, ID: Pacific Press, 1940.

- White, Ellen G. *The Southern Work.* Legacy of Light, 2000.

- White, Ellen G. "To Our Church Members in Australasia," *Australasian Union Conference Record*, 11 March 1907.

- White, James. *Review and Herald*, 3 Oct 1878.

- White, James. *Review and Herald*, 29 Nov 1877.

- White, James. "The Judgment," *Review and Herald*, 29 Jan 1857.

- White, James. "The Time of the End," *Signs of the Times*, 22 July 1880, 1.

- Wilcox, M.C. *King of the North.* Mountain View, CA: Pacific Press, 1910.

- Wilkinson, Benjamin G. *Truth Triumphant.* Mountain View, CA: Pacific Press, 1944.

- Wohlberg, Steve. *End Time Delusions: The Rapture, the Antichrist, Israel, and the End of the World.* Shippensburg, PA: Destiny Image Publishers, Inc., 2004.

- Wolfram, Herwig. *History of the Goths.* Berkeley, CA: University of California Press, 1979.

- Wolfram, Herwig. *The Roman Empire and Its Germanic Peoples.* Berkeley, CA: University of California Press, 1997.

Internet Sources

- http://en.wikipedia.org/wiki/European_Union.
- www.Aloha.net/~mikesch/pope_to_seek_forgiveness.htm.
- www.americancatholic.org/Messenger/Jun2000/feature2.asp#F4.
- www.butler.edu/clergyproject/religion_science_collaboration.htm.
- www.careinternational.org.uk/careswork/where/ethiopia/ethiopia_stats.html.
- www.catholic.com/library/eastern_orthodoxy.asp
- www.cc.org/about.cfm.
- www.census.gov/main/www/poplock.html.
- www.christianchurchestogether.org/default.htm.
- www.cia.gov/cia/publications/factbook/geos/ez.html.
- www.firstthings.com/ftissues/ft9405/articles/mission.html.
- www.gem-werc.org/resources.html.
- www.islam.about.com/library/weekly/aa120298.htm.
- www.jeremiahproject.com/prophecy/ecumen01.html.
- www.ldausa.org/.
- www.newadvent.org/library/docs_jp02tc.htm.
- www.phrasebase.com/countries/index.html.
- www.phrasebase.com/countries/index.php?variable=people_religion.html.
- www.promisekeepers.org/faqscore21.
- www.promisekeepers.org/faqscore22.
- www.promisekeepers.org/faqscore28.
- www.religionstatistics.net/statamer1.htm.
- www.tagnet.org/cbsouth/leo/leo4.html.
- www.tencommandmentsday.com/.
- www.usccb.org/comm/archives/2006/06-003.shtml.
- www.wayoflife.org/fbns/patrobertson.htm.
- www.yuricareport.com/Dominionism/HowCatholicsJoinedEvangelicals.html
- www.zpub.com/un/pope/relig.html.